TY13007743
ARCMW

The Architecture of Change

The Architecture of Change
Building a Better World

Edited by JERILOU HAMMETT
and MAGGIE WRIGLEY

University of New Mexico Press
Albuquerque

18 17 16 15 14 13   1 2 3 4 5 6

Library of Congress Cataloging-in-Publication Data

The architecture of change : building a better world / edited by Jerilou Hammett
and Maggie Wrigley.
      pages cm
  ISBN 978-0-8263-5385-6 (cloth : alk. paper)
  ISBN 978-0-8263-5386-3 (electronic)
1. Architecture and society—Case studies. 2. Social change—Case studies.
I. Hammett, Jerilou, editor of compilation. II. Wrigley, Maggie, 1958–, editor
of compilation. III. Designer/builder.
  NA2543.S6A6325 2013
  720.1'03—dc23
                        2013003011

Cover photo: Painted umbrellas on the fire escape of Umbrella House, a former
squatters' building on Avenue C in New York's East Village. For years residents
have created the display to celebrate the survival of their building, which they
now own as low-income housing. (Photo by Maggie Wrigley)

Book Design and Production: Peter Scholz

(Photo by Byron Baker, courtesy of BASIC Initiative)

THIS BOOK IS DEDICATED TO KINGSLEY HAMMETT (1944–2008),
TO HIS LIFE AND HIS WORK.

Dearest King,

I must write the dedication to your book, the one Maggie and I and Peter have been putting together, the one you first thought about doing with me—The Architecture of Change.

How, my love, do I tell them all about your uniqueness, your beauty, the incredible journalist you were. How do I tell them how much you cared that the stories you wrote did something good for those you wrote about and those who read them. How do I tell them how you knew every story was a human story—not facts, not reports, but about the human beings affected by whatever was happening. How do I tell them about the love you carried in your heart as you wrote those stories, how you loved people, and words, and the act of putting the lives of others down on paper so that they would come alive.

Because they did come alive—the people, your words, your stories. And especially your values and your belief that a better world was possible. You had so much faith in what people could do for each other, what they could create and build, how they could transform misery into hope and put their talents together to improve lives. You wrote from your heart and from the pureness and simplicity that was you. You truly saw all people as equal and you treated them that way. What a gift that is. You envied me for my deep convictions but I envy you for your ability to put yours into your relationships with other people. The respect and kindness you showed them was the same spirit you brought to your stories. And those stories touched so many hearts.

You were a unique one, King Hammett, a jewel, a treasure. Thanks for all you've left us with, for all you were, for your example, for your love and kindness, for your talent and wisdom, for your care and respect, for the light of your spirit, for your innocence. Thank you for touching our lives.

Jerilou Hammett

CONTENTS

The Architecture of Change: Building a Better World
is a compilation of articles from fifteen years of
DESIGNER/builder magazine, whose objective
was to change how we see the world.

MICHAEL SORKIN

FOREWORD

WHAT IS THE MEANING OF A CONSEQUENTIAL ACT? FOR
Jerilou and Kingsley Hammett, the decision to found *DESIGNER/builder*
was motivated, clear and simple, by a sense of conscience and everything
followed from that. Surveying the field of architectural media in the United
States, they found it wanting, myopic, distorted by a trivializing parochial-
ism and by a fundamental failure of empathy, of politics. What they did was
to start a magazine that loved the possibilities within the built environment
not simply to create spaces of comfort and beauty or to goad arcane style-
wars but to repair the planet and to be a tool for social justice. And, they
recognized from the get-go that this project was plural, not simply in its
means and meanings but in the multiplicity of individuals and publics it
necessarily engaged and served.

And what a service *DESIGNER /builder* has performed! Part of a long and
noble tradition of "little" magazines, founded outside the routines of major
media production, publicity, and profit, it has taken on a remarkably
empowering mission. The title itself speaks not to a passive, aestheticized
approach but to something that sounds very much like part of the DIY
ethos that links it to other authentically popular magazines, and especially
to those with an idea about service, about *liberation*. This can't be stressed
enough, the conviction that the environment in all its physical and social
ramifications is something that should and can be subject to democratic
control and change and that individuals of all stripes are not simply entitled
to create the future but have the fundamental competence to do so. Of
course, *DESIGNER/builder* had ambitions beyond the kind of home-building
and hobbyist magazines with which its title invites comparison but it cru-
cially shares their desire to naturalize access to the tools to take the world
in hand and change it, repair it, improve it, share it.

This fight was also for an identity for architecture beyond celebrity, so far beyond this banal view that one read issue after issue of the magazine and thought with increasing joy that our architecture really could be something altogether different than what the conventional apparatus of dissemination and publicity presented. Look at the mix of subjects that kept turning up: public housing, racism, health care, community organizing, adaptive re-use, global warming, squatting, property rights, corporate control, gentrification, a critique of green-wash, homelessness, the real character of "natural" disasters, pedestrianism, Pyongyang, the settlements in the West Bank, big boxes and shopping malls, and, always, the stories of people and organizations at the forefront of the struggles for environmental justice at every scale and every kind of place. This especially: over the years, *DESIGNER/builder* brought to its pages a remarkable cadre of citizen-practitioners whose focus was on doing good, on inventing and evolving strategies of form and practicality that began from the dream of uniting use and equity, from the idea that form could be the instrument of fairness. Like no other journal, *DESIGNER/builder* understood the reach and constituency of architecture inclusively, as so much more than the terrain of aesthetes and patrons and practitioners simply eager to see the latest bauble. Instead, the magazine addressed itself to the needs and possibilities of the poor, the mentally ill, of kids in school, the homeless, of women in the projects, of old folks, of everyone who found themselves on the short end of the stick.

Because of this, *DESIGNER/builder* has been a remarkable force for de-linking architecture and privilege, for an inclusive idea of the built environment and its creators. Many know the celebrated 1964 show and book by Bernard Rudofsky, *Architecture Without Architects: A Short Introduction to Non-Pedigreed Architecture*. This was a foundational text for many who came of age in the sixties, as Jerilou and Kingsley (and I) did. While the book was a sumptuous revelation of the formal wonders of "vernacular" architecture around the world, it also empowered a larger idea, suggesting that building of sophistication and refinement could be produced outside the professionalized system of architecture (and, indeed, recognized that "architects" are involved with less than three percent of the built environment). This idea was very sympathetic to the striving for self-empowerment by so many young (and old!) people at the time who were seeking forms of community liberated from the mentality of "getting and spending" against which they were in rebellion. This meant a search for other forms of authenticity, patterns of life that did not simply depend on the exploitation of others but which could make positive contributions to their own and society's liberation.

Many in those days were also inspired to by another seminal, if more explicitly political text: Henri Lefebvre's 1968 "Right to the City" was both a stimulus and an outcome of that great year of insubordination and rebellion and a succinct embodiment of the sweep of its aspirations. While hardly the first to arrive at the formulation, Lefebvre's work extended the idea of rights—to free expression and assembly, to decent housing, to a democratic polity, etc.—to something more speculative and prospective. Lefebvre asserted that within the field of rights there should not simply be the freedom of conventional physical and social access to the city but the right to imagine the forms and practices of the kind of city in which we wished to live, in which we could find an environment in which to flourish. As David Harvey has put it, this was no less than the "right to change ourselves by changing the city."

DESIGNER/builder, in its mission to inculcate the field of building with the principles of social justice, has wonderfully merged these two streams, joined ideas of practicality and everyday empowerment with the highest hopes for aspirational imagination. By rooting itself in the palpability of space and the reality of lived lives, the magazine discovered and shared site after site at which hope could become instrumental, celebrating the citizenship and creativity of practitioners from every walk of life. What truly distinguishes it, though, is that while fearless in critique, the magazine was truly dedicated to telling the stories of people and practices that were genuinely constructive, loving in particular those who struggled against the odds to secure better lives for their communities, often communities of neglect, places where conventional wisdom never imagined architecture could flourish.

So many of the articles written in *DESIGNER/builder* were by Kingsley Hammett, gone tragically before his time. Our community deeply mourns the loss of a good neighbor to so many both within and beyond it. His crystalline conscience, direct prose, and obvious love of both people and place set a bar for engaged journalism that will inspire generations to leap, in imagination and caring, very high. *DESIGNER/builder* is his—and his dedicated collaborators'—irreplaceable testament of sharing.

• • •

Michael Sorkin is a deeply committed and influential architect and urbanist whose practice spans design, criticism, and teaching. He is a prolific writer. He is Distinguished Professor of Architecture and Director of the Graduate Program in Urban Design at the City College of New York.

(Photo courtesy of Shelter for Life International)

INTRODUCTION

MANY OF US GREW UP IN THE 1960s BELIEVING THAT
the world could be made a better place, and that our part in collective efforts would make that happen. We saw it with our own eyes.
We integrated schools and lunch counters, we stopped the war
in Vietnam, we forced large institutional investors to pull their
money out of the apartheid regime in South Africa, we watched
the women's movement grow, we helped build the United
Farmworkers' Union, we worked on Amnesty International campaigns against torture in some of the world's most notorious prisons,
and we felt strong and powerful and hopeful.

Then somewhere along the line something happened, and it
seemed like no one knew any longer what it meant to come
together and struggle. Suddenly anti-war marches began to feel
more like street theater and public celebrations. The outrage
wasn't there anymore. Demonstrations became more like isolated events than statements of resolve.

Those of us who believe that so much needs to be done, to
be confronted, to be exposed, to be called to account, and to be
remedied, are painfully frustrated.

So what happens when inertia sets in and apathy sucks out
hope, and we look around and there is nothing to connect to?
That's when we have to get really creative, stop waiting for some
new entity to materialize, and begin to make it happen ourselves.

Over a fifteen-year period, through the stories we've covered in *DESIGNER/builder* magazine, we have marveled at the
power of personal initiative—of people who refused to accept
that things couldn't change, who saw the possibility of making
something better, and didn't hesitate. *The Architecture of Change*
is a collection of their stories.

These essays profile architects, designers, artists, activists, and
ordinary people who have challenged the status quo and made
exemplary contributions to innovative housing, neighborhood

revitalization, alternative education, public art, and community empowerment. This book demonstrates how professionals, individuals, and groups can contribute to societal change irrespective of their economic status and political power, showing that one needs neither fame nor vast financial resources to make an impact. Running through these examples is a constant theme of social justice as an underlying principle of the built environment.

Take, for example, Lily Yeh, a classically trained Chinese artist who showed up with a shovel and a hoe, a big heart and a small grant on an abandoned lot in North Philadelphia, an area of derelict housing, flourishing drug trade, and trash-filled streets. She gathered around her anyone who wanted to help, whether they were children, addicts, or aimless youth, and started a process of transformation that in the ensuing years turned four inner-city blocks of utter devastation into joy and beauty. What became known as The Village of Arts and Humanities reclaimed abandoned houses and converted more than 250 empty lots into twenty-four enchanting parks, gardens, and orchards, where mosaic angels gaze down from a rowhouse wall, concrete tigers and baboons guard a tree farm, and undulating Malian walls define spaces. The Village developed a leadership program, youth theater, rites-of-passage ceremonies, and harvest festivals, all of which helped restore pride and hope to an area long written off as beyond salvation.

All the people in these essays are heroes to us. They weren't waiting for things to change; they changed them. These are stories of innovation and inspiration. They demonstrate the spirit expressed in the motto of the World Social Forum: "Another World is Possible."

Jerilou Hammett and *Maggie Wrigley*

(Photo by Steve Rasmussen Cancian)

KINGSLEY HAMMETT

SIDEWALK LIVING ROOMS

ALL OVER THE COUNTRY, LONG-IGNORED MINORITY NEIGHBORHOODS are being threatened by the forces of gentrification and displacement. Rising property values are shifting the racial demographics, driving out original residents, and destroying the cultural and social context of well-established communities.

In most of these low-income neighborhoods, the street pulsates with a rich social life where the local population, be it African American or Latino, gathers on favorite corners and in front of stores to sit, visit, talk, trade news, and play cards. But what is valuable to local residents can be offensive and frightening to middle- and upper-class gentrifiers, who believe the proper place to gather is in homes or back yards and see people on the street as a sign of low-class activity and trouble.

The challenge for those trying to preserve the integrity of these newly desirable neighborhoods is to institute improvements that appeal to residents but repel developers. It is a challenge that motivates the work of California landscape architect Steve Rasmussen Cancian, who has come up with an answer that is cheap, socially engaging, and effective: build sidewalk living rooms furnished with permanent benches, sitting boxes, and planters so neighbors can claim their right to public space while at the same time discouraging those who would like to see them gone altogether.

For nearly thirteen years after graduating from college, Rasmussen Cancian worked as a political and community organizer on behalf of such progressive candidates as Jesse Jackson and in support of Los Angeles public housing residents. After helping tenants develop low-income co-ops, he became interested in the field of design. He then moved north to Berkeley to get a graduate degree in landscape architecture, believing that would provide him with new opportunities to get involved in participatory community projects.

"Realistically, after a couple of community meetings, people can't go out and build a building," he says. "But with one or two community discussions people have all the tools they need to go and build street furniture and create the shared space of community living rooms."

While back home in Los Angeles on a school break he broached the idea to some of his old organizing buddies to launch a major tree-planting and sidewalk-improvement project in some of the neighborhoods he'd worked in earlier.

"Let's make the most of the urban landscape," he told them. "Their response was, 'If we do that, aren't we just rolling out the carpet for gentrification?' They knew on a gut level they'd just be improving the curb appeal of those properties."

He took that question back to Berkeley and tried to solve the core dilemma of gentrification: Low-income inner-city communities have a great need for improved environments. But improving the environment sets people up for displacement. How could they achieve one without the other?

Rasmussen Cancian found less support than he expected within the Berkeley design community. Even those with good politics often were locked into conventional thinking. They felt that gentrification was a problem beyond their scope and power to resolve and told him, "Steve, you're right to worry about it. But you can't do anything about it. You're in design school."

"Designers have self-edited themselves out of many roles. They mainly serve governments and people who can afford to pay," he says. "But if designers accept that they do have a social role and do have some control over the impact of their work, then they have to look at the work they're doing. A lot of their work would not be defensible if you asked, 'Is this serving any social good?' So figuring out how to learn to be a designer, to still be socially responsible, and to make a better neighborhood for the same neighbors is challenging."

Rasmussen Cancian was struck by the fact that nearby West Oakland, a community of beautiful old Victorians, had not been gentrified long ago. It offers gentrifiers the last BART station before a twelve-minute subway ride to San Francisco's financial center along with great weather, ocean breezes, and views of downtown Oakland. But it was the birthplace of the Black Panthers and the Pullman Car Workers Union and remains a proud African American neighborhood. He concluded that what had saved it from gentrification was the racism of gentrifiers. If there is no one on the streets, the area, with a convenient subway stop, might look like a great site for potential development. But when the streets are filled with black people in a society where it has been statistically proven that a majority of white Americans won't move into an area they perceive to be 30 percent African American or 50 percent Latino, gentrifiers tend to keep on driving.

"Gentrifiers and the diverse longtime residents they displace have very different ideas about what makes an inviting, attractive neighborhood," Rasmussen Cancian says. "Experience and studies show that working-class urban residents

(Photo by Steve Rasmussen Cancian)

Before and after. (Photos by Steve Rasmussen Cancian)

view the street as the center of the neighborhood, the place to hang out, to socialize, and to watch the passing scene. In contrast, most middle- and upper-class gentrifiers are looking for a quiet street as a gateway to their homes."

According to Rasmussen Cancian, gentrification unfolds in three well-understood phases. First come artists and alternative folk, who are looking for a cheap place to live in a diverse, interesting urban neighborhood. These are the "risk oblivious" who are willing to take a risk and invest in an affordable house in a multi-cultural, multi-racial community.

Next come the "risk prone," often young, white professional couples and families with more traditional suburban appearances and values. They are betting the neighborhood will "improve" and that they will wind up with a historic house in a fashionable neighborhood they bought at a great price. They trigger the onset of displacement as landlords begin to evict longtime tenants in the hope of higher rents.

Finally come the "risk averse," who want a safe investment in a quiet, homogeneous, upper-middle-class suburbanized neighborhood. They signal the kickoff of mass displacement as a large number of landlords sell rental homes for renovation, apartment buildings are converted to condominiums, and empty lots are filled in with new construction.

Hoping to intervene in West Oakland before it was too late, Rasmussen Cancian sought strategies that would improve the neighborhood and discourage developers. As a designer-in-training he saw that people already were creating informal sidewalk living rooms by pulling chairs out onto the sidewalk, flipping over milk cartons, setting up a card table, and using the street as a social center. What if these became permanent fixtures throughout the area?

Through a mutual friend Rasmussen Cancian was introduced to William "Big Will" Horace and George Paul Wolf, who for three years had been running the West Oakland Greening Project, a street-based community garden group. Horace was a master in turning found objects into art. He was a natural at working the street to get people involved as volunteers. And when he had money he hired local youth. Rasmussen Cancian thought that if the trio could institutionalize the idea of residents building permanent street furniture, they could institutionalize local ownership of the street and the neighborhood and make clear that it was not just a set of buildings, but a community of people. Their guiding philosophy was that everyone was welcome to join, even newcomers, but only if they were willing to become part of the neighborhood as it was and wanted to remain.

"Will thought the idea would work and saw how it would serve as an organizing tool for him," Rasmussen Cancian says. "By going out every Friday and building a bench, people would see what we were doing and we could then recruit more people."

The three scoured the neighborhood for found wood from construction sites. They looked for traditional hang-out corners or the fronts of Laundromats and stores where people already were gathering and where there was a lot of activity. They'd talk up their plans to see if the neighbors thought some permanent street furniture was a good idea and try to get some of them involved. If those they met were supportive, they'd open the doors to their van, pull out tools and materials, and start building a bench.

"By the time we were done we'd have an impromptu christening party in this new community living room," Rasmussen Cancian says. "I think people really appreciated taking ownership, creating some permanent furniture that was theirs, and claiming the space."

From a design standpoint the idea was to build an outdoor living room that included a couch and end tables (a bench flanked by planter boxes), ottomans (sitting boxes that could be moved around to create space on the sidewalk), and other seating (three- or four-step stoops that didn't lead to doors but sat up against walls or fences).

In West Oakland the city code clearly prohibits putting anything "functional" on a sidewalk or in a parkway (the space between the sidewalk and the curb). That included planting food gardens or fruit trees or putting out anything to sit on. Rasmussen Cancian and his new friends decided to forgo submitting a permit request they knew would be denied, and moved ahead, accepting the fact they might lose some furniture in the process. They soon saw their project was effective when on one corner a landlord complained that he couldn't rent his apartments across the street from a popular sidewalk living room. The city came and took the furniture away.

Rasmussen Cancian and his friends replaced the lost furniture and left a note for someone to call and explain what was going on. They soon got a call from someone at the city who said the building owner, who had kicked out the previous tenants, renovated the building, and jacked the rent three times higher, had complained about people hanging out on the street and demanded the city come and remove the living room.

"The caller, who couldn't say who he was, said he didn't want to remove the furniture and would avoid doing so when he could," Rasmussen Cancian says. "So we continue to play a game of cat and mouse." But he knew the sidewalk living room project was finding success when people adopted benches, watered plants, kept the areas clean, drove away drug sales, took ownership, and when others asked the Greening Project to build on their corner.

Rasmussen Cancian graduated from UC Berkeley in 2003 but continued to work with the Greening Project, which is now led by a new generation of young men with street legitimacy who continue to build more street furniture. At the same time he looked for opportunities to bring the living room project to Los Angeles. While the Oakland project was (and remains) a guerrilla, nonpermitted, community-based effort to improve a neighborhood and directly fight gentrification, his subsequent work in Los Angeles also included projects endorsed and supported by elected officials, city departments, and established nonprofit organizations.

He first hooked up with friends from his days as a community organizer, and from there the sidewalk living room idea began to blossom on a number of different tracks. ARTScorpsLA, a local arts, community, and environmental organization, resonated with the idea of furnishing the entire Latino Temple-Beaudry neighborhood, much of which had been torn down for a high school that was never built and was suffering under intense gentrification pressure. ARTScorpsLA members bring art to everything, and, using the guerrilla approach, they built sidewalk living rooms they turned into canvases, painting colorful murals of cacti and religious icons across walls and down benches to the sidewalk, bringing with them a pronounced Latino aesthetic.

Another project was the Fifth Street Living Room Rasmussen Cancian helped build with Stephanie Taylor and the Central City Neighborhood Partners (CCNP) along with the Los Angeles Conservation Corps. This was the first instance of a nonprofit organization using the land directly in front of its building both to create positive social space and to blunt the influence of gentrification.

"A lot of nonprofits have control, either literally or de facto, over some land in the city," Rasmussen Cancian says. "CCNP saw it could use its sidewalk to improve the neighborhood for the current residents and to counter the creeping gentrification."

The Fifth Street Living Room led in turn to two other significant initiatives, starting with CCNP's Positive Places Project. Working with four different community organizations, CCNP had gathered 1,000 surveys from bus riders, which revealed their biggest complaint was inadequate bus stops, some marked only with a

(Photo by Steve Rasmussen Cancian)

(Photo by Steve Rasmussen Cancian)

Before and after. (Photos by Steve Rasmussen Cancian)

sign. One of the answers was to build sidewalk living rooms at key bus stops in areas facing gentrification. The first site chosen was the sidewalk in front of the offices of Justice for Janitors, the Service Employees International Union local. This is a major bus stop for a transit-dependent population and the center of the predominantly Latino Pico-Union neighborhood. Unfortunately the union has sold its building to a condo developer. But before the condos go up, the neighbors will build a living room down the entire block to claim the space and claim the neighborhood.

The second initiative was the Teen LEAD Project, where CCNP worked with teenagers from the YMCA in downtown Los Angeles. Together they toured the neighborhoods and used census and other demographic data to identify where gentrification was taking hold. As a group the teens then determined where to build sidewalk living rooms to fight those ominous changes.

"This was a chance to make concrete the idea of gentrification to teens," Rasmussen Cancian says. "But it wouldn't have worked if they were not able to get their hands dirty and build something. One teen had been evicted from her home to make way for the Staples Center. Now she's living in an area surrounded by new live/work lofts and sees herself as potentially getting evicted again. I wasn't bringing anything new in terms of experience to these kids. But I was able to bring information about similar experiences people were having in other cities and what they were doing about it."

The sidewalk living room effort got a further boost when Mayor Antonio Villaraigosa, himself a product of underserved ethnic neighborhoods where street life is appreciated, got involved with the Verde Coalition. This collection of community, environmental, and labor organizations was working to create more open space and parks in low-income communities of color. The mayor lent his financial and political support to the group's plans to build sidewalk living rooms in each of the city's seven planning districts.

"While elected officials are unlikely to get up and overtly fight gentrification," Rasmussen Cancian says, "the mayor is very happy to get up and say we should support positive street life and give all communities places to gather."

Rasmussen Cancian's work demonstrates that the impact of building a sidewalk living room reaches far beyond its utility as an anti-gentrification device. It also provides residents with the opportunity to take control of their neighborhood, which in some ways is the most concrete form of empowerment.

"It's not empowerment in an abstract sense," he says. "It's actually using your power to physically change and take control of your neighborhood. That kind of empowerment can lead to bigger and broader actions and raise people's expectations so they think they will be able to both improve their neighborhood and preserve it for themselves and their families. They realize it doesn't have to be a tradeoff where they give away a block of the neighborhood in order to get ten units of affordable housing."

Sidewalk living rooms are also a positive form of tagging and provide residents with a way to reclaim their right to being active participants in their city. They allow people to see that in fact they can take ownership and create space for themselves in their neighborhood, that they can force city officials to say yes, and that they can do it in an amount of time and for an amount of money that's completely within their reach. And when people see a living room going in, it stimulates other groups to follow suit, or, as happened in one case, go on to raise $220,000 and build an entire park.

"They recognize they have the power to actually build their own neighborhood on their own terms," he says. "Today there's a lot more talk of neighborhood participation, but often the talk is hollow. More often plans are developed and then brought to workshops where people can only respond. What's so important in this work is to start with a blank slate except for the idea that a community gathering space is a good thing. Neighbors choose where to build, what to build, and how to maintain it, sometimes with municipal support, but always with community control."

• • •

This story first appeared in the January/February 2007 edition of DESIGNER/builder magazine.

The People's Grocery brings fresh, healthy food into the unserved area of West Oakland. (Photo by Scott Braley)

KINGSLEY HAMMETT

PEOPLE'S GROCERY GETS ROLLING THROUGH WEST OAKLAND

EVERY TUESDAY AND SATURDAY, A BRIGHTLY PAINTED REFURBISHED postal van cruises the streets of West Oakland, California, hip-hop music thumping from its oversize speakers. As it pulls to a stop, the three-person crew rolls up the rear door and pulls out a ramp, and the People's Grocery is open for business. Inside, the customers find a refrigerator and stainless-steel racks and wooden bins filled with fresh vegetables and fruits and bulk and packaged foods for sale at prices below those charged at distant groceries.

In fact, most everything is far away from West Oakland, including jobs, transportation, hope, and grocery stores of any description. This neighborhood of 30,000, which is largely black and Latino, suffers almost 80 percent unemployment. It has poor bus service, and only about half of the residents own a car. It has only one grocery store worthy of the name and thirty-six convenience stores pushing alcohol, tobacco, candy, and junk food at prices almost double what they'd bring elsewhere. If ever a neighborhood needed access to healthy, affordable food, to say nothing of economic empowerment, economic self-reliance, and social justice, it's West Oakland. And that's exactly what Malaika Edwards, Brahm Ahmadi, and Leander Sellers set out to provide when they formed a nonprofit called the People's Grocery.

"Our original idea was to start a youth-run grocery store," says Edwards, who had been working with Ahmadi in another organization leading social and environmental justice camps for high school students in which Sellers was a participant. "We wanted to use food as a first step toward economic empowerment. I had traveled around the world studying the impacts of globalization and saw how local economies can narrow the gap between rich and poor."

When she landed in West Oakland, in the heart of the progressive Bay Area in the state that leads agricultural production in the richest country in the world, Edwards found people without access to nutritious food. Major grocery chains had long since redlined this particular neighborhood out of any expansion plans, forcing West Oakland residents to spend their food dollars far from home. So it became obvious very quickly that the neighborhood needed a conscious grocery. Anxious to get something started yet aware that none of them had any experience in operating a full-line grocery store, they shifted their thinking to Plan B: taking groceries directly to the people.

"If you are a mother with a family in need of good fresh fruits and vegetables," she says, "you can spend half a day getting them. And the seniors have no way to get out at all. That leaves the corner stores or one of forty neighborhood food banks that give away emergency food."

West Oakland is the classic disenfranchised inner-city neighborhood, segregated from surrounding towns by freeways and mired in both physical and spiritual depression, Ahmadi says. During World War II, it was a thriving port and railway terminal that drew many blacks up from the South. And despite the economic collapse the area suffered after the war, into the 1950s it still supported a vibrant community of some 1,500 black-owned businesses along what's now known as Mandela Parkway. But eventually, that entire commercial strip was seized by eminent domain and everything was ripped out to make way for the Cypress Freeway (the one that collapsed during the earthquake of 1989), and the neighborhood never recovered.

"Ironically, Mandela Parkway has become the funnel into Emeryville, a small boomtown to the north that has been very successful in luring high-tech firms," Ahmadi says. "The population there doubles in the daytime and shrinks at night. And much of its poorer population has been forced into West Oakland."

The expansion of Emeryville toward West Oakland is almost cancerous, he says, and no one seems to have much concern about where those displaced by gentrification will find a place to live. Now some of the big developers are calling West Oakland South Emeryville and have become blatant about their intentions to expand the corporate-oriented strategy. They are trying to annex that part of Oakland and make it part of Emeryville.

Ahmadi and his colleagues want to work with residents of West Oakland to provide access to fresh, affordable foods that are nourishing, vital, and life affirming, something middle-class communities take for granted. But somehow it seems acceptable that low-income communities should be able to subsist on junk food or on the canned and processed foods distributed by food banks.

"We're trying to go beyond those basic emergency concepts," he says. "Many of the poor are not getting enough food, in part due to resistance to the outreach strategy the food banks use and the gaps such strategies leave. There are also complex

Two shoppers grateful for the nutritious food made available
by the People's Grocery. (Photo by Scott Braley)

issues around people's dignity and their preference to avoid the food bank and remain hungry rather than take a handout. We see the food bank as perpetuating a model of dependency on free food that does not compel the community to move forward to greater self-determination and self-sufficiency."

Nor does it encourage the innovation and entrepreneurship necessary to address food in a different way, Ahmadi says. He and his partners see food as an organizing tool and an opportunity for the community to develop jobs and microenterprises, to get out of the handout model, and to look toward self-employment models that can address food-access issues while building a local economy.

"While we see there is a need to increase access to quality food," he says, "we also see there are deeper things going on and that access to food is really an indicator of deeper material deprivations within the community."

One of the inspirations for the rolling People's Grocery was the Coca-Cola Street Team, a new marketing scheme ripped from the hip-hop community.

Well-dressed young people drive through the neighborhood in a souped-up Suburban decorated in flashy Coke graphics blasting tunes from large speakers and starting impromptu street dance parties where they pass out free Cokes. By combining the edginess of the Coke approach with warm memories of the Good Humor Man, the idea for the People's Grocery truck was a natural.

The nonprofit People's Grocery is supplied by Mountain People, a natural foods distributor, and Rainbow Grocery, a San Francisco cooperative that passes on its volume discount. That allows the People's Grocery to buy bulk and packaged goods at below wholesale prices, savings they pass along to their customers. Many of their fresh fruits and vegetables come from small-scale area farmers and a string of four urban gardens tilled by local young people who work with the People's Grocery Collards-N-Commerce Youth Program.

"That is focused on the idea that urban agriculture is a growing market opportunity throughout the world and is providing viable alternatives for employment," Ahmadi says. "Right now about 20 percent of global food is produced in inner-city environments, particularly so in Asia. We see West Oakland as a prime place to try this kind of model. Seven percent of the total land area spread out over 500 lots is abandoned or absentee-owned property. Our climate and soil are excellent, and we have a workforce that's both available and comes out of an agricultural tradition."

Ultimately, they hope to participate along the entire food chain, from educating and growing to wholesaling to restaurants, retailing direct, and adding value through creating products. Inspired by examples in Havana, Cuba, and the southern United States, they're also looking at forming an urban farmers' cooperative among hobby gardeners and consolidating them into a single entity under a recognizable brand to increase revenue by providing technical, financial, and labor assistance. "That's kind of the big scheme," he says.

To get the People's Grocery project rolling, they bought an old postal-service truck at government auction for $3,000, which they immediately parked for almost six months, stymied by how to accomplish the necessary conversion. Particularly vexing was how to install stainless-steel shelving that required the skills of a tig welder. But a short piece in *Utne Reader* about Edwards and her activities in West Oakland caught the attention of San Francisco architects Paul McElwee and Jane Wason, who happened to be both socially progressive and experienced tig welders and who offered their services pro bono.

"I called to see if they needed help with their store," says McElwee, who for six years lived in downtown Oakland and was all too familiar with the problems across the highway in West Oakland. "They said they weren't ready for a store but that they were working on a mobile market and could use help with a design and welding. It seemed like a tremendous cause, an excellent concept that works on many, many levels."

McElwee and Wason took photographs and measurements, drew up some sketches to see what could fit inside the truck, and decided to focus on three main components: stainless-steel shelving with clip-on wooden vegetable bins that hang from both sides of the interior of the truck while leaving a three-foot-wide aisle down the center, a pair of swing-out rear doors behind the roll-up door that holds more shelves, and a pull-out ramp with handrails.

The wire shelving was donated by the Treasure Island Job Corps, located on a former naval base in San Francisco Bay that has warehouses stuffed with surplus furniture and fixtures. They did their metal fabrication (and received help from fellow members) at an artists' collective called Cell Space, a nonprofit center that has a performance venue, artists' studios, and a metal-working shop. A company in Chico installed the photovoltaic cells to power the refrigerator and sound system. Others were paid to do auto body work, install the stereo system, and paint the truck in attention-grabbing graphics. And McElwee and Wason have since added an awning.

"Architects have to be involved in their immediate surroundings," McElwee says. "Part of the apartheid evident in West Oakland is manifest in the built environment. Architects are in the unique position of being able to change that and make it better. It's an obligation for architects to take the problems at hand and come up with solutions."

He concedes that Edwards and Ahmadi would have gotten their People's Grocery truck built one way or the other, and he knows that he and Wason would never have come up with the idea on their own. But they were happy to play a role, to get the job done quickly, and to be partners in such a worthwhile project.

"If we have more partnerships like this where people working in the community have a vision and need help, it's really positive," he says. "As architects, that's what we can do. We're the ones who can give these organizations the resources to realize their vision. The People's Grocery has its truck rolling around now, and it's wonderful. And we feel we had a part in helping it happen."

• • •

This story first appeared in the September/October 2004 edition of *DESIGNER/builder* magazine.

Advisor Jared Barbick with High School for the Recording Arts students. (Photo by Tomás Leal)

KINGSLEY HAMMETT

HIP-HOP HIGH GIVES DROPOUTS A SECOND CHANCE

WHILE MOST PUBLIC SCHOOL BOARDS AND ADMINISTRATORS REMAIN resolutely tied to a curriculum that relies heavily on math and verbal skills taught in conventional classrooms in hard chairs under bright lights, leading educational thinkers today realize that this model fits only 20 percent of the population. They have come to understand that the rest of us think and learn in different ways and respond to different stimuli. The message seems clear: If we are to reach the vast majority of students with a meaningful experience, we had better come up with relevant alternatives to this old, narrow approach.

One preeminent progressive educator is Dr. Wayne Jennings, who has been pushing the envelope throughout a fifty-year career as teacher, principal, superintendent, and elected school board member in the Minneapolis-St. Paul area. He readily acknowledges that public schools have failed to respond to how the majority of people learn. The brain is constantly trying to understand the world around it, he says. But it wants to do it on its own terms and not those set by some curriculum committee back at headquarters. And there is a wealth of research that cries out for a reassessment of how we teach, how we learn, and how we design schools.

"The work of Howard Gardner is one good example," Jennings says. "We used to think there was just one kind of intelligence, measurable by an I.Q. test. But Gardner suggests there are nine different kinds of intelligence and that each of us are smart in different ways."

One kind of intelligence is verbal/linguistic, which describes people who are good with words—writing, reading, and expressing themselves. Second is logical/mathematical, which includes those who are quick with numbers. The 20 percent of the population who are strong in both of these areas find school reasonably easy to handle. That leaves the other 80 percent in varying degrees of discomfort.

From left to right, Randy Fielding, David Ellis, Dr. Wayne Jennings, Tony Simons. (Photo by Tomás Leal)

Among those are people who are strong in seven other categories of intelligence: musical (singers, musicians), spatial (artists, architects), interpersonal (sales, public relations), intrapersonal (someone such as Oprah Winfrey), bodily kines-thetic (athletes, dancers), naturalist (scientists, environmentalists), and spiritual/existential (philosophical types).

"We are all a mixture of these things," Jennings says.

Rita and Kenneth Dunn have researched the factors that affect the learning environment, such as bright or low lights, hard or soft furniture, music or silence. And Leslie Hart has documented the four major contributions to enhanced learn-ing: an orderly environment absent chaos and threat; input to the brain from our various senses and the importance of environmental stimulation; the opportunity to learn by experience, to try our own wings, test our own skills, and do things; and feedback, or the input the brain needs to judge how it's doing beyond the delayed and indirect forms of report cards and marks on papers.

There have been a number of attempts of late, particularly in the charter school movement, to put this educational research into practice. One of the most exciting stories is that of David Ellis, creator of the High School for the Recording Arts in St. Paul, Minnesota. As a graduate of St. Paul Open School, an experimen-tal public school that Jennings founded some years ago, Ellis seemed an unlikely candidate to become head of a very successful alternative high school. He comes from the inner city of St. Paul and lived a life typical of his environment and back-ground. Diagnosed with Attention Deficit/Hyperactivity Disorder and dyslexia, he had a very rough time getting through school at all and was kicked out of three traditional high schools before winding up in the St. Paul Open School.

"That was a last resort for me," Ellis says. "Some of the kids were geniuses while others were more like me. They just clumped us all in together."

The Open School was nurturing and project-based and Ellis was encouraged to get involved in what was going on. But for the first year he chose not to, and spent most mornings asleep in a carpeted loft space. He was rebellious, looking for trouble, and too often found it. But he did not get kicked out, and one day a teacher asked if Ellis was interested in a new class on how to protect his rights and money and to become a part of a consumer protection agency housed within and operated by students at the school. Because Ellis already was angry at society and its racism, the idea struck a note somewhere deep within him.

"That woke me up and triggered me into realizing that learning wasn't just about facts," he says. "We actually took on the cases of community members who had been cheated or treated badly by businesses. We investigated these cases and wrote letters to the state attorney general, and it invigorated my mind and taught me what education was all about."

He learned how to do research, how to write reports and letters, and found an outlet for his young, rebellious energy. After graduating from the Open School, Ellis earned his pilot's license, enrolled in college for a stretch, worked at the Minnesota Pollution Agency, and recognized that he had the skills to solve any problem thrown his way. But none of that stopped his slide into drug and alcohol addiction and three tours through rehab, during which he turned to rap music as his bridge over troubled waters, since music was something he knew a good deal about. He played the drums and had grown up with Prince, and one of his sisters sang in Prince's first group.

"I was always trying to get Prince to incorporate rap and hip-hop into his music," Ellis says of the recording artist. "He wasn't initially amicable to that, but in the meantime I was writing this rap called 'True Confessions.' And when I was done I never used drugs or alcohol again. That transformed me, and when Prince heard it he was moved to give me a record deal through his company."

Ellis began working at Prince's studio and went on to produce several records for him and others until Prince broke from Warner Brothers. With the split went Ellis's contract, so he opened his own recording studio in downtown St. Paul, an area teeming with footloose kids ditching school who hung out in the warmth of the city's building-connecting Skyways. Before long they found their way to Ellis's new studio, anxious to record their own raps.

"They were so good I couldn't believe it," he says. "They were better than anything I had ever done."

With their pants hanging down, doing their best to look like a collection of young thugs, the kids were nevertheless highly motivated to learn about the intricacies of the music industry. They hounded Ellis for information on how to publish, how to secure a copyright, how to wire a studio, and that's when the light came on in his head: if these kids could get as motivated by the recording arts as he had about consumer rights, then they could develop the skills applicable to any phase of life and find themselves. He called Dr. Jennings, his former principal at St. Paul Open School, who was then in the process of opening charter schools.

"I told him I had about ten kids hanging out every day begging for studio time; what do you think should happen?"

Dr. Jennings came to take a look and was immediately impressed. He offered to enroll the kids in the St. Paul Family Learning Center, a K–12 charter school that was then operating only at the elementary level, which allowed him to collect state aid on Ellis's students and earmark the money for Hip-Hop High. They hired a few licensed teachers, and within six weeks the program swelled from an initial fifteen kids to a waiting list of fifty.

The students then wanted to get on the computer and learn Microsoft Word and Excel, to learn about graphics and how to design album covers, to learn how to create PowerPoint presentations to communicate their ideas, and to learn how to join the world successfully. Some who came in to rap gravitated to the mixing board, while others who accompanied rapping friends as their "managers" wanted to learn about the business end of things. It was time to put together a more formal program.

"That's when I began to design the Studio 4 model to integrate the recording arts with the project-based learning system," Ellis says. "The 4 stands for Family, Respect, Community, and Education."

He started by staggering the activities for the kids because all of them wanted to be in the studio at the same time. For the initial curriculum he had the students read the newspaper every morning, pick three articles out of the World/National section and another three from the Local/Metro section, and summarize each. After that, they got a pass to work in the studio. He used their newspaper summaries as ways to discuss English, grammar, spelling, and social studies. As they went along, he tried to incorporate math into the music. Then came the business of music, where they learned about production, engineering, publishing, copyright, marketing, promotion, art, graphics, and contracts. Twice a year, Ellis tears the studio completely apart and puts it back together. Some kids discover an interest in electricity, electronics, and engineering, and two have gone on to become journeyman electricians.

"They come in thinking they want to be the best rapper in the world," he says, "and some end up wanting to be a sound engineer or an electrician."

Jennings and Ellis applied to the State of Minnesota for an independent charter and officially launched the nonprofit High School for the Recording Arts five years ago, which then contracted with Studio 4 to provide the integrated recording program. The staff now includes an education director and teachers of English,

Phil Winden scheduling studio time with students. (Photo by Tomás Leal)

science, math, history, and social studies. Every Sunday morning at 8 a.m. the students broadcast "The Fo' Show" for a half hour on the Twin Cities' main hip-hop radio station, featuring music from the kids at the school. The school's record label has released five CDs, and today there are 200 students enrolled in the High School for the Recording Arts and a waiting list of many more.

"We're getting a lot of national attention as well as visitors from as far away as China," Ellis says. "Now I am lending technical advice to a school in Las Vegas that is adding a studio to its program, and we are discussing our operating a recording arts project in that school next year."

After the building Ellis originally occupied was condemned and torn down, he found a new home in a former mattress factory in an industrial area. He started out with 5,000 square feet in the factory's office area and has since added 15,000 more from the former warehouse. Architect Randy Fielding, who with partner Prakash Nair has built a practice devoted to studying and designing alternative schools, designed the new space to work more like a school than simply a commercial recording studio. The facility now has two recording studios, a pre-production area, offices, and classrooms.

"As soon as Randy saw the school he could feel the love," Ellis recalls. "He hung out with the kids, took a lot of pictures, asked them what kind of spaces they wanted and what they would do with it. He came up with an awesome plan. Everybody loves it."

They turned the drab warehouse into a riot of color; made a performance space with a stage that doubles as a lunch room; and set up six advisory areas where each student has his own desk, chair, computer, and a place to secure belongings. Scattered around the facility are comfortable couches, tables, lots of lights, and exposed wood and brick. Large garage doors with glass panels divide the advisory space from the performance space.

Fielding planned the space with the belief that the best learning results from students who feel alive, who are learning and growing and producing, and who are stimulated by three important kinds of components. First is the collaborative, which means sitting together in a coffee shop or around a table conversing, sharing, bouncing ideas off each other. Second is the kinesthetic, or spending part of the day making something, building something. And the third component is the individual—spending part of the day writing on your computer, e-mailing, writing a song, recording music—assimilating and creating something on your own.

The ideal school, therefore, provides spaces for these three separate activities. At Hip-Hop High, the most flexible is the collaborative area where at any given time kids may talk, eat lunch, or create individual or group projects. If they are launching a new CD, for example, they may use the space to spread out, sort, and fold printed materials and fill boxes. Or they may use sewing machines to make banners. Or they may share what they have learned regarding a black history project.

"So that collaborative group is a flexible area where lots of different things can happen," Fielding says.

Students in the recording studio at High School for the Recording Arts. (Photo by Tomás Leal)

When it comes to traditional learning in the areas of reading, math, and science, fifteen students make up a single group, which has its own advisor. They spend time in individual workstations, using computers in small teams. Since many of the students have poor learning skills, the school employs a carrot-and-stick approach to encourage academic improvement as a way to earn recording time. While the scores on statewide tests are lower than average at Hip-Hop High, they have to be weighed against the alternative. As Ellis makes clear, if they weren't enrolled at the alternative high school, they wouldn't be enrolled anywhere and would wind up on drugs, in jail, or dead.

"Instead, they're getting a high school diploma, they're graduating with the skills equivalent to having had two years of music school in the recording arts, and their test scores are higher certainly than they would be in a traditional high school," Fielding says. "People who are against charter schools will use the club of standardized test scores as a critique against them. But what's the alternative?"

And as Jennings is quick to remind his critics, "Do you want them back?"

The Minneapolis public schools are now encouraging Ellis to create another similar school in the city, but by now he is all too well aware of the bureaucratic difficulties he is bound to encounter.

"I would like to do that," he says of expanding within his hometown, "but it is so tough. There are so many people and organizations that are trying to sabotage charter schools. Then you have all these compliance hoops you have to jump through. They force us into a box, and even though our test scores have gone way up they want us to look like them. It's so stressful. It's almost a fluke that we are here."

Ellis is working on another program that will allow him to introduce recording arts programs to established schools rather than re-create Hip-Hop Highs elsewhere from scratch. It's an Internet web-based studio recording arts project where kids from all over the world can join Another Level Records Worldwide, a label he created. Any enrolled students at participating schools can go to the website, set up a template with a photograph and bio, create storage for their own music, take classes in the business of music, talk to other kids, and share each other's music projects.

"I want the Internet project to be a community where students from all over the world can join our record label," Ellis says. "Then I want to get some tour buses, convert them into mobile recording studios, travel from school to school, maybe park in one place for up to two weeks, and kids who are members of Another Level Records can come out and record their projects."

• • •

This story first appeared in the March/April 2006 edition of DESIGNER/builder magazine.

Little Village residents protest the desperate need for a new high school. (Photo by Michael D. Rodríguez)

KINGSLEY HAMMETT

POWER TO THE PEOPLE

LITTLE VILLAGE HUNGER STRIKE YIELDS NEW HIGH SCHOOL

IT'S A RARE DAY WHEN A WORKING-CLASS IMMIGRANT COMMUNITY can win a major fight against the power and might of an insensitive and intransigent bureaucracy that throws in its way all manner of obstacles. But as the story of Chicago's Little Village neighborhood demonstrates, if you don't give up and you refuse to take "No" for an answer, you can achieve amazing things.

In the late 1990s Little Village had a major problem. This Hispanic low-income neighborhood on Chicago's West Side was the most densely populated and youngest community in the entire city, with half of the residents below the age of twenty-four. It had more than 4,000 high school-aged kids and the local troubled Farragut High was serving just half of them. The rest had to travel well beyond the neighborhood, sometimes up to an hour, to get to school, in turn overpopulating those schools as well. And forty percent were dropping out.

"There was no argument regarding the desperate need for a new neighborhood high school," says Jaime de Leon, director of the New Communities Program of the Little Village Community Development Corporation. "Everybody was in agreement, including city and board of education officials, which is why they made the commitment to build a new school in Little Village. At the same time they decided to also build two selective enrollment or magnet schools in other neighborhoods of the city. All were supposed to be open and operational by the year 2000."

School officials began by buying and clearing the land for the Little Village high school and putting a fence around the site. But there it sat with no movement, while the school board turned its attention to the magnet schools that would serve mostly white, high-achieving students.

"At that time our organization was fairly new, and as we went around engaging in block organizing, knocking on people's doors, asking them what they were concerned about, most were talking about the school and how they weren't getting what the city had promised," de Leon says.

Out of that came an education committee made up of block club leaders and parents, mostly women, who began to strategize around how to pressure the Chicago Public Schools (CPS) to make good on its promise. The Little Village Community Development Corporation helped facilitate meetings with city officials, organize neighborhood meetings, and get signatures on a petition. For the next eight months they were told repeatedly that the school board had run out of money, even though it was documented that $30 million from the state legislature had been allocated to the city for the Little Village project.

"What we learned later was that that money had been used for the other high schools, which had gone over budget," de Leon says. "So we kept hitting a brick wall with the school board. All they would do was invite us down to Springfield to lobby the state legislature for some more money. Our reasoning was, 'No, you were already given the money. It's documented here in this capital improvement budget.'"

Little Village residents finally got fed up and decided something more drastic had to be done to capture the eyes and ears of the city. Somebody threw out the idea for a hunger strike, a radical method employed throughout history to give a voice to and champion the causes of marginalized and disenfranchised peoples. Folks in Little Village were familiar with how successfully the tactic had been used by United Farm Workers president César Chávez. So they set out to create some transparency by which neighbors could see what Chicago Public Schools had done to their community. They thought such a protest might last four or five days and maybe get some play in the local press. Their argument was simple: CPS promised to build all these schools, it had the money, it built ones for predominantly white students, and basically told Little Village it wasn't worthy of a new school.

"Once folks hear they aren't deserving, that's what fuels the anger that gets them to act," de Leon says.

The Little Village community launched its hunger strike on Mother's Day, 2001, with four strikers, their families, and ten supporters. They pitched a small tent city, dubbed Camp César Chávez, at the front of the lot where the school was to be built. They saw themselves as being part of a collective fighting not only for bricks and mortar but to create a new sense of community marked by human dignity, respect, justice, democracy, and equality.

Over the next nineteen days the number of hunger strikers swelled to fourteen, the majority women, ranging in age from seventeen to seventy-two. On any given night they were joined by 300 to 400 supporters from Little Village and other communities around the city, along with businesses, churches, and members of other organizations who brought them broth and cases of water and wood for the fires. The carpenter's union built a stage and during the day the protesters held rallies, teach-ins, open mikes, Spanish rock concerts, and church services conducted by local pastors, all the while enduring weather that fluctuated from unseasonably cold to very hot and humid. And the media showed up every day to cover the protest.

The strikers also brought their fight downtown to CPS. They took 100 protesters to the board's monthly meeting, causing a ruckus. And they began to follow Mayor Richard Daley around the city, getting in his face every chance they got. "Nothing like this had ever happened in this neighborhood, nor recently on that scale anywhere in Chicago, a city known for its organizing and movements," de Leon says. "We were on the news almost every night and everybody in the city knew what was going on. It was a combination of mobilizing folks in our community by setting up this camp and then taking people to the bureaucrats downtown."

Before the strike was terminated after nineteen days (due to health considerations), Paul Vallas, the CEO of Chicago Public Schools, and board president Gary Chico resigned. At a later meeting Chico admitted publicly that the money for Little Village had been spent elsewhere.

"Then we had to think about how we were going to deal with this new administration," de Leon says. "They weren't necessarily the bad guys, but they were part of the system. So we opened a dialogue, and about a month later CPS allocated $5 million to finish cleaning up the Little Village site and to hire architects as a gesture of good faith to show they were moving forward with the school."

Nearly half of the Little Village students were then dropping out and most of the schools across the city with a predominance of black and brown students were under-performing. A facilities design committee of Little Village residents was formed to be at the table with Chicago Public Schools and take part in all the decision-making to ensure they got what they wanted: a good school that would set a standard for something different. They embraced the school-within-a-school concept with four small schools operating autonomously while housed within a single multiplex structure. They settled on four distinct divisions that would allow for some crossover: Multicultural Arts; World Languages; Math, Science, and Technology; and Social Justice. Through their work the committee developed an excellent relationship with the architects, engaged in an eight-week process with the design team, and helped develop the entire floor plan and even chose the interior wall finishes and the colors of the chairs in the auditorium.

"The architects gave us disposable cameras in order to take pictures of buildings and culture and people that reflected what we wanted to see in our building," de Leon says. "And we visited other schools and brought back what we wanted to use. We give a lot of credit to that particular architect team. They didn't just do this because they were being told to do it by Chicago Public Schools, but because they saw value in the community's participation."

During the planning process, de Leon says, Little Village was advised by CPS that, because of integration mandates, 30 percent of the students at the new high school had to come from the neighboring African American community of North Lawndale. "'O.K.,' we said, 'that's fine.' So we reached out to our friends in North Lawndale in order to counterbalance the historical obstacles that have been designed to disempower and divide our communities. We got some participation, but not the level we wanted because we were dealing with hundreds of years of divisions among folks. People were distrustful and it's still a challenge. The student body is now maybe 25 percent African American. But it's hard to get the parents to participate and for the kids to stay for after-school programs."

One problem is that the black students have to cross gang boundaries on their way to school, which forced the neighborhoods to address issues of violence. But once the Lawndale students are within the school, the relationships are more peaceful, thanks to outreach workers and violence-prevention initiatives. In one gesture of goodwill that bridges both cultures, Little Village Lawndale High School named the art wing after Elizabeth Catlett, a noted black artist and sculptor, who spent most of her adult life working and living in Mexico with her husband, artist Francisco Mora.

When it opened in 2005, the Little Village Lawndale High School wound up being the most expensive school Chicago Public Schools had built to date ($72 million). It included a range of amenities that are shared by all four divisions: a swimming pool, a weight room, two gymnasiums, athletic teams, a library, a state-of-the-art 500-seat auditorium, a dance studio, a distance learning lab, adult education programs, a child-care center, and a school-based health-care center with four examination rooms that serves the larger community.

The finished product grew out of the community's belief in self-determination and conviction in the right to a quality education. Today it serves as the center of community life and has become the highlight of the Chicago Public Schools system. Dolores Huerta, a leader of the United Farm Workers, attended the grand opening, and the school has hosted appearances featuring the governor of Illinois and representatives of the Mexican Consulate.

"The attendance rate has been great," de Leon says, "hovering around 90 percent for all four programs. There is a separate principal for each one, and when Little Village Lawndale High School is at capacity each program should have 350 to 400 students. But the battle goes on for continued funding, for an adequate number of teachers, and to resist pressure to make it into a single school by eliminating three principal positions. Every year or so CPS comes out with a new policy that negatively impacts the school. So it's about building community and being ready for whatever comes."

• • •

This story first appeared in the May/June 2008 edition of *DESIGNER/builder* magazine.

Jose Rosado tries to re-create everything. In his apartment in the Bronx he painted bricks in his hallway. He has spent hours staring at the Brooklyn Bridge just to create this miniature version. (Photo by Pam Parlapiano)

KINGSLEY HAMMETT

THE CURE FOR HOMELESSNESS IS HOUSING

THE INDUSTRY THAT HAS SPRUNG UP TO DEAL WITH PEOPLE WHO
are homeless and mentally ill commands ever-increasing amounts of public resources
yet delivers few substantive changes in the condition of homelessness. In most
instances the prevailing system is highly regimented, gives its clients few options, and
is little more than a revolving door between the institution and the street.

The traditional system forces the homeless mentally ill into hospitals, shelters, or congregate-living programs where they are required to eat, sleep, and
wake when told, watch preselected television channels, observe curfews, and
restrict guests, all while being forced to earn privileges by proving they are sober,
taking prescribed medication, and staying fully under control.

There is one program in New York City, however, that gives the homeless mentally ill the one thing they crave most: a home of their own. Pathways to Housing
has taken the path less traveled and reversed the order of priorities typically practiced by those trying to help the homeless. It recognizes the fundamental fact that
many of the homeless mentally ill are fully capable of taking care of themselves
most of the time, and that they would rather see a landlord to discuss ways to allevi-
ate their housing crisis than see a psychiatrist for their long-standing mental illness.

"One of the hallmarks of mental illness is denial," says Pathways founder and
director Sam Tsemberis. "People often behave as if there's nothing wrong with
them—and for the most part, this is actually true. They can learn to live their lives
and cope. Symptoms come and go, and none of us are in a distressed state all the
time, and certainly not forever."

Few know that better than Pam Parlapiano, a photographer who teaches the
gift of the camera to Pathways clients. The first recipient of the Gordon Parks
Humanitarian Photography Award, she has been with Pathways from the beginning.

"What I love about Pathways is that from the very moment people have an encounter with Pathways, they start being talked to like individual human beings," she says. "That's what's so different from other programs. There's much more asking, 'Who are you? What are you looking for? Do you like this apartment? Do you like this neighborhood?' It's not, 'Here's your apartment. Here's your key.'"

That difference allows people to see the homeless mentally ill as individuals and not as a category, she says. And from that very first moment, Pathways clients start guiding their own destinies.

"They don't have to be drug compliant if they don't want to be," she says. "They don't have to be in a drug program if they don't want to. Sam's concept is that people have the right to direct their lives. The more you have, the more you're going to do the right thing to keep it."

Certainly there are those who fall and lose what they have gained, she says. Drug addiction has an irresistible pull for many people, and it can take many tries to beat it. But if they don't lose their homes, don't wind up in jail, and don't get into big trouble, they can turn things around quicker.

"To get off drugs can take several attempts," she says. "But because people have their apartment and are working with their service coordinators, they have someone to go to. They're no longer alone and they know it."

And that's enough for Pathways clients to keep coming back, even if they've fallen off the wagon, stopped taking their medications, or lost their apartment and want their money to go out and buy drugs. "They come back because Pathways becomes their family and their lifeline," she says. "Sam is totally non-judgemental."

Tsemberis recognizes that in many cases the homeless mentally ill had, somewhere along the line, been evicted from housing they'd once enjoyed, often through no fault of their own. He believes that the major reason for the rising rates of homelessness in the last twenty-five years is the elimination of federally subsidized housing. The federal government reduced construction of subsidized housing units in the latter part of the 1970s and virtually eliminated them when Ronald Reagan took office in 1980, after which the number of new units of subsidized housing went from approximately 350,000 per year to less than 50,000 per year. In the early 1980s, this loss was coupled with a very strong real estate market that was busy converting affordable housing units into co-ops and condominiums for affluent buyers. The poor were left homeless when relatives could no longer support them. For those with the least support, especially the mentally ill, America's streets became their home at alarming rates.

"There is a certain degree of sympathy for the mentally ill because people can recognize they didn't choose it for themselves," Tsemberis says. "However, when homelessness and mental illness are coupled with substance abuse, the public's perception shifts to believing that the person is primarily an alcoholic or a drug addict and is homeless because of weak character or bad choices."

The result is a system that blames the victim and demands clients be clean and sober before obtaining what they most need: housing. Consequently, those who are homeless and have both psychiatric and substance-abuse problems are the least likely to get into existing housing programs and most likely to get evicted and end up on the streets.

Tsemberis's attitude is a sharp departure from the more familiar approach. Pathways provides clients with immediate access to independent apartments, moving them directly from the streets into homes of their own, and, wherever possible, ones located in the neighborhood of their choice. Apartments are furnished with the essentials and the client is accompanied to shop for the amenities.

"People are overjoyed to have a place of their own," Tsemberis says. "They love having a key to open and close their own door, deciding when to sleep and when to wake up, choosing which channel to watch, or using the phone when they like and being able to leave a call-back number. People personalize their places beautifully. They are very resourceful with very little money. Once people are off the streets and safe and secure, they can relax and begin to consider their next step."

Pathways is funded by government contracts and pays most of the rent on the apartments. Clients, in turn, must meet two program requirements: (1) contribute 30 percent of their income (usually a Social Security Disability check) toward the cost of rent, and (2) meet with their service coordinator twice a month. Pathways is the representative payee for most clients, and service coordinators have monthly budget meetings to help clients pay their bills. Whatever money is left over is the client's to keep, and he's free to live his life as he sees fit. Furthermore, about 30 percent of the Pathways staff are in recovery from homelessness, mental illness, or substance abuse, and they speak to clients from a place of experience.

"People would tell me, 'I want a place of my own and I want beer in the fridge and when you come over I don't want to have to hide the beer,'" Tsemberis says. "How could you not listen to that?"

He and Parlapiano listen to it all the time and they are continually astounded at what they hear. Peter Price, one of Parlapiano's photography students, had been homeless for twenty years, had a severe drinking problem, and was highly manic and fairly volatile. But he was very quiet when he first came into the program and one day he and Parlapiano started talking about Federico Fellini.

"He not only knew about Fellini," she says with amazement, "he knew everything about him—every film he ever made, everyone in the cast. And when I asked him to explain film development he explained emulsion and how it's mixed. He knew all about the architecture in New York and he was an amazing mathematician. Every time it came to the science section of the *New York Times* on Tuesday

I called up Peter to cipher it out for me. Everybody in Barnes & Noble knew Peter, who would sit on this one couch with a gigantic math book checking the problems just to see if they had done it right."

One day Peter lost control and Parlapiano convinced him to check into the hospital for a few days. The doctor asked if interns could sit in on the intake. Peter agreed, and the doctor started by asking him if he knew who the president was.

"He not only knew who the president was," she remembers, "he knew every president and what years they served!"

When the doctor asked if Peter could count from 100 to 1 backwards, he responded, "In increments of seven?" When he asked if Peter recognized the saying, "Those who live in glass houses shouldn't throw stones," Peter told them not only what it meant but where in the Bible it came from.

"It was a humbling experience for everyone," she says. "The interns could have learned that even if people have extreme emotions it has nothing to do with them being smart or not. But the interns didn't get it. Peter died in his late seventies of a heart attack in his home, in his apartment, in the program, with people who cared about him and he knew it. I don't think Peter missed having a full life."

Parlapiano has always loved teaching photography to people who might have a special need, she says. She's comfortable in that role and knows that people who have special situations also have special creativity. She has traveled the world photographing leprosy victims and is the author of *Quest for Dignity: Personal Victories Over Leprosy/Hansen's Disease*, which formed the core of a major photographic exhibition at the United Nations in 1997. She also teaches photography at Empire State College in Manhattan, where much of the time she is encouraging people to discover their creativity, to find out what they feel about things. But her students from Pathways are people who are already dealing with extreme emotions and their feelings are right on the surface, requiring little coaxing.

"We all know art is in the extreme," she says. "I know if someone has that particular talent, they have that other component—they are out of the norm, they have that extreme emotion. If I can direct them into photography I'm going to see some great stuff. I also have an opportunity to give them a chance to see what they're able to do after living by themselves as 'unable' for years."

And by putting a Nikon around someone's neck, she says, even if the people they encounter recognize that they're a little different, they have a common denominator—a camera—if a stranger wants to strike up a conversation.

"Then they would find out how brilliant Peter was because he could tell them everything about the mechanism of the camera," she says. "So you have this equal thing everybody can talk about with respect. What you are now is something other than a category. And if you are a category, you're a photographer, not someone who was homeless."

Jerome Dinkins was finishing the tiles in his new apartment and installing great lighting. (Photo by Pam Parlapiano)

While working at Pathways, Parlapiano has met any number of gems of human beings, like Bruce, a brilliant artist who knows all about Michelangelo and every other Renaissance artist. "He should be teaching at a university," she says.

Jerome is a Pathways client who, when he's not on drugs, is brilliant. When he is on drugs, he's one of those tenants who gets his apartment, loses his apartment, gets his apartment, loses his apartment. And every time he gets a new apartment he puts down new tile and installs wild lighting himself.

"Every time he loses an apartment he creates a new one," Parlapiano says. "He's a different kind of success story. He's not in jail, he's not on the street, and he never quite lets go completely. Sam just went to give a talk about housing. Who did he take? Not the angel. He took Jerome."

Jose is an artist who is very precise. His apartment in the Bronx was not in great shape, so he painted the bricks on his wall. He sits in front of the Brooklyn

Bridge for days and days at a time and re-creates it in miniature form out of anything he has. "Everything about him is meticulous," she says. "He's immaculate in a starched shirt."

What people have to know is that behind the category are a lot of individuals with amazing stories and a lot of gifts to give because of what they've been through, she says. They involuntarily became different, and in doing that they lost some things and gained some things.

"What I want to see is not the story of their loss, but the story of the gains," she says. "Behind these faceless statistics we're always talking about is the perception that mental illness is bigger than the person. It's not. Human individuality usurps everything."

Tsemberis's thinking about how to help the homeless mentally ill began to evolve after he completed a doctoral program in psychology at New York University in 1983. Well-intentioned professors had taught him how to identify, classify, categorize, and diagnose people with stigmatizing labels as a prelude to delivering treatment. Upon graduation, Tsemberis worked in New York City's psychiatric hospitals. Then he ran an outreach program designed to treat people who were homeless, living on the streets, mentally ill, and possibly posing a danger to themselves and others. He and his colleagues could assess up to thirty people a day, and those who met the clinical and legal criteria were taken to Bellevue Hospital—involuntarily, if necessary. Some of the people they got to the hospital were in bad shape, with severe medical problems such as infections, frostbite, and pneumonia. If they received the necessary medical treatment, Tsemberis felt he had done them a useful service.

"Ultimately, however, this program was very disappointing," he admits. "People we had anguished about taking to the hospital with the hope that they would get treatment and be discharged to a decent place to live would, within a very short time, be right back on the street."

Many people they reached out to would say, "Leave me alone. I don't need to see a psychiatrist; I need to see a landlord. The problem is obvious: I'm homeless." His efforts probably saved a few lives and amputations, but the experience primarily taught him how to listen to people and understand their problems. Nevertheless, he remained frustrated that he couldn't get people off the streets and into permanent housing.

By the late 1980s the agenda concerning the homeless mentally ill shifted from clinical needs to housing. But the official focus was trained on creating more places of congregate housing—forty to sixty residents, single rooms, common kitchen and dining room with treatment services on-site. Each facility was essentially a mini institution, but many of those assigned there couldn't take the regimentation and found themselves back out on the street.

People felt their program routines were demeaning, that they were being treated very poorly and were forced to compromise their dignity, autonomy, and self-determination. Many people found a way to cope with the restrictions, Tsemberis says, "but from my perspective as a street outreach worker, I could see that approach was not working for those who remained on the streets."

There remained a desperate need for an alternative to this "treatment first" approach to scooping people up off the street and taking them to hospitals. So Tsemberis and his team started opening drop-in centers where people could take a shower, get a meal, and speak to a friendly face—which to those on the street seemed like a wonderful break from the chaos outside. If someone had a broken leg, Tsemberis explains, you'd get him a cast, a cane, or a wheelchair. The handicap doesn't end his life and debilitate him completely. In the same way, Tsemberis and his colleagues began to work around the disabilities posed by people's mental illnesses and to get them to focus their abilities on ways that they could cope.

"Instead of the clinician saying, 'I think you need this or I think you need that,' it changes the entire relationship by asking clients, 'What do you need?' or 'How can I help you?'" he says. "It becomes much more a service-oriented approach to working with people and giving them a greater voice in what will happen to them. In fact, they begin to drive the intervention as opposed to having the intervention imposed on them. Then people start to have a different conversation with you."

In 1992, desperate to provide housing for those successfully engaged in the psych rehab drop-in center, Tsemberis took the leap. He obtained $500,000 from the New York Office of Mental Health, a supported housing grant with which he could pay rent and staff, and began to give his clients what they had been requesting for so long—independent housing with no pre-treatment requirements. This first grant provided for rents and case-management services for fifty clients.

At that time the program cost approximately $9,700 per person a year, compared with the $15,000 annual cost of a cot in a homeless shelter, or the $35,000 to $45,000 expended annually for each bed in congregate housing. This allowed him to demonstrate that supported housing is not only more desirable for clients, it is also a far cheaper alternative for New York State.

"It's still the cheapest program around," Tsemberis says, "about $22,000 per person per year, while homeless-shelter costs have risen to between $25,000 and $30,000 a year and the congregate-housing cost is close to $50,000."

Once Pathways clients get their apartments they are very grateful, he says. Then, after a few weeks, they want to find jobs, the next issue, after housing, that people are very motivated to do something about. That sent him on a mission to find additional money for support services. Today the program has expanded to include enhanced clinical services and vocational counseling for more than 400 clients, and the annual budget has risen to $7.2 million.

Ben Matthews with his flag table cloth and photos of his brother
in the service and a favorite rap star. (Photo by Pam Parlapiano)

"Every year the program has grown in terms of more people housed and more services offered," he says.

Seventy of 400 clients are working, some of them full-time, many part-time within the agency—painting, helping to fix up apartments, etc. While the agency houses primarily single adults, its roster includes at least thirty families, and in several cases parents have recovered enough stability to have their children returned to them.

The demand for an apartment through Pathways is very high, as is the retention rate: 85 percent of those who have obtained their own homes have maintained independent apartment living. The agency keeps a waiting list of 500 people anxious for a place of their own, anxious to return to a lifestyle that many take for granted.

"We want to support people so they can make lives for themselves," he says, "but the continuum-of-care congregate-housing enterprise is growing astronomically compared to our housing-first program. It's a pity, because that system continues to build architectural structures that inhibit the development of complex lifestyles."

Mental illness coupled with homelessness is often a very isolating experience, Tsemberis says. On the one hand the homeless person doesn't want to bring shame to his family, while on the other hand the family rejects the idea that one of their own has mental illness because of all the stigma and fear attached to it. There is thus a mutual pulling away. What sets Tsemberis apart from his colleagues is that in his gut he trusts and accepts the experiences and beliefs of those who have mental illness.

He also tries to remain responsive to the individual needs of his clients, as he demonstrated in the case of one of his first, a homeless man named Glen Lee. Mr. Lee was about sixty-five years old, had been sleeping on the streets in the vicinity of Fifth Avenue and 40th Street, and spent much of his time at the nearby New York Public Library. He believed New York State had robbed his family, possibly of Native American origin, of a great deal of land. So he would travel to towns with names like Glens Falls, Glenville, and Glenvale and take photographs with a Polaroid camera to build a case to sue the state.

"He was exhausting himself," Tsemberis says.

"When I met with him I immediately offered him a place on 50th Street. He said that he would consider my offer. A couple of days later he returned to say that the offer was appreciated but he had made some inquiries and understood that the money funding our program came from the New York State Office of Mental Health. Under these circumstances he couldn't accept the apartment because it would put him in a conflict of interest with the lawsuit he was building against the State."

Tsemberis asked if Mr. Lee would consider accepting the place not as an apartment but simply a place to serve as an office space for all the papers he was carrying around, and he agreed. So Pathways furnished the apartment like a law office—file cabinets and desk along with a convertible couch. Mr. Lee lived there for several years until he finally made contact with his family, who took him back to Pennsylvania.

"This example demonstrates the way you have to think if you hope to meet people on their own terms," he says.

At one point Tsemberis had been asking his Pathways clients how the program had changed their lives. Many said that now they could rest, they could dream again, they could have their own thoughts for the first time without having to worry so much about their survival. But when he asked Marvin, a very spiritual individual, if he sensed himself changed when he got a home of his own, Tsemberis got an unusual answer.

"He said, 'It's like the path of the sun: in the morning it's low in the sky, at noon it's high overhead but seems smaller, and then in the afternoon it's large in the west. But isn't it the same sun?' That tells me that homelessness is a transient condition. People are who they are and sometimes they are homeless and sometimes not, but let's not treat them differently because they are in one condition at one point in time."

After ten years serving the homeless mentally ill, there are two issues that continue to drive Tsemberis. First is the agency's mission to serve people who are still living on the streets: how many apartments can he find, what grants can he get, and how can he ensure that his growing staff share the agency's radically client-driven approach. But more importantly, he struggles with how to change people's minds about what mental illness means and the true capabilities of people in that condition.

Tsemberis has found that it's difficult to find mental-health professionals to do the work of Pathways. There's a tremendous amount of risk-taking and authenticity required for the job. They can't play it safe like in an office setting— they're not behind a desk, they're not controlling the situation, and they're not selecting their clients. And most professionals don't want to spend 80 percent of their time going out to visit their clients in their communities. So it's not an easy sell. But the fact that his approach works better than any alternative is incontrovertible.

"If we can change mind-sets we can begin to create programs like this one all over the place," he says. "People have been trained in the traditional system and it's very hard for them to believe you can practice your craft in a different, more useful, and more rewarding way.

"I'm not pushing them into anything," he says of the people he is committed to serve. "I'm letting them pull me. Our slogan is Love, Respect, and Creating Possibilities. It is in that spirit that our services exist. It's compassionate, it's pragmatic, and it's about creating an environment where people are free to pursue their dreams."

· · ·

This story first appeared in the May/June 2003 edition of *DESIGNER/builder* magazine.

Detail of *Victims' Journey*, 3065 Germantown Avenue, Philadelphia.
(*Healing Walls: Victims' Journey*, © 2004 City of Philadelphia
Mural Arts Program. Designed by Cesar Viveros &
Parris Stancell. Photo © Jack Ramsdale)

JANE GOLDEN

WRITINGS ON THE HEALING WALLS

WHILE I ALWAYS SAW MYSELF AS A VERY TOLERANT PERSON, I WAS nonetheless judgmental toward people in prison. Every time I read an article about a terrible crime I would think, "When that person gets caught, they should receive the maximum sentence." If I heard about someone committing a crime after being released from prison, I thought, "Why were they let out?" When I thought about murders that were particularly brutal, I felt that the perpetrators should be executed. It was very simple in my mind—there was no justice for someone who took a life. I had never thought about prison, life after prison, or what led a person down the path to prison.

It did not seem logical to me that I harbored this kind of stern judgment. I was not a stranger to this world of criminals. As director of the Philadelphia Mural Arts Program and the Anti-Graffiti Network for twenty years, I had worked with young people at risk. The vast majority of my work was in neighborhoods decimated by crime and violence. I had worked with many kids who had been involved in crime, ranging from petty to serious. This had been my life's work; why had I not seen a connection between these kids and people in prison? Is societal stigma about prisoners so deep that even socially minded people, like me, cannot sympathize with adults who have come from troubled backgrounds?

I received a call in the spring of 2001 that changed the way I see the world. Will Ursprung, an art therapist at the Pennsylvania State Correctional Institution at Graterford, invited me to the institution to give a talk. Graterford is the sixth-largest maximum security prison in the country. It has the reputation of being a tough place—I thought of it as foreboding. There were serious criminals there—people I had read about, people I had judged.

I thought about Will's request for several weeks before I called him back.

Graterford was far away … it was scary … I was busy. Eventually, I agreed to go. The night of the talk I drove out to Graterford with my colleague Ariel Bierbaum. It was raining hard, lightning was illuminating the sky, and thunder rumbled all around us. To make matters worse, we got lost several times. These were not good signs. By the time we arrived we were ready to leave. Yet we did not turn around—we met Will out front, shook his hand, and proceeded through the front door. We were processed by the guards and followed Will down what seemed like an endless corridor.

There were thirty men in the class seated in a circle. With much trepidation, we began our talk. When we were finished, there was an awkward silence and then came the questions—good questions. They were followed by something I was not expecting: appreciation. They thanked us for our passion, our enthusiasm, and for our commitment to kids. They told us repeatedly, "If I'd had an Anti-Graffiti Network or a Mural Arts Program, I might not be sitting here today."

I thanked the men, and as I headed for the door they responded by asking me when I was coming back. This led me to agree to do a mural in the prison. At first, I told my staff and the men that it would be a six-week project. After about twenty-four sessions I began to stop counting. I am not exactly sure why I kept going back to the prison, but I did.

In the beginning, the class was not easy. We met in a hot room, and some of the men were suspicious. I could not figure out the system—how to get on "gate memos" or how to get art supplies approved. Guards searched our bags, they opened our paint; everything was mysterious. To get into the prison, I had to check in with the guard, get my hand stamped, go through a metal detector, and walk down the long main corridor. Everything about the prison was stressful.

We persisted. Eventually the men in the class—assisted by my colleagues Kristen Goddard and Gyan Samara—created a mural in the auditorium. We went on to paint several other indoor murals. By this point, I was noticing changes in the class. I could see the impact that mural painting had on the men. Conflicts were diminishing; men who had mistrusted each other seemed to bond. Instead of talking about the streets, there was talk about saving kids' lives. We also saw first-hand how the murals affected not just the inmates, but their families as well. Some men encouraged their young relatives to sign up for our after-school programs; others urged their family members to attend our events or request a mural in their neighborhood. While these changes were unraveling, something very personal was happening to me as well. I started to see the men as human, as people with talent and intelligence. I noticed that if given a chance, these men could be productive. Was this wrong? Was I being duped? It did not seem so. Their efforts seemed sincere.

Art seemed to be having an impact. What I find so interesting about art is that

Inmates' Journey, 3049 Germantown Avenue, Philadelphia. (*Healing Walls: Inmates' Journey,* © 2004 City of Philadelphia Mural Arts Program. Designed by Cesar Viveros & Parris Stancell. Photo © Jack Ramsdale)

it sometimes flourishes in the bleakest settings. People can be inspired to create by an incredible feeling of powerlessness. If these men could face their demons, their struggles, and their pain; if they could attempt to articulate remorse, and make themselves vulnerable and empathic, could this be bad? In my mind, it was not. Redemption can, in some cases, be possible. It may not always happen, but the potential exists.

When I started working at Anti-Graffiti in 1984, many young men told me that they expected to be dead or in jail by the time they were twenty-five. I began to imagine the men in my class as these children, and imagine the young people in our after-school program as adults. There were so many connections I had not initially seen; now I noticed them everywhere.

As we were painting the indoor mural, the men in the class told me repeatedly that they wanted to give back to the community. I concluded that the next step of this unfolding journey would be to challenge the men to design and paint an outdoor mural. That was the beginning of the Healing Walls project.

We selected a neighborhood in North Philadelphia that many of the men in the class had come from and had helped to destroy. We found empty walls, and we began to hold meetings with all of the stakeholders. Barb Toews of the

Pennsylvania Prison Society joined the team to advise us and introduce us to those on the other side of the issue: victim advocates and those who had lost loved ones. The murals were to serve as a bridge between victims, offenders, and the community at large.

We held meetings at the prison between victim advocates and inmates. We created two mural designs: one from the viewpoint of offenders depicting the journey toward rehabilitation and reconciliation, the other from the perspective of victims of crime and their families focusing on the journey toward healing. Over one hundred inmates, victims, and victim advocates participated in the creation of these murals. Once the two murals were completed, I drove by Germantown and Glenwood and parked my car and got out to get a closer look. As I stood there, someone came up to me and asked, "Are you the person I should thank for these murals?" "No," I said, "not me. Thank all the participants that came out to the prison, the men who are in my class at the prison, and the community members who agreed to be involved in a difficult and risky project."

The majority of the murals were painted by the men in the prison on panels of poly-tab "parachute" cloth. Once-a-month paint days were held at the prison where victims and victims' advocates were invited to participate in morning discussion groups, which were followed by afternoon paint sessions. Additional community paint days were held both at the Mural Arts Program's headquarters at the Thomas Eakins House and at neighborhood churches. The sessions resembled quilting bees, where the participants began by focusing on the task at hand but gradually began to talk with one another about their personal experiences.

At some point over the previous year, while we were working at Graterford, I decided that our organization needed to play an active role in facilitating discussions about the impact and consequences of crime. We would then transform this dialogue into action. After working in neighborhoods where many men have been killed or incarcerated, with kids who have fallen through the cracks, and with prisoners, I was determined to bring a closeted issue out of the shadows and into the public eye. In our society today, we rarely reflect, in a conscious manner, on the broader consequences of crime. We do not think about the loss of human potential or the cost in tax dollars or the long-term effects on public safety. The Healing Walls project could create such dialogue.

We hope to use public art to facilitate a dialogue about the impact of crime among people who, because of socio-economic and geographic differences, rarely interact. We are trying to raise awareness about the current criminal justice system, its implications and true costs. We are also creating art involving people with diverse experiences.

Murals are perfect vehicles to explore this terrain; they are big, bold paintings that reside in our communities. They speak to our past, our heroes, and our

Victims' Journey, 3065 Germantown Avenue, Philadelphia. (*Healing Walls: Victims' Journey*, © 2004 City of Philadelphia Mural Arts Program. Designed by Cesar Viveros & Parris Stancell. Photo © Jack Ramsdale)

dreams. Murals in this city have come to be a part of the phenomenon of hope and transformation, of seizing change from the jaws of defeat. They are about taking rubble and debris and turning spots of turmoil and blight into places that people stop and admire. Murals are done by the community, for the community. They document the community's journey.

What started out as a single lecture has turned into a formal part of the Mural Arts Program. Now the program at Graterford is a formal work program; the men in the class are paid to create murals for schools all over the city. Although their pay is only 51 cents an hour, they paint with dedication and drive.

In addition, we are continuing our Healing Walls project. Now we are working with young people in detention, the men at Graterford, and a community group in Lower Kensington to design and paint a mural about Balanced and Restored Justice. We know these special projects are not easy—they are difficult and challenging. The original project had moments of tension and conflict. But in the end the spectrum of opinions, ideas, and voices was heard, respected, and used as the backbone of the murals' design.

While working in Philadelphia's neighborhoods, I have met women who have one child who is dead and another who is in prison. These mothers understand the deep sadness wrought by a society that cares little for education and promotes incarceration. The sadness in their eyes helps drive our work. We at the Mural Arts Program stress that we work with the community. For us, "community" means everyone, including not only children and families but also adults who are incarcerated.

Working at Graterford has given me hope. I hope that we can learn how to save children's lives. I hope that rehabilitation can occur. I hope that communities will be safer because the men and women getting out of prison may have been changed. What I see through my work is that human repair seems to be taking place. This happens in spite of widespread cynicism. I have changed how I think about prisoners, and how I see the problems of crime and violence. We can break the cycle of violence. But first we need to see the connections between our kids, our prisons, and our society. It is all too easy to blame the men in the prison or to blame the prisons themselves. The real truth is far more complex. The many broken lives we find in prison were not created there, but instead were created by communities and neighborhoods long forgotten by the politicians of this nation.

My journey in my work with the City of Philadelphia has taken me into prisons and then back out into neighborhoods that suffer from substandard housing, high rates of violence, and poor schools. In the vacuum that is created, prisons step in. What I did not know before our work at Graterford is that we need to work with everyone impacted by crime. Healing this world is a common task. Breaking the cycle of poverty and violence is a task that belongs to all of us. There is much work to be done. Please join us in our efforts. We can no longer close our eyes to the violence that plagues our streets—it costs us too much as a society not to care.

• • •

This story first appeared in the September/October 2006 edition of *DESIGNER/builder* magazine.

Patricia Moore disguised as a middle-income woman
with moderate mobility and normative aging.
(Photo by Bruce Byers, courtesy of Patricia Moore)

KINGSLEY HAMMETT

DISGUISE

GOING UNDERCOVER TO EXPERIENCE LIFE AS AN ELDER

AS A CHILD GROWING UP IN BUFFALO, NEW YORK, INDUSTRIAL DESIGNER/ graphic designer/gerontologist/sociologist Patricia Moore gave hints early on that she was destined for a career helping the handicapped and the elderly. One day, when she was just starting to walk, she left her mother's hand to toddle over to a smiling woman in a wheelchair. As her mother recalls the encounter, she reached out to gently stroke the woman's leg and, with a very intent look in her eyes, asked what was wrong.

"Nothing," the woman said through her tears. "I just didn't feel like walking today," and the two rode off around the store.

Since that encounter more than forty years ago, Moore has carved out a leadership role in the world of universal design that goes far beyond ramps and wide doors. She has devoted her professional life to understanding what makes people so afraid of growing old and what the design world can do to ease that inevitable transition.

"I recognized back in the 1970s that designers would become the anthropologists of our time," she says. "And in taking responsibility as that gatekeeper, designers would have to become versed in a number of different languages and disciplines. We would have to understand the lifestyles of others without making judgments. And I think architects and designers have to recognize that it's not so much their own dreams and visions that are consequential to end users, but rather what they can do to understand the lifestyles of people in order to make a difference by design."

When you are Superman riding in a horse race one minute and a quadriplegic the next, she says of Christopher Reeve, the architect you call in to help is no longer designing a house for a superstar. Now he's responsible for this person's life and the life of his family, which will be profoundly affected by the design solutions the architect develops. His challenge is to give that client increased capacity and open pathways rather than create roadblocks.

Moore was raised with her grandparents in her home in Buffalo. At seventeen she went off to college at Rochester Institute of Technology, where she experienced a world of design made up of "them" and "us" in which it was acceptable to exclude certain people. If, for example, an older person could not utilize a certain household appliance, her fellow student-designers felt comfortable in saying, "If Grandma can't use it, then she's broken. I still can, so it's a good product."

"That audacity and arrogance found its way into the built environment where it was assumed that just because someone couldn't ambulate by putting one foot in front of the other, then it was reasonable to say, 'Well, this domain is not for them,'" she says.

Moore found that attitude unacceptable and began to push for more barrier-free products. She found support among those who, in the aftermath of the Vietnam War, saw that the country could no longer accept barriers in the built environment and forced the barrier-free movement to become a feature in architecture. She wanted to see more integration among architecture, product design, and graphic communication design—menus, highway and airport signage, instructions that come with appliances—any material, iconic or verbal, that gives users direction, be it in self-care and health, entertainment, or travel.

"We need a multidisciplinary approach to all design solutions," she says. "For example, the architect focuses on designing the edifice called home. The product designer focuses on filling it with furnishings, appliances, entertainment, and communications features. And the graphic designer somehow communicates with the TV guide and the instruction manual and the keypad on the security system. When all three are doing all this in not necessarily disparate but not very homogeneous ways, it's no wonder the end user, the consumer, is left adrift, trying to make sense out of three basic languages."

If the users cannot translate those languages successfully, then their independence and quality of life are in jeopardy. Yet designers often respond arrogantly that if someone is too old or too sick or too unable, then that's his problem. "Normal" people, "regular" people, "real" consumers can manage all that complexity; therefore there is no design flaw.

Good design looks at the life-span needs of the consumer, Moore says, including all members of a family, from babies up to great-grandparents. We want communities that appreciate the presence of all those diverse individuals and their diverse capacities, whether they be related to normal aging, birth anomaly, injury, or illness. But when traditional designers design for the typical seven-year-old they see him playing soccer, reading, and playing computer games. The child who is blind or without legs, however, is automatically eliminated as a child-consumer.

"I've been telling the collective design community that we ought to be looking at that child as part of our scenario and not exclude them," Moore says. "And that when we build features into an environment on all levels—the structure itself, the products within it, and all the information-communication vehicles—and accommodate that handicapped child, then we've probably benefited people in late life and anyone else who has limited capacity. That's what universality is all about—the recognition that we have coexistence of all abilities and all ages and that the product relationship is such that we have to meet the needs of all those people as equals."

It's often erroneously assumed that Moore operates out of Phoenix because it must be a hotbed of great ideas and applications. But sadly what she finds is a wealthy elder population that forms the leading edge of what she terms the "denial of aging," a movement that follows the dictum "nip it, tuck it, liposuc it."

"As long as all 76 million of us baby boomers embrace that sensibility as graceful aging, it's no wonder we're not coming up with great ideas about design," she says. "To me it's akin to a very Hitlerian attitude that says you are somehow better, more acceptable, more lovable, more beautiful, more handsome if you are convinced to cut up your body and reshape it into someone else's image of acceptability. We know we can cure this aging thing! But we're worshiping all the wrong aspects of life. I have a real problem with that."

Every day Moore hears horror stories from people who were hurt or knew someone who got hurt trying to navigate the world most people take for granted. In one letter she received, a son told the story of his father, who was leaning down over a kitchen counter, using a knife to open a box of cookies. The knife slipped and the man lost an eye.

"Too many people respond, 'Well, if he didn't have the physical capacity to open the package then he shouldn't have tried.' But it was the package designer who failed to consider this man's vision level, strength level, coordination level. If it had been a child of five everybody would have been screaming. But because it was an elder we have the added prejudice that he was too old and therefore shouldn't have been trying to get himself a snack."

After graduating from college in 1976, Moore moved to New York City and took a job as a product designer with the international firm formed by Raymond Loewy, the father of industrial design. She was the only woman on a staff of 350 and soon became frustrated, watching as architects and designers used their creativity on behalf of society's most able, beautiful, and wealthy. Her interest was to understand product design in relationship to how the human body moved and functioned, something that excited the medical professors in her master's program in biomechanics at the Rusk Institute at New York University. But such an approach left her fellow product designers scratching their heads. If we're not designing for all the others, she asked repeatedly, then who is? She wanted to come up with a way to design a refrigerator, for example, that might have a foot pedal or a quick release on the door that would permit someone small or frail or with full arms to open it with no hands. Her supervisor looked at her and said in all seriousness, "Pattie, we don't design for those people."

To see what "those people" needed, Moore developed a three-year research project for her work towards her third degree, this one in social gerontology at Columbia University. Ten days after meeting Barbara Kelly, makeup designer for NBC's *Saturday Night Live*, the twenty-six-year-old Moore was on an airplane disguised as an eighty-five-year-old woman on her way to Ohio State University for a conference of architects examining how to meet the needs of elders. All her capacities had been altered with cinches and splints, and she couldn't see, hear, or move very well.

To keep her research pure and avoid any entrapment, she wasn't allowed to initiate conversations. She could only respond and let the encounter build from there. Over the next three years she traveled to more than 100 cities and sought answers to the question of why this is a racist society, a society with gender bias, and one with all kinds of intolerance. "Above all else," she says, "I wanted to know what was making us ageist, because ageism embodies all of those prejudices."

She was surprised at Ohio State to see how rude everyone was to her. Despite wearing a name tag that said "Pat Moore, Columbia University," no one even noticed she was there. As she approached the conference hall, someone holding a door for others let it swing in her face.

"What was most irritating is that these were the very people who were at the conference to say we want to design better housing for our elders," she says. "'Physician, heal thyself.' The practitioners who claim to be addressing all these issues are the worst offenders. All the end users just become statistics and people forget to look into their hearts and minds. Unfortunately, the people we need the most are failing us due to their prejudices."

Moore came out of her disguise on the second day of the conference and the whole tenor of the gathering changed to "Shame on us!" What her colleagues learned was that they didn't know their constituency because they were afraid to get near them. They were not comfortable enough to live what their would-be clients face every day. She forced them to look inward and ask why they were so fearful of tomorrow and how they could possibly do a good job today.

"Nobody wants to be in that form," she says of the elderly and frail. "But until as a society and culture we can embrace all forms, all features, and all people as equal, we will not be doing our best work."

Between May of 1979 and October of 1982, while Moore crisscrossed the country designing jet aircraft, she traveled to 116 cities in a range of disguises. She would spend one day of each trip posing as one of nine different characters in three separate categories of the aging woman: the homeless bag lady, the middle-income woman, and the very wealthy society matron. Within each category she portrayed three levels of health, from being wheelchair-bound to walking freely.

"I didn't try to pose as a different race," she says, "but I knew the guy who saw an old woman and let the door swing in her face was the same guy who would

Patricia Moore disguised as a middle-income aging woman.
(Photo by Bruce Byers, courtesy of Patricia Moore)

see a black person and say, 'She doesn't belong here,' and let that door go. People would be happy to say they had black friends if they were Bill Cosby and Michael Jordan. But would they say the same about the guy down the street pumping gas? Probably not. This is sadly where we're at."

Every day people go about their business in a world that demands they have the physicality and cognitive ability to bathe, feed, and dress themselves and go off to work or play under their own power. Yet some need to wrestle with the complexity of a wheelchair, while others face the demands of getting six kids off to school. Design is the only thing that can level the playing field.

"When we don't have the means by which to easily and safely do these things," Moore says, "we have been robbed of an opportunity for a helpmate that makes sense. And those helpmates will be products and environments that embrace us prosthetically and make us able. People don't need to be reminded of what they can't do. I would rather look at this from a proactive side that asks, What is a person's ability level, what are their capacities, and how can I enhance and embellish those so they can do the most for themselves?"

Everything about the home environment that is static can interface with us tragically, she says. Why not a refrigerator that senses our presence and with a slight touch of our palm slowly swings open? We need smart technologies in the home, like the faucet in an airport restroom that opens when you pass your hands underneath it. We want homes that are intuitive, with a front door that will speak to us when we approach it, recognize us, and open automatically.

"With fixed solutions in our homes, the interface fails," she says. "I ask people to imagine Captain Kirk and Spock coming

Patricia Moore as herself.
(Photo by Helen Marcus,
courtesy of Patricia Moore)

up to a door that has a round handle they have to fiddle with. We should be going in our future to where the *Enterprise* has already gone."

Standing in the way of such progress are professional associations that want to make sure the American economy doesn't render obsolete certain items, like hard-to-open tin cans, and replace them with more convenient packaging. In Moore's experience, too many ideation design meetings that are supposed to come up with new concepts are loaded with like-minded people who don't stop to consider people who are different from themselves.

"When I'm invited to come into a company on a project, I put together a design team that is made up of non-designers," Moore says. "That's where all the best ideas come from. My clients are always amazed at the quality of the outcome, but for me clearly it's because we invited everyone to the party."

In her travels in disguise Moore encountered every walk of life, every job description, and every consumer relationship that offered situations that ranged from abysmal to glorious. There was no area that was all bad, nor was there any one that escaped criticism. Even when visiting churches she found people's antennae went up at the sight of a stranger.

"You had to establish your credentials, you had to identify yourself," she says. "We have created a world where nobody is automatically embraced any longer."

Through it all she tried to tease out any distinctions, any correlates that might explain why we have ageism. What became most obvious is that people are defined by their presence or absence of money. At the low end of the scale, the poor and infirm either draw out someone's charitable nature or cause him to turn his back on someone who is not their kind. When sitting as a bag lady in a doorway watching the world go by, she met people who would go down to the deli on the next corner and come back with a bagel and cup of tea. One day a man in an Armani suit on his way to work paused to give her a ten-dollar bill. But sometimes she would pass whole days when nobody addressed her, touched her, or even smiled, leaving her either very angry or sad and withdrawn.

"Colleagues who are handicapped, particularly those who travel a lot, tell me that people put themselves out roughly half the time," she says. "Unfortunately, it's not higher. People are so unsure as to what is appropriate that they often err on the side of doing nothing."

Above all, Moore found a strong fear of tomorrow. The assumption of most folks is that the future holds nothing but bad: we're going to be less attractive, less rich, less able, and therefore less individual. We know all too well what this culture celebrates and worships and that's why we're afraid. And that's why baby boomers walk around with platinum American Express cards, strong investment portfolios, and teams of good doctors, determined not to become like their grandmothers.

"That is not graceful aging," she says. "What troubles me as a designer on the business side is that we have robbed ourselves of precious time and resources in getting ready for tomorrow. Generations X and Y, which are tiny compared to the baby boomers, are going to have to bear the load of their parents and grandparents who have not come up with good design options, assisted technologies, and remediations that will allow everyone to nest and age in place."

The leading edge of the baby boomers is already in trouble, she says. They are in their mid-fifties and all they can do is brace and hope for the best because there has been no corporate response to the obvious need for universally designed products and homes. Moore is proud to have been on the Smart Design team in the 1980s that came up with Oxo Good Grips. They never identified the line of kitchen utensils, with their large, black, soft rubber handles, as something for "gimps and geezers." Instead they fashioned a beautiful piece of kitchenware that sold itself.

"Incredibly, this has become the icon of universal design," she says. "But we need a little bit more than a good potato peeler. I see the indictment going out simultaneously to architects, designers, planners, builders, city officials, and politicians people rely on to do more than meet the minimum requirements. Design should be about excellence. I see them all as racehorses lined up waiting for some starting gun to begin addressing the pressing needs of diverse populations, and no one is leaving the gate. What are we waiting for?"

• • •

This story first appeared in the July 2000 edition of *DESIGNER/builder* magazine.

Group effort raising beam formwork. (Photo by Byron Baker, courtesy of BASIC Initiative)

KINGSLEY HAMMETT

DESIGN/BUILD PROGRAM BROADENS EXPERIENCE

One challenge facing virtually every architecture education program is how to give students a sense of the real world beyond the classroom. Several schools operate community design centers where students can work with the neighborhood on design issues. But one of the most successful programs—where students can get their hands dirty and learn how buildings actually go together—is the design/build semester the University of Washington offers in Cuernavaca, Mexico. Every winter students spend ten weeks helping Mexicans build schools, libraries, and clinics, gaining valuable practical experience in building, design, and working with clients along with a priceless intercultural experience that many have found life-changing.

The founder and co-director of the program (along with Steve Badanes) is Sergio Palleroni. He grew up in Patagonia, in southern Argentina, did his undergraduate work at the University of Oregon, and earned a master's degree in architecture at MIT. From 1981 to 1984 he worked for the Nicaraguan Ministry of Culture during the administration of the Sandinistas, an experience that sparked his interest in the creation of architecture as a cultural process.

NICARAGUA WAS TRYING TO RECOVER A HISTORY THAT HAD BEEN denied a long time through the colonial process when the country had essentially become one giant agricultural state for General Somosa. There remained very little sense of the past except for the official history. The Sandinistas were trying to give people a sense that there was a lot to be proud of. They started poetry and music festivals and promoted local artists. My job was to build museums with communities and to celebrate local events that were important. For instance, we built one where Sandino was born, which became a community center as well as a museum. These facilities couldn't just be places to store artifacts;

they had to be places where people could meet and talk about their history and have cultural events.

We began building a museum of colonial history right on the border between Costa Rica and Nicaragua. But it was never finished because by then we were right in the battle zone. So we moved north onto the agricultural plain to create a museum near León, which is one of the two traditional capitals of Nicaragua. León is a site where a very early settlement by the Spanish had been destroyed, much like the city of Pompeii. The people wanted to build a museum of the early colonization and talk about the political history of Nicaragua. We worked there for three or four years, and the work raised several issues that led me to return to school to see if I could figure out some of the answers. I needed to know what the early cities meant, why they were so highly ordered, and to understand the policies of the Spanish government and the Church toward the indigenous people.

Palleroni returned to MIT to get a research master's degree in history, theory, and criticism, which was in fact a license to study anything he wanted around architectural and urban issues. His studies eventually took him to Spain to work on the history of the colonization of Latin America and to understand how a uniform policy had been applied to every country in Latin America. The Spanish government, after hundreds of years, was opening the archives in Seville, where he spent two years poring over ancient documents. He was interested in exploring the many issues, both moral and cultural, that arise when one country decides to take over another people, and how those issues are resolved. He wanted to find out who made those decisions and what ethical issues they encountered. What were the conquered people like? Were they like the conquerors? Was it right to colonize them? In 1985, shortly after he returned to Cambridge, Mexico was struck by a massive earthquake.

One of my professors at MIT had an offer to go down and consult on the reconstruction. I went down the next year in what was called Phase Two, a period following the initial shock and immediate rebuilding, when the government began to ask, "Could this be more organized?" They gave out jobs to different architectural firms and hired consultants to come in and help them out. We were hired as consultants to help two architectural firms deal with standardization of housing and how such standards might be applied.

One of the firms I worked with was headed by a man named Carlos Mijares, an extraordinary architect who had been working in the villages all over the countryside, and especially in the State of Michoacán, northwest of Mexico City. He had been working with indigenous communities and individual craftsmen, building churches and cultural centers and trying to recapture their historical cultural memory. He had been looking at issues similar to the ones we had faced in Nicaragua, specifically the proposals drafted by Bartolomé de Las Casas, the first archbishop of Mexico, for chapels that would address the native needs.

When I went down to Mexico I rediscovered architecture. It just blew me away the way Carlos was working so closely with communities and the craftsmen themselves. He was looking at brick, the simplest material, which in Mexico is like a work of art because it's handmade and semi-irregular. Every region has its own version. And since it's modular, brick has a lot of architectural possibilities. Carlos was looking to see, beyond the barrel vaults with concrete and brick that they do now, what other things could be done with brick that had to do with the cultural ideas that Bartolomé de Las Casas had outlined. He was trying to build these open-air chapels that de Las Casas had proposed, where native people worshiped under the open sky because that was significant to them. And it had to be a public meeting space as opposed to a normal Catholic church. I was interested in the way Carlos made the connection between culture and architecture. Eventually I became his partner and published a book on his work.

> Palleroni was invited back to the University of Oregon to teach a studio, and for a while he commuted between Mexico City and Eugene. While teaching that studio in 1989 the idea of the design/build program emerged. After showing his students slides and giving a lecture on the work he and Mijares had been doing in Mexico, several of them said they wanted to go down and participate. He explained that all fieldwork in Mexico was donated, so there would be little that would be like their future careers in the United States. He also explained that architecture in Mexico is held in the highest esteem among all the professions. Consequently, architects enjoy a high level of respect and a great deal of mobility to move among villages where the people feel architects can help find solutions, as opposed to working in the United States, where there's always a doubt about the architect's role.

As I talked about this they got all excited and said, "No, no, we want to go." At the time I was working on a library in a little village and I told them they could come down and help work with the local craftsman. That was the first design/build program we did. We didn't have any expectations that the class would finish the project at that time. But they organized themselves and made the trip, which surprised me because I wasn't sure they would show up. We went through the design and met with the community and started to understand what the people needed, not just in terms of building but what their lifestyle was like.

From the very beginning we were engaged in some of the cultural studies that I had been working on since Nicaragua. We talked to the community about the way they lived and what they thought and what their daily cycle was about. We had them do these cognitive maps—drawings people created in groups—about what happened during the day and where they stopped and who they talked to—anything that happened that was significant to them. In that way we began to figure out where the library fit into this mental map of what was significant in the village. It helped the students understand the place of the library, and it also helped the community feel like people were listening to them. The mapping and the conversations created a kind of bridge of understanding.

The Mexicans of course are master builders, so as they helped the students there they developed a reciprocal relationship where each was learning from the other, which is one thing that I realized right away that was important. After the studio ended the villagers finished the project in their traditional way. But I realized that the students had made a big impression on the community. The villagers remembered them very well, and the students had played an important role in the acceptance of the building.

In 1993, when I moved to Seattle, I brought the work/study model with me to the University of Washington. By then the model had evolved further. The design/build part was still in its early stages in the sense that we hadn't figured out how to get a studio group to build a significant building in an academic semester. But what was evolving by then were questions of what ideas do you expose the students to, how do you integrate them into the society, how do you interview the communities, how do you get them to feel like they are companions in building this project together, and how do you get them involved in this cultural exchange that's so significant to both cultures? To accomplish this the cognitive mapping that I'd been doing in my own practice became more and more involved.

We found accommodations right in the heart of Cuernavaca, and we started working in a squatter community. We felt that rather than working in the indigenous villages, which are more intact, it would be better to work within the contemporary conditions of Mexico, where the current economic situation is displacing people, thanks mainly to the United States. The free market is pushing people around, and a lot of campesinos are leaving the rural areas and coming to the cities because they can't make a living through farming the way they have for thousands of years. Native villages are centered on traditional crops, family, religion, community organization, and a distinct way of life. When the peasants are forced to move to the city, they have to leave all of that behind. The question was, could we help them in that transition, could we help people find not only a decent way of living in the city, but also help them retain a sense that who they are is okay and still significant?

Sergio Palleroni discussing the Zapata School project with neighbors and volunteers.
(Photo by Terry Wild Studio, courtesy of BASIC Initiative)

Palleroni and his students began to work with very impoverished communities around the Cuernavaca industrial center. The residents live on the margins in a giant squatter community of close to 800,000 people who suffer all the problems of extreme poverty. They don't have social services. They don't have any infrastructure. They don't have health services or educational facilities.

Years ago we restructured the design/build program to use it as an opportunity for American students to better understand the condition of the Mexicans while giving them an opportunity to build the kind of infrastructure—schools, community centers, medical facilities—that the squatters normally can't build. You can squat your own home, because Article 27 of the 1910 Constitution gives people the right to occupy land that's not being used. But there's no mechanism, even within squatting, for producing public buildings.

So we started working with a couple of communities that needed a school, because schools are the heart of any community. The first thing Mexicans want, after they squat their own land, is to build a school. They want to make sure their kids are better off than they are. Building a school also puts them in the middle of the political process and makes their presence known. So we thought we could bring resources to build a school, introduce some new ideas of sustainability into that school, and at the same time have our students learn from the Mexicans about how to build and how building is a cultural activity.

In Mexico the whole community gets involved in building, and as they build, they build an identity as a community. They get to know each other, they exchange ideas, they learn what each can give to it, and they build social capital and a very strong social fabric that establishes a kind of resource bank for very poor communities. Social capital is one of the most important resources that gets built in these squatter communities. If they build a road, the act of building the road together creates the social bonds of the community. I wanted my students to learn about that aspect of Mexico and how poverty finds resources to build communities.

The University of Washington students are immersed in Mexican community culture by documenting the way people live. They get the adults to write about their community and the children to draw maps and sketches of what happens on their way to school—where they meet, what they find significant in the fabric of that area. They do the same with every social group they can identify and ask them to make maps of their visions of the community that detail the things they do along the way as they go about their daily activities.

We started handing out disposable cameras, getting people together for giant parties to do drawings, and it was fabulous. They did beautiful maps. After we compiled all this information, we were able to figure out that even though one street was bigger, this other one was more significant to them, and that there was a path that went beside the school that was very significant to the community and thus an element to retain. We learned a lot about how they saw the site as opposed to how we saw it as outsiders.

So the first step in the design/build studio is identifying all the things that should be considered in the design process. The Mexicans have a very strong sense of ritual. They look at a site very differently than we do, and are keenly aware of historical, physical, and cultural facts that create their landscape. We try to bring the students in tune with things that might be of importance to the Mexican landscape while at the same time teaching the Americans something about a different way of constructing architecture. It's an educational process as well as an exercise in getting in tune with your clients.

The language barrier is always a problem, but we don't use translators. Maybe 25 to 35 percent of the students speak Spanish and they pre-select themselves in a way. I put them out in the middle of the squatter community, and after they are there for a while, working fourteen, sixteen hours a day, everyone learns to communicate.

At the same time, Mexicans are amazing about reaching out to people. I had a project doing some housing in Chiapas in an area where they spoke a Mayan dialect that we couldn't understand. So drawing, which is supposed to be a fundamental act in architecture, and the cognitive maps became the means of communication. It's more important, of course, to have language because it's such a complex communications tool. But sometimes you can do a lot of important exchange through drawing and other means of communication.

Once you put the students in this mix they quickly realize that not everybody speaks English, and that if they are going to get the project done they are going to have to force themselves to reach out. And when they come back home, they always cite that experience of reaching out to the people as the most significant thing that happened to them.

My number-one priority is the educational experience that happens in both directions, for the Mexicans as well as the American students. By putting themselves in a position that is not in their normal realm of experience, and doing something that they would normally not be engaged in, the students have stepped out of their normal circumstances and must reevaluate where they are. That creates a change in them. I put them in places of poverty where they don't see the view of Mexico one traditionally sees, and they return with a different view of Mexico, a different view of architecture, a different experience of architecture as a kind of cultural/political/social act. And a significant number of them have followed up and set up their own design/build firms.

But that's not really the point. The point is this: when they go back to school, maybe they view the human subject that's involved in the design process very differently, and maybe they have a different idea of what Mexico is. I look with pride when we're back in the United States and somebody says something which is culturally inaccurate about Mexico, and the students will say "No, no, no, the Mexicans are the hardest-working people on earth." They also understand the Mexicans as complex individuals with this incredibly rich history behind them.

As Americans, we never go to Mexico thinking that we're next door to an Egypt, you know. Yet it's one of the most ancient cultures with some of the great achievements of human history. They have the most extraordinary kind of understanding of the cosmos and mathematics. But you also have to pay tribute to the Mexicans when you walk into the greengrocer's part of your supermarket. Here is a culture that built an entire religious and cultural understanding of the world on the basis of the agricultural miracles they were performing in the landscape. The students get that by the end.

Six days every week the design/build students commute via public transportation to work a long day at the site. Their home base is a campus in the center of Cuernavaca with dormitories and studios built around the principles Palleroni has tried to instill. They capture their own water, treat it three times, and use it for bathing and washing.

Design charrette in the treetops studio at the program facility in Mexico.
(Photo by Jared Polesky, courtesy of BASIC Initiative)

Steve Badanes, my co-director, and I just kind of literally designed it on a napkin, but it turned out much better than we imagined napkin architecture would ever turn out. We had a piece of land that was left over in the middle of a lot that was given to us that's about 20,000 square feet. We've built a garden that surrounds two blocks of buildings, which are two stories, and then on the third story of one of the buildings we have a giant loft studio space up in the branches of these trees. It's open to air circulation, is solar heated, and has all these roofs that capture the rainwater. If you stripped the gardens away, you'd realize there is this incredibly complex set of biodigesters and water-processing catch basins, etc. The water gets used three times over and eventually becomes the irrigation for the gardens.

It's very nice construction and we built it for $14 a square foot. The University helped us some. The Kellogg Foundation helped us. It's two-and-a-half blocks from the Zócalo, on Calle Leyva. At nine o'clock at night, when we finally let the students go, they have a chance to have beers and decompress. You've got to have some time for them to hang out and relax. They need time to reflect and not feel like they're being brainwashed.

Every student works five days a week, and because we stagger the schedule, we're on the site six days a week. Everybody's there on Sunday, to show respect for the Mexicans' communal workday and to make sure that we're involved with the community. Sundays they have a big meal in the middle of the day, which is the way they celebrate coming together to build their communities. So it's not just an act of building. It's also a cultural act that says we are a community. It's identity-building, both for the Mexicans and also for my students, who begin to feel like part of the community and are becoming architects for the first time.

Then everyone gets one day off where they can do anything they like. On the other free day, usually a Thursday, we take a cultural trip. We might go to Mexico City to the theater or the museums, or to an archaeological site. We make these short, one-day excursions to do things and expose them to ideas.

We also take two trips during the quarter. One is a three-day trip, usually to Oaxaca, where my brother's been working on the museum, or to Michoacán to show them the work we used to do up in the highlands. At the very end I take them for ten days on a bus tour through Mexico to get to know other communities.

For the first three years working in the industrial quarter of Cuernavaca, the students built a school that also served as a cultural center for three different colonias. It is built around an open plaza, which they didn't have, and it has a kiosk and music area where people get married and enjoy musical concerts and cultural activities. The school includes a small library for the children of the area and a cistern that is used by several surrounding communities.

Then we helped a group of women who for fourteen years had organized themselves to provide health services, which were absent in the squatter communities. They made an enormous effort to get training in both traditional and modern medicine. But they needed a facility to both provide services and do community education. In two years we built a clinic, which turned out to be like a little hospital, along with an instructional kitchen where people could learn how to incorporate some of the new dietary information. One of the problems the squatters have as they switch to the city is that the foods aren't the same, the waste cycle is not the same, they're totally misplaced, and they become more of a burden than even the traditional urban dweller because they don't even know how the world works in a city. So the women try to teach the new settlers how to survive in the urban environment. They try to incorporate kitchen gardens and show that they can still raise crops. They help people figure out, okay, given what you can get here, how do you give a nutritional meal to your children, how do you do preventative self-care.

Next we built an auditorium so they could have classes and hold large meetings in the community. In many ways the Mexicans are far more progressive than we are. They actually have a really good school program where if a kid is having a problem they look to see if it is linked to his home environment, to his nutrition, or to his ability to learn. Now the medical schools of the University of

Washington and Southern Methodist University are sending residents and doctors down there every year to work in this counseling center to help kids deal with all these issues.

We just finished a school in a very poor community. The first school was for about 360 kids and this one is for 200 kids. It actually has an ecological park for the kids to learn about the local ecology. We convinced them not to pave part of the native flora and fauna, so we have an area that has to do with native plants, edible plants, herbs, etc. They have a program there that we coordinated with the clinic, and when a native herbalist comes, she teaches classes. It is a six-classroom traditional school. The bathrooms in that one and the one before also include biodigesters. There are offices and meeting spaces, and areas for community meetings.

With a ten-and-a-half-week program, a lot is asked of the students who dive into a building project ten days after they arrive. They find that the total cultural immersion happens very quickly. The students start dealing with the clients the first day they arrive, and ten days later they participate in a huge community celebration, bury a pre-Columbian and a Christian god in the first slab poured on the site, and the building process begins.

We try to be sensitive about the materials we build with, but my attitude in all these things is that we should build from materials that are available in the communities. We give them options of different ways to incorporate passive cooling, water catchment, and biodigesters. What I'm really interested in is that the people in the community begin to understand the consequences of some of their acts, which they would have understood in the villages, but don't understand once they move to the city. In a village, everybody is connected to the waste cycle, and if you eat something and it goes through your body, it comes out and gets incorporated into the land, and it's a very conscious act, because the village has survived for thousands of years being aware of it. But when they go to the city they can't translate that consciousness into their new urban life where waste streams are handled by flush toilets and water comes from a tap. They don't understand that misuse of graywaters or black waters in the area has dire consequences for the water resources and everything else. We also try to make them aware of how to filter the water they catch from rain on their roofs, which can provide them with water for most of the year, and ways to filter the waste stream.

In order to ensure that the program has a continuing impact, an office is maintained in Cuernavaca year-round.

You can't just drop out of the sky once a year. So we have an agency called Comunidad, which acts both to find funding for projects and to coordinate the work. Some of the funding comes from Mexico; most of it comes from the United States. In the office we have an anthropologist and sociologist, who work with the community all year long to prepare them for the projects, to do the follow-ups, to see what works, what doesn't work. Otherwise you don't make an impact.

• • •

This story first appeared in the May 2001 edition of *DESIGNER/builder* magazine.

DESIGN/BUILD PROGRAM BROADENS EXPERIENCE

ONE DC Executive Director Dominic T. Moulden pounds the pavement for equitable development in Washington, D.C. (Photo by Gloria Robinson)

DOMINIC MOULDEN

ONE DC

Dominic Moulden is the executive director of ONE DC (Organizing Neighborhood Equity DC), a community organizing effort in the Shaw/U Street area of the nation's capital, a prime downtown location that is facing the challenges of gentrification. The goal of ONE DC is to retain the local population and reduce the displacement that is destroying so many poor and working-class communities around the country.

ONE DC focuses on solutions stemming from an in-depth analysis of race, power, and the economic, political, and social forces at work in the city. It stresses popular education, community organizing, and alternative economic projects. What makes ONE DC unique is its understanding of the incredibly rich and vital resources, especially the people power, that make up its neighborhood, which can be mobilized to strengthen local control and to develop equity. In its literature, ONE DC quotes a Japanese proverb that reminds us that "vision without action is a daydream and action without vision is a nightmare."

WHEN I WAS BORN IN 1961, THE BLACK COMMUNITY IN WEST BALTIMORE had its own theaters and small churches, and several of my uncles owned and operated small shops and convenience stores. As a boy growing up in the housing projects, I absorbed the rich and enduring qualities and values that marked African American life. When we didn't have something, we didn't go to the bank and get in more debt; we didn't go begging to a stranger. We went to our neighbors. With so much grace and dignity people would tell their children to run to so-and-so's house and get whatever was needed. That's a big thing we have lost: the ability to trade with each other on an equal basis. These days what we've gotten tied to is more indebtedness rather than respect.

Another thing we have lost is the "we" concept. All of us have needs and we were just sharing and supporting each other. Before I went to school I had some consciousness of being of African descent and not being a traditional person from the United States, not overly patriotic, not overly convinced capitalism works. I played sports because it was teams, always about the "we." We were always knocking on doors and asking whomever if they wanted to play. All of that is lost. That's why I love organizing so much. It's about knocking on doors and building relationships.

Now we assimilate into the mainstream culture. Children don't do any door-knocking or relationship-building for fun. Now it's about getting out of the neighborhood.

I think there's a deep level of confusion among most people in this country when they hear African Americans say the old days were better. I think they misconstrue the fact that what we mean is that when you have a healthy sense of self, when you work from the "we," from the concept of mutual support, you are a lot happier and more comfortable than if you go into the mainstream culture that is desegregated but where they hate everything about you and want to force you to buy into their values. My mother always said if something good happens, if I win the lottery, I'm supposed to divide it nine ways among all the people in our house. That's the culture that we lost and that's some of the profound goodness of being segregated and being in your own culture.

You have to ask, "Why would we want to acquiesce to a system structured to keep us down and oppressed?" From the schoolhouse to the church, it's focused on consumerism and capitalism, rather than the church being the most radical place where you learn to organize and change society and to become self-sufficient.

We have always valued education, but not the kind of education you have to quantify with standardized tests. Do you know how powerful the illiterate people in our neighborhood were? They were wise, they had relationships, and they shared that wisdom. Today you have all these people with all these degrees who can't solve a problem because they don't know how to relate to anybody.

The larger Anglo community has a lot to learn from the values of the traditional black community. I still remember during my childhood that when someone in our community was a little different, you always treated them special. If you discovered someone was homosexual, transsexual, or developmentally disabled, you would get punished severely for treating those people in an inhumane way. That's what people can learn from us.

The other thing is a deep level of forgiveness and respect for people who have hurt you and tortured you. I think that comes from the mere fact that we believe in more than the material world. In the end, our lives are really about a radical transformation and that's why there are so many people who have done extraordinary things in African American culture. The mother of friends of mine fed every single person who came into her house, whether they were a drug dealer, a drug user, a stranger. That woman was so powerful. I don't know if she ever went to school, but she was brilliant and she was powerful. She knew who she was. And she told people you couldn't disrespect people because they had less than you. But these days black people have bought too much into the Anglo line.

Our goal with ONE DC is to re-institute these values and this knowledge within the African American community. Until I was fifteen, I never lived outside segregated neighborhoods. When I went to school, there were three things that we as African Americans had to embrace that were horrible for us. First was individual success over the collective and community responsibility. That's produced the notion that you should not worry about your community, but leave people behind and step out on your own. We learned that through integration.

The second thing I noticed is there is a deep level of mythology around Anglo education being superior to African American education. How was it possible for enslaved people to risk losing limbs or being killed because they hungered for education and gathered in a single room to learn how to read, how to write books, but more importantly, how to think, how to cultivate, how to maintain their culture? Then we go into integration and we have no sense of our intellectual or cultural capacity because it doesn't mimic the mainstream society. We lost our own way of thinking.

The third thing I realized when I left my neighborhood was that I brought my culture with me. People were surprised I had high moral standards; I always had a great sense of my history, sense of respect. I refused to study for standardized tests. I refused to speak standard English, and I wouldn't let them change my speech. A lot of people, when they hear me, try to figure out how come I understand Descartes, Dostoyevsky, the people of African tribes. I knew who I was.

The fundamental thing we have to come to grips with is that through these three aspects we lost a deep sense of dignity and respect for who we are. That's why I can't stand *The Wire*. Through programming, starting with Black Entertainment Television, we were anesthetized to our own sense of respect for ourselves and we believe that we were always drug dealers, that we always had provocative nasty music rather than provocative revolutionary music. You get this whole impression that we've always been gutter people, that we've always been addicted, we've always been selling drugs. I'm forty-six years old and when I was growing up this wasn't the dominant theme of our neighborhood. Now younger people have no historical context and people aren't teaching them historical context.

You will never hear me say the word "ghetto," you will never hear me say I come from a bad neighborhood, you will never hear me say my people are bad. So ONE DC is trying to get people to understand that this is an ongoing struggle. Like the struggle to keep people enslaved for 400 years, it will take the next 1,000 years to deconstruct this because this is a system.

I came to Washington in April 1986 to do organizing for my church. In Baltimore

I had been part of the Industrial Areas Foundation youth organizing program called BUILD: Baltimore United In Leadership Development. In that spirit I noticed a lot of people in D.C. were uncomfortable with people organizing themselves.

At ONE DC our mission is to do just that, to exercise the political strength to create and preserve economic and racial equity. This actually came from the people. In the Shaw/U Street neighborhood they said their goal was to preserve the history, culture, and heritage of the people who live there. The only way to do that is to fight for rights around housing, land, and jobs. They used to call this area the Black Broadway. Howard University is seven blocks from the U Street area. Our office is two blocks from the Dunbar Theater and one block from Howard Theater, a stop on the chitlin' circuit. All classes of people used to dress up and enjoy the entertainment on U Street.

About twelve years ago new people started moving into the neighborhood. Manna, the group we grew out of, had purchased and developed more than 500 units of housing—all affordable homeownership. The first thing we said was we wanted to organize people to preserve the value that was here because we always looked at this as a good neighborhood. You won't see anything in our literature about our neighborhood being a ghetto. We don't use that term. Yet it's a neighborhood that has experienced generations of disinvestment, redlining, disenfranchisement when it comes to the political process, and the neglect of public education.

We evolved and needed to become separate from Manna because we began to focus on change as a collective responsibility, as institutional change, and not just part of the system we're trying to tackle. We're trying to tackle the whole system: what happens to public land, people's right to housing (even if you are disabled or make low wages, you should have a place to live), and jobs (you shouldn't just have a job—you should have a good job and a living wage). That's all about what we call equitable development: development of people and place, and not just development of place. We don't believe it when they say the neighborhood will be better when they bring in Dave and Buster's, a Starbucks, or a stadium. Actually, it might not be better. All those things might be horrible for our neighborhoods because they don't develop our people.

We realize our people have the answers. One of our theories is that we are interested in resident-led change, resident-led development. We provide people with the skills and the talent to evaluate the inequity in their neighborhood. This is not about service. This is about systematic change that's focused on inequity around land, income, and housing.

We don't consider what we do avant-garde or chic. What we're doing is building a movement for future decades. We just became a membership organization and established what we call our LEAP Academy: Leadership Education for Action and Power. We're teaching people about jumping into the movement.

Members can sign up for a monthly training in the values of ONE DC, the values of movement building, the values of learning what community organizing is, and learning about the different social issues through peer learning coordinated by staff. We've held trainings on deconstructing capitalism.

We use popular education methods where people tell their stories, identify the problem, then break into groups and try to solve the problem. What should the community have? What should each community look like? How should we treat people in those neighborhoods? How should relationships be different? Then we have people illustrate with drawings what they want their neighborhood to look like.

Verizon Sports Center is a fifteen-minute walk away, city museums are ten minutes, there's a Metro stop across the street, there are bus lines, and you can get to the courthouse and downtown in ten minutes. The neighborhood has suddenly become very desirable and houses are now going for $500,000 and $600,000.

What we're experiencing is an influx of new people. We're not fighting against that. What we're fighting for is the right of our people to stay here.

A colleague told me of a conversation he overheard in a neighborhood coffee shop, where two white residents were talking about people of color in disparaging terms. He asked the two white men, "Do you know any of these folks?" Of course they didn't but they were strategizing about putting an iron fence around a park where black people congregate. Some of these new folks feel they have a right to move us out of the city. And that's why this is an issue of rights and equity.

We are organizing around union jobs at the new convention center hotel, which is within walking distance of U Street. It is attached to an $800 million convention center. We got legislation passed for a $2 million training fund to prepare residents for union jobs with good benefits. The city council asked us where we were going to find the 500 to 600 people to train. Well, there are 170,000 working poor in this city and they wonder where we're going to find the people?

We have a staff support program called "appreciative inquiry," where we emphasize and appreciate people's strengths and don't start with criticism. I model my leadership on Ida B. Wells, Sojourner Truth, Harriet Tubman, Denmark Vesey, Gabriel Prosser, and David Walker, whose appeal to the African people said they would always be part of the colony of the United States until they rebel and migrate back to Africa because they would lose all their souls and all their values here. And that's where we're headed.

ONE DC was started because the residents and the staff noticed there were few opportunities for longtime residents of Washington's Shaw neighborhood to have their voices heard in a positive and constructive way. Most community-based organizations and most community development corporations focus on bricks and sticks a lot more than people. Our preference was to focus on organizing people so they could exercise leadership with regard to the social changes happening in their neighborhood.

As an organization, we don't know where we're going to end up. As we evolve, the residents will help us focus on issues related to our housing needs, not the housing needs of the marketplace. They will help us focus on our job needs, not the Mickey Mouse jobs we get from these stadiums and convention centers. They will help us focus on our right to decide what happens to public land in our neighborhood. But at some point they might say, "Hey, you need to focus on the issues that are stopping the movement and do something about the drugs, crime, violence, incarceration, and community health." Some of these things are starting to rise up.

Our constituency will continue to be the people at the bottom, and when their lives get better, it will be their responsibility to remain socially conscious and go back and work with the other people who are at the bottom, because that's where they came from. We're not trying to recycle people into middle-class values. What we're trying to do is organize people for permanent social change and the continual struggle for justice. We're not trying to create an organization like the Urban League or the NAACP that becomes classist.

We went knocking on doors in Southeast D.C. with our youth partner, Facilitating Leadership in Youth, to recruit the adults to help prevent the government from moving them out of public housing. A woman opened her window and said, "I like what you all are doing and I appreciate you knocking on my door on Saturday morning, but I don't come out for anything except for church." And the guy next to me knew that I wanted to yell to her, "We're doing church right now!" If I knew the woman I would have said that.

Growing up in public housing were the best years of my life. But that was before work disappeared and before the government allowed the drug trafficking in our neighborhood, and the abandonment of these communities by the churches, other institutions, and everybody else. They convinced us that all our people are the bad people and so people wanted public housing torn down. This is how they change society: they just get rid of all the bad people, who just happen to be the people of color and low income. Then they import all the good people rather than saying, "Wait a minute, what is dysfunctional about our economic system, where people go to work every day and still can't pay their rent, don't have health care, can't afford public recreation? Could that be the reason we have so many social issues?" I say, do you think it's strange there are so many drugs in certain places in this country? People refuse to examine the deeper issues and the idea that you need a certain group of "bad" or "despised" people to make this capitalist machine work. Our position is we need to deconstruct that idea and to organize and educate as many people as we can to make social change.

We don't buy into this theory that if everyone looks like they went to an Ivy League college, everything's going to be OK. We believe you need fundamental institutional change and individuals who move from an individual mission to a collective mission of people working together. That's what we're trying to promote. We're trying to be radical. We're trying to get to the root of these issues: the history of discrimination, the history of enslavement, the history of disenfranchisement. The real work is to help the people educate themselves.

I've got this term I'm trying to develop that I call "organized history." We have been so brainwashed we haven't organized our own histories, we don't have the pathway to tell the truth about who we are. So I'm trying to figure out how to teach people to organize their stories. If you want to solve the drug and crime problem, just talk to the young people. They can tell you what's happening. They know what's going on.

I still believe our children have gotten way too conservative. They subliminally and unconsciously have become swamped in the belly of the beast called capitalism and focus only on their humanity through the lens of whether they can be commodified or sold, and they're always worrying about their image, about pleasing people, and what they need to get next.

Where I'm hopeful is that slowly, through the work we and other groups are doing, the movement is coming to life again. There is some flickering of hope. And some people are beginning to grapple with the grotesque nature of our dehumanized, monetary-driven society. So they are saying to themselves I can go to school not to make money but because I love art, I love people. A lot of people are starting to realize a sanitized neighborhood is not real.

My goal is not to be the mouthpiece, but to be one of the voices with the voices. We're looking for support to change the world and to get people to be authentic to who they are. We do a lot of this popular education to raise people's consciousness to deconstruct the miseducation they've been given.

We want to lay out the richness, the values, and the strengths of traditional black community life, the vast self-help networks that once flourished, the wonderful institutions—churches, clubs, newspapers, sports, businesses—that made up for the ones from which blacks were barred because of race.

We had the strength of the educational values, the respect for seniors, the fabric of extended families, the respect for all classes of people. We made room to include those deemed challenged in one way or another, the way people bought and prepared food versus the fast- and junk-food diet of today. This is the richness of the values at the core of the black community.

• • •

This story first appeared in the September/October 2008 edition of *DESIGNER/builder* magazine.

Lily Yeh in The Village of Arts and Humanities.
(Photo by Christopher Connell)

JERILOU HAMMETT AND KINGSLEY HAMMETT

THE VILLAGE OF ARTS AND HUMANITIES

AN INTERVIEW WITH LILY YEH

One day in 1986, Lily Yeh, a classically trained Chinese artist, showed up on an abandoned lot near 10th Street and Germantown Avenue in North Philadelphia, an area called the Badland for its blocks of abandoned housing, flourishing drug trade, and trash-filled streets. She brought with her a shovel and a big heart, and the results have been nothing short of amazing.

In the eighteen years since, Lily and her band of paid and volunteer workers at The Village of Arts and Humanities have turned four blocks of devastation into beauty and joy. They have converted more than 250 abandoned lots and properties into twenty-four enchanting parks, gardens, and green spaces where tile angels gaze down from a rowhouse wall and concrete tigers and baboons guard a tree farm wrested from the site of an abandoned Westinghouse plant. They have launched a range of projects, including a core leadership program, youth theater, numerous programs with Philadelphia public schools and community groups, comprehensive environmental and hands-on health programs, and many family-oriented activities. They have produced fourteen original theater performances and held seventeen community festivals in addition to rites-of-passage ceremonies and other events that exhibit the boundless talent and accomplishments of the residents of North Philadelphia, all of which have helped restore pride and hope in an area long written off as beyond salvation.

DESIGNER/BUILDER: Could you define The Village of Arts and Humanities—when it started, where it started, why it started, and a brief overview of its history?

LILY YEH: I started it as an art project in the summer of 1986. There was an abandoned lot next to where Arthur Hall operated his African American Dance Ensemble. He had seen my work with interior gardens and invited me to come help him build a park. And so I got a grant and came in very naively. Two critical things made it possible. I convinced Jo Jo (Joseph Williams), who lived in an abandoned house next to the park, to join me. He helped me to anchor the project in the community. And also he protected me. I didn't know that, but looking back I realize he was protecting me. The second critical thing was that because of him, children came, because the children knew him. So from the start it was not just people from the outside trying to do something in the community; it's always been with the people in the community, adults and especially children. I think that made people feel relaxed.

Originally I came for one summer, and even that was very hard. I almost didn't go in, because everybody said you can't go in, it's too difficult, you don't have enough money, you don't have the knowledge, the kids are going to destroy your things, and so forth. But I knew that somehow it was critical to my growth as an artist and as a person that I had to do this park. At first I wanted to run away, because the one little abandoned lot became eleven lots after ten houses next to the lot were taken down by the city because they were dangerous. I felt maybe it was time to rethink the program. At that critical moment a voice within me said, "You have to rise to the occasion; otherwise, the best of you will die and the rest will not amount to anything."

DESIGNER/BUILDER: And from that first little park in 1986, can you tell us what The Village of Arts and Humanities grew into?

LILY YEH: It's hard to define The Village now because there are so many parts to it. Basically, it's a very comprehensive program in education through the arts and land transformation, which includes turning abandoned lots into parks and gardens. Up to now we have converted more than 200 abandoned lots into twenty-four parks and gardens, painted passageways, and numerous green spaces where we just plant trees and grass. We also have a two-acre tree farm and, with a gift from the Philadelphia Eagles' Youth Partnership in 2000, we turned thirty-two abandoned lots into a beautiful playground. In addition to a very handsome grant, the whole team family of 150 people, including all the players, came one day to actually construct the park with us and with the people in the neighborhood. It was tremendous.

We work under contract with the city's Neighborhood Transformation Initiatives to turn abandoned lots into green spaces as part of our income-earning activities and job training for our adults and teens. We don't tear houses down, but we go in, clean and seed the lots, plant trees, and make them beautiful. Where there is abandonment, that's where we go, and where there are people with no skills, no jobs, we organize them, we teach them work skills, and at the same time transform the land into something lovely. And so you have multiple levels of transformation happening at the same time.

We also transform buildings into usable space. We have renovated six abandoned buildings. Now we have space for our offices, for our clay studio, rehearsal spaces, an education building where we do performing arts activities, and space for meetings of Narcotics Anonymous. This is very formidable. There are three or four groups—the oldest is over fourteen years—and they meet there three times a week. That's where people fight for their lives. It's a very valuable social service. In addition to the six buildings we renovated, which are the core of The Village, we also worked with HUD and the Redevelopment Authority to build six new homes for first-time, low-income-family home buyers.

DESIGNER/BUILDER: So in one case you reclaim the land and buildings, and in another you reclaim lives?

LILY YEH: Yes, community building takes several different kinds of transformation. The first—the physical transformation—is the most visible. The second is really mental, to build self-esteem and pride, reclaim the history, understand who you are, your family, see deficits as resources, and have the courage to embrace the difficult and the challenging. And through the act of embracing, then they become part of the forces that do the rebuilding. That's what The Village is about.

Much of this is done through theater. We had nothing to start a theater. I was not a theater artist, but five years into the project, in the summer of 1991, I felt the community stories of many people began to unload on me. They were so powerful, and many of them were very dark, human tragedies. We held them in shame and secrecy. And so I said, if we held them inside of ourselves they would continue to destroy individual families and communities. I realized the way we could heal ourselves is to listen, to bring them out, to share them, and to incorporate and eventually understand those experiences. And so I thought the best way to do it was through art and through theater. I see it almost like cleaning up water, through an aeration process. You can't isolate the dirty water by itself. You have to stir it up, you have to air it, you have to look at it, you have to analyze it, and eventually it becomes clean water. It's the same with those tragic, dark, and shameful experiences. The reason we have to do theater is for our survival. We have to understand and embrace those dark experiences.

DESIGNER/BUILDER: How did the theater project get started?

LILY YEH: The theater began innocently. I just knew we needed to do theater, and this theater would not be like any other kind of theater. It was not to teach young people skills; it was not to entertain. It was about our survival. And it was us telling our story to our people at our community place. It was almost like the old-time village theater. I found the people who began to tell me stories, the most powerful experiences, and I sat them down, interviewed them, and from the interview incredible, authentic, original human experiences were revealed. As an artist, with my open arms, I just saw those powerful experiences like jewels, like things that spilled into my hands, and I said, "My God, I have a responsibility to those experiences. I must respect and honor them." And that's how I found a theater director who would understand what I was trying to do.

I had the good fortune to find H. German Wilson, who brought in a playwright, and the three of us transformed the interviews into theater. We were commissioned to produce a piece for the Mythos Festival at the University of the Arts. We performed first at The Village and then we took it downtown, and all the dark and powerful experiences that wanted to destroy us were transformed into jubilance and joy. That's alchemy. That's a chemical process. I call it urban alchemy. We turn lead into gold. That's what The Village is all about.

Designer/Builder: Give us a sense of the other kinds of programs that fit into the educational and the experiential.

Lily Yeh: I can continue to list the programs we have. But the magic of The Village is that it's multifaceted, multilevel, interconnected, broad-based and community-based, and through a process of distillation under the guidance of people like artists and educators, we deliver a high-quality product. For example, the gardens are all fabulous, the theater is at the professional level, and we publish our own materials. We have exhibitions. Our teens travel. And on and on. But they are all connected. That's where the magic is. It's in The Village. It's in a ten-square-block area, but it sponsors programs in schools and public places throughout inner-city North Philadelphia. I have traveled to close to forty cities and to seven or eight different countries talking about The Village and how community transformation through art can happen. The Village is forever emerging, it's alive, it's like a living flame. And it is not about one flame becoming a huge torch, like corporations. But it's about helping others to light their pilot. So across the land, we all burn the light inside of us, and that's our divine light, our creative imagination, given by God, and nobody can take that away.

Our education program is what we call Learning Through the Arts. The core leadership program includes fledglings—ages six to twelve—and teens, from thirteen to eighteen. We see them five days a week, and often on the weekends, where they do visual and performing arts. We have painting, drawing, creative writing, urban greening, and garden design. We also have computer learning. Dance is very big here. And for teens we have digital music, documentary filming and editing, and job training. Another very big part is homework help. Parents want us to help them stabilize their children's study habits and so forth.

We also have a paid internship program, so every summer we hire a lot of teens to maintain the gardens, tend the trees, work with the staff in administration, do carpentry and repair work, and work with the younger children as tutors and teachers.

A big and very powerful part of the teen program is the youth theater. Every year we create an original play that's performed in Philadelphia's Painted Bride Art Center. We've also performed in Boston, Atlanta, New Hampshire, New Mexico, and other places.

DESIGNER/BUILDER: What is the leadership program?

LILY YEH: The leadership program is just for people who make the commitment to come on a consistent basis. The youth theater, for example, is the most intense. They literally become transformed. People who are very shy come, and often they don't write. Soon they have a presence, they speak, they write their own monologues, they perform on the stage, they look at the audience, they understand teamwork, and through that they become leaders. This coming year we're going to get them to organize and initiate teen-run talent shows and other activities. Just to give you an example of our success story, we have a young girl from the neighborhood who has been here from the very beginning, from 1986. She was seven and a half years old. Her name is Ora Eldridge. Her family was at risk. Now Ora, a fabulous performer in dance and theater, is studying at Temple University and doing modeling jobs. She's also the youngest member of our board and serves as its secretary. She volunteers. She will help with anything. She's on the fund-raising committee. It's just amazing! Her commitment is so deep.

DESIGNER/BUILDER: What about those who are less committed?

LILY YEH: Some of the families and children are not ready for the structure or for the commitment, so we have open workshops and what we call Village on the Move or outreach. People can select which they want. They can come for dance lessons, ceramic lessons, and computer skills. They can help us do soil treatment and recycling, or do mosaics and painting.

But open workshop is not only for the people in our neighborhood. We have many, many requests from public schools in Philadelphia and from colleges all over the country to come and do community service. For example, just this year we had students from Brown University, Ramapo College in New Jersey, and Wayne State in the Chicago area. Especially around Martin Luther King's birthday we receive many requests from volunteers to come and do something for us at The Village.

DESIGNER/BUILDER: They are obviously coming there for something that they need to learn and understand. What do you think that is?

LILY YEH: What a wonderful way you frame the question. Most people say what can we do for you, and what kind of help do you need? But I see that they walk away with incredible life experience and growth. What The Village provides is a powerful bridge. We see our society as split into the haves and the have-nots. There are plenty of people who have a lot and plenty who are struggling to get through their days. Many of the struggling people live in inner-city environments. While such areas are often broken off and disenfranchised, they contain beautiful energy and human resources. To create a wholesome society, these various portions need to reconnect. The foundation of our society lies within grassroots communities, which hold the heartbeat of the people, their energy and emotions. I think many students and volunteers come to us wanting to get in touch with those roots that hold immense humanity and creative power.

DESIGNER/BUILDER: So these people are coming to you to get in touch with that raw, basic energy, what it means to really be alive, because you have nothing else but your life. Can you describe that?

LILY YEH: Yes, I can. I realize what I experience here is the realness of connecting with people. That doesn't mean that we are always smiling. We're not. But the scope of human experience, from pain to joy, from poverty and abandonment to aspirations and inspirations, is totally real. And when life is so challenging, there's something split open that one can look through and see what life reveals. It was so powerful, even when I didn't want to come back, that I couldn't forget it. It would haunt my mind every day. Then I said, there is something here for me. I have to be here. And to be here means to be at the beginning, at the fountainhead of creativity. There's a tremendous life force surging forth, sometimes in creative form, sometimes in powerfully destructive form. But there is that realness, truthfulness, and authenticity that I feel I need to be fully involved with. People from the outside wonder why anyone would even think about coming to the inner city. I think it's because they feel a sense of incompleteness, a longing for something they can't figure out but something they can sense.

DESIGNER/BUILDER: What do you think that is?

LILY YEH: We're in the inner city and we have it all: drugs, violence, abandonment, trash on the streets. And yet, what you see is this vibrant color and life and beauty that dares to announce its own confidence and its own value, despite the whole society that crosses us off. We have the confidence and the courage and the joy to celebrate ourselves and to tell the world who we are, what is our value. In the face of death we bring life forward. And that's what draws people here. The power of art is all inclusive. You just have to be willing to come and join us, in that moment, in that time. And that's the beginning.

I am an immigrant, so when I came, there was the immigrant dream that there's a tower there up in the sky bathed in glory. That's where I wanted to go. As an artist my desire was to exhibit in galleries and, even better, in museums, have somebody, a powerful critic, write affirmatively about my work, and have my work sold and make big bundles of money. That was my dream. I didn't want to go into the inner city with African Americans, Latinos, and Asians—the down-and-out people. I'm an immigrant. I'm already out there. I am going to the other place, the hill. That was my erroneous, limited, and untested dream at that time.

Then I met Arthur Hall, and I always admired his talent as a dancer and what he did for the community. So when he asked me, I was open, I was curious, and more than anything, I was looking for another space to do my art. There was this opportunity in North Philadelphia, but when I was ready to step in, I was totally frightened. I didn't want to come in. I was scared. I said, this is nowhere for me to do my art. I wanted to go away. But I came for a deeper reason. And after two months we did wonderful things. We did the beginning of a garden, but I had no intention of coming back. At that time I was thinking, Okay, I did this project, it was very difficult, but it was successful. I'll write a report and move on to more glamorous places.

Then the project took hold of me. The life experiences took hold of me. I couldn't forget it. It would surge into my memory. Something was so deep that nurtured me in a way that I was not nurtured in my other experiences in my professional life. I was teaching and had a very respectable position at the University of the Arts. But gradually I was haunted by this place. More than that, I was pulled back. I knew there was treasure there! There was a gift there! I knew I must come back and understand what that was about. And so that began the journey of coming back, and eventually staying, eventually giving up my "golden rice bowl," a tenured professorship at the University of the Arts, so that I could totally dedicate myself to this project. In that darkness of the human spirit something shone in a way that I had never seen before. That's my experience. Why do people come here? Probably they are drawn by something similar to what I experienced.

Designer/Builder: What are the myths that keep us separated as a society and that keep us afraid of the inner city?

Lily Yeh: First, I would really not like to use the word "myth" because "myth" has a whole different connotation for me. I would like to say prejudices and a lack of understanding that comes from fear, misinterpretation, arrogance, and bigotry. To begin with, I think the prejudice toward people in the inner city does not reflect the reality of the people who live there. We often associate people who live in the inner city with those who have committed crimes, who have fallen, who use drugs, and so forth. We judge them before we understand their circumstances and their humanness. After all, Christ loved the sinners, and he chose to be with them.

There's good reason, because they are closer to God. We are all human. You know the symbol of Tao, yin and yang? Yin and yang literally mean the sunny part of the mountain and the shady part of the mountain. You cannot have one and exclude the other. You have to embrace both the brightness and the darkness at the same time. When you do that, there is completeness and God is present. As humans we have limited capacity to understand the divine and we only want to embrace the light, things we can see, things in the bright. We are fearful of the dark. Yet that darkness that we don't like in others is the darkness we reject in ourselves. When we make those statements of fear and prejudice, we have a split personality, and that's what causes all the illness. We inflict such pain on other human beings because of our basic inability to embrace the night in us.

DESIGNER/BUILDER: What have you learned since the day you walked onto that site in 1986?

LILY YEH: The most valuable thing I learned is to have faith and to listen inside. We have to pay attention to our feelings. If we don't, we begin to alienate ourselves from ourselves. Then split personalities happen and illness happens. And so the most powerful thing is that despite the world saying no, don't do this, I managed to go, and I found my life unfolding. I would advise a lot of people, especially young people, to pay attention to their inner voices, their intuition.

The second thing I learned is that a person does not have to be fully prepared to take on life's journey. One only needs to be fully prepared to meet the destiny of his or her life when it knocks on one's door. If we miss that moment, it will be of great, great regret. One needs just the desire, the willingness to put oneself in the position and let oneself be guided. When I came here I didn't know anything about building gardens. You see, my gardens were only art and mostly about painting. But now we have a tree farm, we have a vegetable farm, we have so many gardens with so many trees. Do I know how to take care of all of them? No. It's better that I don't. It's better that I don't have a lot of wealth, a lot of knowledge, a lot of strength. Through the creative process in working on this project, my weakness became my most powerful strength.

Because I did not know how to do things, I was weak, I was powerless. That allowed me to step into this broken place and accept the help that was offered. Jo Jo, Big Man, Johnny May, and many people in our community, they were resource-less, they were broken, but in this project they became giants. They came to help me. Jo Jo, especially, began living his dream as an artist constructing masonry sculptures. He was able to take down huge sick trees with simple tools that he designed, a process that would have cost hundreds of dollars and required a tree surgeon. He was also able to solve problems and get children and families reconnected. In this broken community he became a strong entity. Sometimes teens, children, they would come, burn things down, knock down our sculptures, and so forth. I say great: they want to tell us they are here, they want us to pay attention. And those places become the bridges to come together and to make contact and to build together. I learn so much every day, every moment, in everything that we are doing together.

I learned how to organize. I learned, without really thinking about it, a new kind of model that can happen as a community emerges. I learned that through art we can rebuild, reconnect the broken, heal the wounded, and make the invisible visible. Through that, a new kind of urban village emerges, and the people become empowered and reclaim their cultural heritage, and thus can be better prepared to confront this twenty-first-century international community in the global village.

DESIGNER/BUILDER: Did you learn anything about judgment and how judgment constricts and confines the ability to do anything?

LILY YEH: I didn't want to judge—on two levels. I was prepared because of my years of study of Taoism and Buddhism, and I understand the power of openness and embracing. For example, anger. We always say don't be angry if there's something bad. Actually, anger is a powerful form of energy if we don't attach it to destruction. We need to harness that energy to help us build. Also it's just wisdom. As in the story of Beauty and the Beast, you have to confront the difficult, the thing that you abhor, and have the courage to look at it with compassion and to embrace it. And through embracing, magic happens. I experience it time and again and again and again. How can you judge when you experience a deeper level of life revealed to your eyes? I just need time to understand, digest and listen, and try to prepare myself for more.

The second level is more practical. I had an art project. I had a vision. But I couldn't do it alone. I needed people to help me do it. And whoever wanted to step in for an hour, for three hours, for a moment, and wanted to help build I embraced and was full of gratitude. That's how it started. And through art, through building together, we cut through all the problems of class and prejudice and were able to connect with the creative element of the human spirit. Community comes from the Greek word meaning a group of people working together. I didn't come to think about or to look at all the problems—drugs, poor education, abuse, and poverty—I didn't come to look at that. I came to create, to bring a new sense of place, and that's a project. It's in the project, in our mental and physical space, that we can all lay our problems aside, step into the light, and in that moment build together. That's how the beginning of community happens. You don't have to address the layers of history and social prejudice. You just go directly, connect with people, and my God, it is powerful. It's like the painting of creation by Michelangelo when God pointed at Adam. The divine light was transmitted from one to the other, and Adam came to life. It was like that!

DESIGNER/BUILDER: So you didn't have to lay out a plan. You just followed what knocked on your door; you just followed the thread.

LILY YEH: When you read Genesis, God created the universe. I don't think He made plans. He just followed his sense of joy and creative impulse. He just made it. And when He finished the six days, He looked at it and He said, "Oh, this is good! I like it." And on the seventh day He rested. It was like that spontaneity. Our society doesn't trust it, doesn't trust intuition, doesn't trust organic development. But the earth is a spiritual being, and all beings are alive. We learn, we breathe, and God manifests through all life forms. But humans don't trust it. That's our problem.

DESIGNER/BUILDER: And so the lesson is…?

LILY YEH: To listen. The solution begins with paying attention. Listening to our voice inside. Listening to what other people are saying. Listening to what the sun is saying, the wind is saying, living in the moment, and being in touch with that sense of joy.

DESIGNER/BUILDER: And then trust the answer.

LILY YEH: Trust the answer. And try. If we fail, we fail. No big deal. Try again.

• • •

This story first appeared in the May/June 2004 edition of *DESIGNER/builder* magazine.

Students are exposed to all kinds of work, including assisting a chef
at a first-class restaurant. (Photo by Wendy Berry)

KINGSLEY HAMMETT

A SCHOOL AS BIG AS NEW YORK CITY

WHEN IT COMES TO DESIGNING A SCHOOL, ONE'S THOUGHTS OFTEN turn first to campus layout, building design, and internal configuration of space. But when the City-As-School High School was created in 1972 in New York City, the guiding principle was a philosophy rather than a specific structure: put students in a situation where they can learn rather than build a place where they can be taught. Under this model the classroom for students can be unlimited, ranging from sowing crops in city gardens to sewing up cadavers at the city morgue.

It's sometimes hard to imagine—among unhappy teachers, frustrated parents, and alienated students—exactly who high school works for these days. There is always a percentage of young people who find a home amid the traditional curriculum, but an increasing number do not. They need to be challenged in different ways, and a high school as different as the City-As-School appears to offer a successful format for increasing the number of students who graduate.

"One small but remarkable fact about this school is that every teacher not only has a desk but his own telephone, just like so many other adult professionals," says Bill Weinstein, who has worked in New York City public schools since 1969. "When I first came into this building and sat down at a desk with a telephone, blood rushed to my head. I never saw anything like that. I think that's important for architects to know. In the adult world, adults have phones, and teachers need to be treated like adults."

Phones on the desks are not the only thing that separates City-As-School from the typical high school. Here the different is the expected. Students don't have their own desks or lockers. They are granted large amounts of responsibility, respect, and autonomy, and devise their own programs and timetable. They split their time between in-school classes and outside working internships, gaining invaluable experience in the real world.

The school was started in 1972 as a project of the New York City Board of Education funded by a planning grant from the Ford Foundation under the leadership of founding principal Frederick J. Koury. It is housed in a five-story, H-shaped elementary school building built in Greenwich Village shortly after the turn of the last century that it shares with a GED program and an occupational training center for adolescents with developmental handicaps.

The initial planning team consisted of three adults and six to ten students (whose presence has affected the culture of the school ever since). The idea was to create a school structure that would use the resources of the city at large to break down barriers—the cultural, class, and generational divides that continue to beset us as a society—and to demonstrate that learning can take place as validly outside the four walls of a classroom as inside.

"City-As-School has always attracted both students and teachers who have a different idea of what education is like, a different idea of what relationships are like within a school building," says Weinstein, who has worked at City-As-School for the last twelve years. "Many of us did not fit into traditional schools themselves, just like our students. Here there isn't the typical distance between the faculty and students; we're all on a first-name basis."

City-As-School does not take students from junior high schools and cannot recruit them from other high schools. It acts instead as a transfer alternative high school. Typical students have spent one, two, and sometimes three years in a mainstream high school where, in the end, it became clear that their education wasn't working, for them or the school. If they are lucky to hear about City-As-School, they attend an open house, listen to a presentation about the program, and schedule an admissions interview.

Students have come from all of the high schools in the city, be they neighborhood, vocational, or the elites, like Stuyvesant and the Bronx High School of Science. Some of them are brilliant, some bored, others are truant or failing, and some exhibit all of these qualities at the same time. An ideal profile is someone who did well in junior high school and, for whatever reason, is not making it in high school. Or he or she may be holding down a job, which tells City-As-School that the student has a basic skill level to offer the community businesses and organizations that sponsor internship opportunities.

The school is in effect ungraded. While the students might refer to themselves as juniors or seniors, they are in fact simply further from or closer to graduation based on the number of units they have accumulated. They are required to attain a level of proficiency in math and English, science and social studies through a combination of outside working internships and in-house classes that range far beyond the traditional textbook approach. Along with a host of free courses open to students at seven or eight local colleges, some of the in-house classes offered this fall

A student at City-As-School interning at a city daycare center.
(Photo by Wendy Berry)

include "Growing a Business," "Topics in Algebra," "ESL: The Research Paper," "Play Making," "Toni Morrison," "Women's Group," "South of the Border: Music and Dance," "Urban Horticulture," "Urban Ecology," "Gay/Straight Discussion Group," "Smoking?," "Greek Philosophy," and "The Science of Compost."

The school is ungraded in another, perhaps more essential sense: there are no grades other than Credit/No-Credit. This even avoids the notion of pass/fail in that a student who does not meet requirements receives a notation of no-credit; he or she does not "fail" in the literal sense of the term. Many, if not most, of the students coming to the school have already been through a system that labels them as failures. This is a crucial distinction for many and is part of a philosophy that seeks to see the present as a departure point rather than a continuation of the past. The emphasis at City-As-School moves away from labeling and from negativity and in the direction of the future and taking responsibility for it.

Analyzing a new student's transcript, the school determines how many of the required credits he or she has obtained at prior schools and how many more are needed for graduation. Then it looks over the list of the school's 400 to 500 internship possibilities that will take students into real-world work situations all over the city. Assignment to an eight- or sixteen-week internship is based upon the student's interests, the kind of credits an internship might offer, its availability, and the student's schedule. An Advisor (in-house teacher) meets with his or her students in a once-a-week meeting called Seminar, while the Resource Coordinator is responsible for the success of the internship. He meets personally with the students once or twice during the eight-week cycle at the internship site, and stays in touch via telephone and e-mail. The Resource Coordinator, in addition to taking attendance, writes the curriculum for the placement and evaluates how well the student fulfills the learning goals set out in the curriculum.

"We have survived all these years as an external-learning school because we have staff dedicated to being outside the building," Weinstein says. "Resource Coordinators visit their students on-site and make sure everything is on target. This contact with the students is crucial."

Weinstein coordinates the fourteen-member department responsible for maintaining the body of internships that anchors the school's educational character. In addition to receiving a steady stream of inquiries, staff canvass the city's business and nonprofit communities to secure internships that make the school tick. Internship offerings run the gamut from the ordinary to the mind-boggling.

"I had students working on autopsies in the medical examiner's office," Weinstein says. "They were sewing up cadavers and this was my most sought-after placement. I used to go and supervise their work, so it was an education for me, as well."

Others include serving as a photographer's assistant, working at nonprofit organizations, helping to set up displays in a fashion design showroom, serving as a complaint mediator at the Better Business Bureau, assisting a job counselor at the New York State Department of Labor, helping with Hispanic outreach for the U.S. Committee for UNICEF, organizing and cataloging the staff library for the National Action Council for Minorities in Engineering, researching mutual funds as an assistant to a stockbroker at PaineWebber, working administratively in various police precincts ("I make sure they know in advance that they do not get to carry a gun or hunt down lawbreakers," Weinstein says), teaching groups of youngsters at the New York Aquarium, learning about medical administration as a dental assistant, coming to understand the school system and its effect on young people as an education-advocacy assistant at the Urban Justice Center, assisting in the medical care of animals as a veterinary assistant, designing and maintaining web pages at the New York City Department of Administrative

Student intern working in a computer installation/repair company.
(Photo by Wendy Berry)

Services, learning culinary skills in the kitchen of New York City's exclusive Le Cirque 2000, and learning the trade at various print and broadcast media, like *New Youth Connections, Fairness and Accuracy in Reporting, Foster Care Magazine, The Villager, Courier Life News, A. Magazine, The Resident, Chelsea Clinton News*, and WNYC.

Students are free to choose the combination of internships and classes that works for them, depending on credit and scheduling needs. During any given eight-week cycle, some students are taking only internships and some are taking only classes, though the majority mix both kinds of learning experience.

Students attending internships need not stop at school first, but rather have their attendance monitored in the field by telephone. Because of the school's track record and long relationships with placements, Weinstein and his fellow resource coordinators field regular phone calls from companies and organizations that wish to participate and offer internships to City-As-School students.

"They definitely want to be involved in making this a better community," he says. "But if someone wants to be in for the wrong reasons, and if a student is not happy, we learn about it and we'll terminate the internship. If all he's doing is filing all day long, that's just not a learning experience. And then one student might love a place and the next one hate it. So the coordinator has to know what works, how to explain what the student can expect, how to place the right student at the right internship, and how to teach students how to negotiate less-than-perfect situations."

Throughout the internship, the student must meet the requirements laid out in his individual Learning Experience Activity Package (LEAP), the curriculum for each placement. The LEAP is a set of assignments that each resource coordinator develops with each site and each student must complete.

"That's how it becomes an academic experience," Weinstein says. "Depending on the advisor, the resource coordinator, and the site, the LEAP may be more or less flexible and more or less proscriptive with more or fewer options."

About 80 percent of the graduates of City-As-School go on to college. And while some are picked up as permanent employees where they once served as interns, Weinstein tries to avoid promising anyone that will happen. The point of the program is to educate young people and broaden their horizons. It is not a vocational program nor is it a job placement center.

"The atmosphere is different here," Weinstein says of the Greenwich Village facility that has about 500 students and whose location alone connotes freedom. Three other facilities in this program now operate in Brooklyn, Queens, and the Bronx. "The students are given a lot of responsibility and a lot of respect. I just spoke to someone the other day who graduated ten years ago and is now working for a company that wants to take interns. I liked this young man very much and remembered him well. He was into heavy metal music and landed a sought-after placement at *Hit Parade* magazine, which was perfect for him. There was no way he could have found that at a traditional high school."

Weinstein is also the coordinator of the school's effort to disseminate the City-As-School concept to school districts around the country. The school's five-member team has trained teachers and administrators in how to open similar programs in twenty other states. For a fee of $5,500 they will spend three days training up to ten people in how to look at education through an alternative lens and explain why internships work for high school students, what schools must do to make them work, the kinds of difficulties they might encounter, how to anticipate and deal with problems, and provide samples of paperwork. They also role-model the development of three internship sites.

"People generally teach the way they were taught," he says, "so there is a traditional belief that education has to be in a classroom. Then there is the question of the prescriptive nature of state- and district-wide curriculums: in general, educators believe all students must go through an established set of experiences in order to be considered educated. That doesn't leave a great deal of room in the school day to let students have real experiences in the field."

Fortunately in New York City there is a superintendency for alternative schools and a lot of room for experimentation. A student at City-As-School graduates by handing in a portfolio of collected work showing the best of what he has attained, or a spread of work showing improvement. The portfolio documents the student's achievement in classroom study and internship experience and is presented to a committee of three staff and one outside person in lieu of having to take the New York State Regents examinations.

"I've been in this milieu for many, many years, and I am biased," Weinstein admits. "I have always been partial to people who don't fit in. I think the program is enormously effective, and is most effective when the kids can find their own route without being told they have to do this and they have to do that. Alienation is still a theme in modern society, and not every young person will discover where he or she fits. But we offer them an opportunity at City-As-School that they would never get anywhere else."

• • •

This story first appeared in the October 1999 edition of *DESIGNER/builder* magazine.

Members of the Interfaith Community Building Group helped rebuild Rocky Point
Missionary Baptist Church, McComb, Mississippi, 1997. (Photo by Lance Laver)

KINGSLEY HAMMETT

INTERFAITH COMMUNITY BUILDING GROUP

SAINT FRANCIS IS SAID TO HAVE EXHORTED HIS FOLLOWERS WITH the call to action, "Preach the Gospel at all times … and if necessary, use words."

Since 1996 a group of Philadelphians of different faiths has been doing its best to live up to that dictum. Founded by Lance Laver, who is Jewish, and his wife, Mary, a Catholic, and made up of other Jews, Catholics, Protestants, Quakers, and most recently Muslims, along with some secular humanists, the Interfaith Community Building Group has performed good works in its hometown, in the Deep South, and in El Salvador.

"We are part of the reconstructionist movement," says Lance of his own congregation, Temple Mishkan Shalom, "which holds that Jews are both part of an ancient religious tradition and also part of a contemporary community. We try to reconstruct the traditional teachings relevant to our time. For us that means trying to make society more equitable, eliminate racism, and work for peace and justice."

Mary's church, St. Vincent de Paul, is a magnet for Catholics from around Philadelphia who struggle to stand with the poor and has spun off several non-profit outreach organizations in its Germantown neighborhood. As an 80 percent white parish in an 80 percent African American area of the city, St. Vincent's has made racial healing a major focus of parish life.

The Lavers conceived the Interfaith Community Building Group as a one-time volunteer response to the rash of arsons that destroyed a number of African American churches in the South in the mid-1990s. Eighty people showed up at an initial meeting publicized through Mishkan Shalom and St. Vincent's. Ultimately, twenty-seven individuals—singles, couples, some professional carpenters, architects, and others with wide-ranging skills, including some who had done no building at all, ranging in age from nine to sixty-two—packed up some tools and headed south to McComb, Mississippi, in the summer of 1997.

Habitat for Humanity matched up the group with the African American Rocky Point Missionary Baptist Church. Several white congregations in McComb also provided housing and transportation during the week. The group slept on the floor of the community room in a Presbyterian church, cooked its meals in the church's kitchen, and was driven to and from the construction site by volunteers from a United Methodist church. Various men's and women's church clubs provided home-cooked meals for the group.

"By the time we got there the new church had been framed and the roof was up," Lance says. "We built the altar and the stairs leading up to it, framed out and installed new windows, and did a lot of finishing work. In one week we put in more than 1,300 hours."

During its stay the Interfaith Group encountered many unexpected but wonderfully spontaneous moments of interplay between races and religions, he says. "Rocky Point is not a big congregation and most members, many elderly, came almost every day. The daughter of the interim pastor was an opera singer, Sebronette Barnes, who appeared on the last workday. When she sang 'This Little Light of Mine' and 'Amazing Grace,' with all of us holding hands in a circle in the almost-completed church, it was an absolutely magical moment."

At the end of the week all members of the group felt transformed by what they had learned about each other's faiths, about the people of Mississippi, and about interracial relations. There was a consensus that if there were other places where they could do this kind of work they would be eager to do so again. That is not to say they didn't encounter social barriers and taboos. "One time a men's group offered our kids the chance to swim at their country club," Mary says. "We knew this country club had a policy of no blacks and felt that if they knew our group included Jews, both sides might not feel comfortable. We also knew that going to an exclusive place like that was not in the spirit of why we were in Mississippi. So we chose instead to take our kids to a public pool where most of the swimmers were black. We came back and said, 'Well, we integrated the public pool today!'"

Lance had been in college during the Civil Rights movement of the 1960s but never got on a bus and went down South to participate. He was anxious on this trip to see firsthand what the new South was like.

"On the surface, it looks like total integration. You go to a restaurant, there are blacks and whites eating together, and most of the public spaces are mixed. But the churches are almost completely segregated, and even though the population is nearly evenly split between black and white, the public schools in McComb are 85 percent black. The white children go to Christian day schools."

Members of the Interfaith Community Building Group rebuilding a Civil War–era porch for the New Frankford Community Y in Philadelphia, 1998. (Photo by Lance Laver)

But when he thought about the situation back home in Philadelphia, he realized it wasn't much different. "It's easy for northerners to bash civil rights in the South, but we're doing a lot of the same things up here. Maybe we didn't have the lynchings. But there's still a lot of racism in the North as well as the South."

As a result of the intensity of the experience in Mississippi, both on and off the construction site, the volunteers committed to an annual project. In Philadelphia in the summers of 1998 and 2000 they rebuilt an abandoned row house in the Germantown section through St. Vincent's InnDwelling program, which renovates houses for first-time homebuyers; helped rebuild the main porch of the New Frankford Community Y, a Civil War–era building used as a neighborhood recreation center; and worked with the South Indian congregants of Grace Trinity Church in Frankford to rebuild part of their building for day care, computer training, and other services for African Americans and Hispanics living in the neighborhood.

In 2002 the Interfaith Community Building Group put in an exterior underground drainage system and built bookcases in the sanctuary and library at Mishkan Shalom. In 2004 it worked with a Puerto Rican women's organization, Grupo Motivos, to renovate a double row house in the Kensington section of Philadelphia for a future café, a community storefront, and a computer training center. The women, who had previously cleaned up Norris Square Park (also known as "Needle Park"), had taken over an entire city block, started a community garden, and had begun a catering business with the vegetables they produced. They had also built a replica of a 1945 Puerto Rican rural casita adjacent to the gardens.

In January 2006, following Hurricane Katrina, the Interfaith Community Building Group took the first of three trips to New Orleans, where they worked with parishioners from St. Gabriel the Archangel Church to rebuild the church and houses in the Gentilly neighborhood. The church—and a treasured, forty-five-year-old, life-sized wooden statue of Gabriel—had stood under seven feet of water for three weeks. During their first trip, the Philadelphians offered to take the statue to the studio of one of their members, a furniture maker, who restored it. Nine months later they brought it back to New Orleans, where it was rededicated and now stands as a symbol of hope in that ravaged community.

In the past twelve years, 125 people have participated in the Interfaith Community Building Group's projects, in addition to scores of others from the host communities. In 1999 they began doing international projects and made the first of five trips to El Salvador. Through St. Vincent's Church they arranged to work in the rural village of Las Anonas de Santa Cruz in the San Vicente region. They sought to help heal wounds opened by U.S. support of the brutal civil war that raged in El Salvador throughout the 1980s.

"We will never forget standing in the church where Archbishop Óscar Romero was murdered in the middle of saying mass," Mary says. "There are murals on walls all over the country that quote him as saying, 'If they kill me, I will rise again in my people.' We had this palpable sense that many others before us had visited there to be in solidarity with the Salvadorans in the midst of their great pain. It was clear to us that it takes solidarity for the people to reclaim their human and civil rights. We wanted to use our leverage as North Americans, not just to rebuild physically, but to speak to U.S. embassy officials in San Salvador and to work politically when we returned home."

Moving into the international arena was a quantum leap for the Interfaith Community Building Group, requiring people who spoke Spanish and a good host organization to guide them and help negotiate the culture. They found what they needed in the U.S.–El Salvador Sister Cities organization.

"It worked beautifully," Lance says. "Hurricane Mitch had destroyed a lot of stick-built houses in Las Anonas. We worked with the people there to rebuild the houses in reinforced masonry construction to withstand hurricanes and earthquakes. If you have only one week, it's impossible to finish the work. But we managed to get five houses out of the ground and up to about five feet high."

Initially, the Americans wanted the satisfaction of completing at least one house. But the Salvadorans told the group that it was much more important to their sense of equality if all five houses got to the same level. "This message from

Members of the Interfaith Community Building Group and Las Anonas villagers mixing concrete
for the church's foundation in Las Anonas, El Salvador, 2001. (Photo by Lance Laver)

our hosts allowed us to learn from them how a community goes about integrating physical building with knitting together relationships," Lance says. "It's how they all survived the war."

U.S.–El Salvador Sister Cities had warned the Philadelphians not to come as know-it-all Americans, telling the local people to step aside. "Before the trip, they gave us many orientation sessions to make sure we understood the community was in the driver's seat, not us," Mary says. "The first day we got there, the men in the village gave us a lesson in mixing concrete in a group circle right on the ground with just shovels and water. So we stood back and watched and learned how they do it."

The second time the Interfaith Community Building Group went to El Salvador, it helped build a chapel in Las Anonas. This work took a tangible interfaith turn when a member of the group, sculptor Joe Brenman, who happens to be Jewish, spontaneously offered to donate a set of original ceramic Stations of the Cross he had crafted in Philadelphia. They now adorn the walls of the chapel.

Beyond helping to build buildings, the Interfaith Group builds bridges between cultures. On one trip, Mary used her "toolbox" Spanish to facilitate a tearful conversation between a Philadelphia woman who had adopted the child of an American soldier and a Vietnamese woman after the Vietnam War and a Salvadoran woman who had been trying for years to find out what happened to her three toddlers kidnapped by Salvadoran soldiers during the U.S.-supported civil war.

A member of the Interfaith Community Building Group, Teresa Naughton, helps make tortillas with the women of Las Anonas, El Salvador, 1999. (Photo by Lance Laver)

"It's important for people in El Salvador to know there are North Americans who care about them, who are in solidarity with them, and who are willing to challenge their own government's policies on humanitarian grounds," Lance says. "One of the hopes of the rural Salvadoran people is that we can do something to help their situation. When we first started this work, I thought it was about the physical building. I've since completely changed my mind. It's really about building relationships with people."

And in building these relationships, the work has continued to address human rights issues. In addition to speaking with U.S. embassy staff in San Salvador during visits, Interfaith Community Building Group members have published articles in U.S. newspapers, organized walks and programs, and held fund-raising events. While building a community center in El Milagro in July 2007, the group learned of the arrest of members of the rural grass roots organization CRIPDES, with which the Philadelphia group had worked in the last decade, on trumped-up "terrorism" charges stemming from a peaceful demonstration against the Salvadoran president's announcement of planned water privatization in a nearby town, Suchitoto. Upon returning home, members helped organize a rally at Philadelphia's city hall and an effort leading to forty-two U.S. Representatives signing a letter to Salvadoran President Antonio Saca condemning the arrests of the "Suchitoto 13." In January 2008 two building group members, Frank Hollick and Sharon Browning, joined a delegation that met with high-ranking Salvadoran officials and the "13" to advocate for their complete freedom.

This year the Interfaith Community Building Group will work in North Philadelphia with a Muslim organization renovating a former auto-parts factory to create a mosque, school, and Islamic center. Lance made the contact through his connection with the Philadelphia Interfaith Walk for Peace and Reconciliation, whose 2007 walk included 1,000 participants of all faiths.

"Through physical work and spiritual connection," Lance says, "the Interfaith Community Building Group tries to find the divine spark in each of us—with those in our host communities and with each other."

• • •

This story first appeared in the May/June 2008 edition of *DESIGNER/builder* magazine.

As part of the 2003 (Dis)Orientation program, Alan Walks leads a tour of Toronto's Church and Wellesley neighborhood and explains local conflicts that have shaped the area. (Photo courtesy of Planning Action)

KINGSLEY HAMMETT

VOICES OF OPPOSITION

The Plan assumes that planners will be reasonable, developers will be benevolent,
that architects will be brilliant, and that citizens will be quiet.
—Doug Young, Planning Action

URBAN PLANNING TODAY IN MOST CITIES HAS BECOME A TOOL OF a well-connected minority in service to its private interests, while ignoring the needs of the broader population. Shut out of the discussion is the equitable allocation of resources, especially to the economically disadvantaged.

In Toronto, as in other places, city government makes only superficial efforts toward providing affordable housing, improved transportation, support for the homeless and mentally ill, environmental protection and remediation, and the other services needed in less affluent neighborhoods, such as adequate schools and access to fresh fruits and vegetables, recreation, libraries, museums, medical care, and advocacy.

Many architects and planners have long searched for ways to put their years of training to use in support of progressive ideals and underserved populations. In a field circumscribed by time-honored and elitist traditions and rigid rules of engagement, this often takes great resourcefulness and courage. Among those looking for alternatives is Canadian urban geographer and planner Deborah Cowen, co-founder (with Sue Bunce) of Planning Action in Toronto, a group dedicated to advocating for the needs of the voiceless in that rapidly globalizing city.

In 2000, Planners Network, a well-established progressive organization, held its annual conference in Toronto. A group of local planners and architects, including Cowen, who had helped set up the meeting, came away feeling they needed a new organization that would take a more proactive approach to local issues.

Cowen is currently a post-doctoral fellow at York University. During her studies, she encountered various radical thinkers—Marxists, feminists, anarchists—who helped her formulate her ideas of what equitable urban planning could be. She also met a number of people who shared her vision of civic activism, and she realized that while she had no interest in becoming a professional urban planner, she did want to continue her involvement with urban planning issues and address questions of poverty, ethno-racial relations, civil rights, and anti-gentrification politics. A small group began to explore creating a new entity focused on what social justice viewed through the lens of urban planning could do. The result was Planning Action, an all-volunteer organization that has tried to become the voice of those left out of the city's master planning process.

They began by researching similar groups around the world, and found promising models in England and Australia organized something along the lines of Legal Aid. "As one of our members, Doug Young, said, we were torn between being a roving band of radicals and a social service agency," Cowen says. "And neither extreme seemed quite right."

They initially leaned toward lending help in a Legal Aid model and first called themselves Planning Aid, a name they abandoned before they even started because it sounded too paternalistic. They settled on Planning Action because they didn't want to appear to be dropping care packages into underdeveloped neighborhoods.

They started with a series of public meetings, spreading the word through any lists of people they thought might be interested in joining an activist group. At the same time, Toronto's municipal government was being reorganized; a massive new urban plan was in the works; and the forces of neoliberalism, including the privatization of once-public spaces and services, were taking hold rapidly, leading to devastating cutbacks for virtually everything but the police budget.

From twenty-five to sixty people showed up at a series of six or seven meetings over a period of several months. They included students, architects, individuals active in their neighborhoods, members of civic groups, and professionals working for nonprofit organizations. Many were drawn to a Jane Jacobs–style model of middle-class city reclamation and beautification, a legacy that is very strong in Toronto.

"There had been a time when Toronto had a lot to be proud of," Cowen says. "During the 1960s, when American cities were going through radical disinvestment, Toronto looked appealing. But there hasn't been any focus on many of the exciting dimensions of city life that were being celebrated at that time. In some ways it can be difficult to distinguish within the urban planning community between a gentrifying impulse and a social impulse because they are so entwined here due to Jacobs's legacy."

Kanishka Goonewardena of Planning Action and Barbara Rhader of Planners Network tell (Dis)Orientation participants about the work of their respective groups in Toronto. (Photo courtesy of Planning Action)

Toronto also has a strong history of reform activism, which led to some success in stopping highways being rammed through downtown neighborhoods. But even though that saved some areas from destruction, it also contributed to a middle class-ification of downtown and moved industry and working-class jobs out of the city.

Planning Action chose to sidestep mandates and mission statements and moved directly to three areas of action: community involvement, popular outreach, and critical projects. Under community involvement they imagined providing design and advocacy services to individuals and neighborhoods chronically marginalized from the traditional planning and legal systems. They also wanted to support participatory planning that creates alternatives to competitive, municipal- and corporate-driven planning practices.

Secondly, through popular education and outreach, they sought to challenge the professions involved in the planning process to redefine their role in a more critical and responsible way; to build relationships with social justice and environmental organizations, academic institutions, and diverse communities of the city; and to increase awareness, understanding, and involvement among city residents in the planning process.

The third area, and the one where they have had the most success, was critical projects. Here they testified before the city's Planning and Transportation Committee, arguing against the narrow perspective that Toronto's Draft Official Plan took in support of property owners, developers, and multinational corporations.

"The city's plan was a discouraging document," says Cowen, whose group did not want to see its concepts set in stone for the next thirty years. It divided the city into different zones that would allow different kinds of development. There was a lot of pretty language about having nice streets and so forth, but nary a bone thrown to the concept of social justice. The local visioning process was replaced by private consultants and high-profile architects, and the media labeled any local opposition as NIMBYism.

"What we saw coming in these plans was inner-city neighborhoods protected for the middle class, gentrification of avenues and larger-scale streets, and upscale redevelopment of poorer and industrial sections," she says. "That left no provision for anything that met the kinds of problems we were seeing."

Planning Action brought the issues to the fore by writing articles for various community publications. Members also spoke at the showdown at city hall. That they had to follow Jane Jacobs (who wholeheartedly endorsed the plan) was difficult, because she had become synonymous with the best in progressive planning

(Dis)Orientation participants in Toronto's St. Jamestown neighborhood, outside a hospital that recently lost government funding. (Photo courtesy of Planning Action)

that Toronto had to offer. But, Cowen remembers, it helped that Planning Action's approach was funny and crisp in its critique. The presentation opened with the line coined by member Doug Young that "The Plan assumes that planners will be reasonable, developers will be benevolent, that architects will be brilliant, and that citizens will be quiet."

The group contrasted the city's plan with the city's own maps, which demonstrated growing poverty and social polarization, and asked why the two documents weren't speaking to each other. It pointed out the need to start the planning process with the people who were struggling with the problems the city itself acknowledged existed, such as homelessness, social polarization, and racialized poverty. Coincidentally, that same afternoon, a squatter community of several hundred people from the waterfront had been evicted to make way for a Home Depot, and they came bursting into the council chambers.

"That got some city councilors to reevaluate their position on the plan," she says. "Others demanded we give them the policy to put into the plan. But we were so critical of the foundation of the plan that we didn't want to offer one corrective fix. We wanted to make demands for a completely different kind of political process."

Planning Action subsequently made a similar presentation to the city called "Making Waves: Principles for Building Toronto's Waterfront," regarding the lack of affordable housing in the city's waterfront plan. And it conducted a forum on "Public Service for Sale?" that addressed the implications of the World Trade Organization's General Agreement on Trade in Services (GATS). The group questioned the shift of city services to private corporations, placing the city's recreational facilities under the economic development department, massive expansion of police budgets while governments at all levels were crying fiscal austerity, and the municipal amalgamation of local and regional councils that reduced opportunities for public participation.

"In such a big city with so many voices it's difficult to say what impact our criticism has had," Cowen says. "The city's plan was adopted in 2002, but there was some rethinking of affordability. The biggest impact might have been simply to serve as a thorn in the side of the power structure, maintaining an annoying voice, and building counter public entities."

In addressing the city council, Planning Action made some of the same claims as the squatters and anti-poverty coalitions. But because several members in the group had extensive backgrounds in planning and could speak the official language, they couldn't be written off so easily, which introduced a key new element into the politics of planning in Toronto.

Along the way Planning Action has developed a number of tools to strengthen the voices of opposition. One is community mapping, which involves rolling out a map of a given area and working with neighborhood members to identify problems in their everyday lives.

"When people start to think spatially they can see how much more tangible the problems are," she says. "It's a great technique to get residents to start to talk about how they feel about their neighborhoods, and it works well with young people."

Fortunately Toronto is home to three universities with planning departments, which provide an important source of student energy. In contrast to the traditional university "orientation," Planning Action created a program of "(dis)orientation." Instead of the typical introduction to drinking and partying, it organized a process to introduce a whole new crop of incoming students to the concept of critical planning.

"We talked about what was really going on in Toronto," Cowen says. "We introduced them to both Planners Network and Planning Action. We did walking tours of different neighborhoods. And political professors familiar with gentrification and community conflict briefed them on how people talk about planning in the city."

Planning Action has also conducted a training for the University of Toronto planning program on participatory planning, community mapping, and more radical ways of thinking about city planning. The organization now has 140 people on its mailing list and a working group of twenty-five, a number that swells or shrinks depending on the issue at hand.

• • •

This story first appeared in the July/August 2006 edition of *DESIGNER/builder* magazine.

Local residents fought to save the Suba neighborhood pharmacy. (Photo by Martha Cooper)

KINGSLEY HAMMETT

POWER OF THE PURSE

AN AD HOC COLLECTION OF NEW YORKERS ON THE CITY'S UPPER West Side brought a corporate giant to its knees when it forced the national CVS drugstore chain to close one of its stores, on Broadway near West 102nd Street. CVS had paid $1 million to buy out the lease of the neighborhood's only supermarket. But after a seventeen-month boycott by residents who took their business to a neighboring mom-and-pop pharmacy, CVS threw in the towel and closed.

The lesson for the victorious neighborhood coalition is obvious: get active, get organized, get informed, stay involved, vote with your pocketbook, and you can get results. Through its victory the residents reminded themselves that the American consumer has enormous power to direct the fate of unwelcome merchants and the makeup of individual neighborhoods. Exercise that power by withholding spending, and sooner or later the unwanted offender has to bend. As we are told almost nightly by business pundits and economists, this is an economy driven by the whims and wishes of consumers. Regardless of what planners plan and zoning officials approve, the final word ultimately rests with the buyer on the street.

To the casual observer, New York City appears to be an impersonal wilderness of concrete canyons whose residents work to avoid contact with their neighbors. But in fact its residential neighborhoods are highly organized and citizens are well informed and deeply concerned about what goes on at street level. So in the late spring of 2000, when the neighborhood Associated Supermarket on Broadway and West 102nd Street stopped stocking inventory and told customers it was about to be closed, neighbors got alarmed. Two weeks after the store actually closed, they learned to their horror that CVS was planning to move into the space.

"Our stretch of Broadway between 96th and 110th Street is in transition," says history professor and community-newsletter editor John Davenport of the area that in the 1980 census was the most ethnically diverse tract in the entire country. "To lose that supermarket was bad news for a lot of people—an inconvenience for the more affluent, but a real hardship for the less affluent."

The news of the CVS arrival was met with outrage by the neighborhood that already was home to two chain drugstores and Suba, a small pharmacy run by a Pakistani family. The loss of their grocery meant they would have to walk further to one of two nearby supermarkets owned and operated by the Gristede's chain, which, without neighboring competition, were free to raise prices.

"The feeling was we had lost any kind of control over our neighborhood," Davenport says, "and we were prey to forces beyond our control. In the case of CVS it was just a bunch of people from Woonsocket, Rhode Island, who didn't care about us."

The CVS expansion was all part of a larger struggle going on within the drugstore industry all over the country, Davenport says. Baby boomers are now approaching retirement age and will be drug-dependent at a time when drugs are getting more and more sophisticated and the industry has a drug for every ailment. The drug business, both prescription and over-the-counter, is very profitable, much more so than supermarkets, and the major drug chains are all fighting to see who can force out the competition and end up being number one.

"It's essentially a gladiatorial combat, a free-for-all," Davenport says. "Whoever wins will be well positioned to dominate a whole retail industry that's highly profitable."

Davenport's block association accounts for about 2,000 apartments in the area between West 102nd and 103rd Streets, from Broadway to Riverside Drive. As editor of the quarterly newsletter he's often pressed to come up with news about an area so small. But the editorial he wrote about the closing of the Associated grocery and the coming of CVS touched a nerve among his readers. They began their organizing with a meeting at the office of Ed Sullivan, their state assemblyman, where they devised a plan to gather signatures on a petition to send to the landlord, to CVS, and to a few politicians, including a city-council member.

"When you're in a bomber and you drop some bombs you don't really think about whom you are killing 30,000 feet below," Davenport says. "That's the way CVS was operating, thinking like generals running a region-wide campaign. They weren't thinking about this single store. They didn't care coming in and going out. It was all bottom line, and that's what was so infuriating."

Davenport and his neighbors took to the streets every day after the supermarket moved out while renovations were going on in anticipation of CVS's arrival. In a two-pronged strategy they gave out leaflets urging people to boycott the coming store and to buy instead from Suba, the type of fast-disappearing neighborhood store that would special order anything that a major drug chain wouldn't have. To Suba they offered a compelling argument: if you want to hang on in the face of three major national chain competitors right here in the neighborhood, undercut

Support for Suba documented in the pharmacy's windows. (Photo by Martha Cooper)

them on prescriptions and we'll go out into the street and encourage so many people to come in that you can make it up in volume.

"And that's what he did," Davenport says. "So he's become the prescription guy along our stretch of Broadway. We saved his business, and that was very gratifying."

The neighborhood coalition got 4,400 signatures from those who agreed to boycott CVS. They continued their picket after the store moved in around Labor Day 2000 and held a few rallies out front. After one of their community meetings broke up, everyone took a piece of chalk and went to the sidewalk in front of the store where they could write how they felt.

"It was amazing," Davenport says. "The entire sidewalk along Broadway was filled with their scrawling. CVS had just opened and the manager was royally pissed. But what could he do?"

By Thanksgiving the daily pickets had petered out but the boycott remained strong. CVS managed to hang on from September 2000 until January 2002, but the dearth of business finally forced the company to concede defeat and move out.

"There's power of the purse," Davenport says. "And if there are thousands of us we really have economic power, particularly when we have something to focus our attention on. History in the last fifty years has been changed by ordinary people taking to the streets, and the Civil Rights movement wrote the playbook for all subsequent protest movements: stay focused, get the attention of the media, and don't give up."

• • •

This story first appeared in the March/April 2002 edition of *DESIGNER/builder* magazine.

Bullet Space circa 1990. (Photo by Maggie Wrigley)

MAGGIE WRIGLEY

BULLET SPACE

HOME AS AN ACT OF RESISTANCE

IT WAS WAR IN THE NEIGHBORHOOD. A HOUSING WAR ON THE Lower East Side of New York City that lasted through two decades, three mayors, countless legal challenges, and pitched street battles. It was decided, finally, with victory for the community of squatters who had settled the abandoned buildings of a neglected neighborhood.

At one point in the 1980s there were about thirty squats in the downtown Manhattan area known as the Lower East Side. People in search of affordable rents, artists, families, and low-income locals moved into abandoned and crumbling buildings and worked to repair, restore, and revitalize a neighborhood. The city often responded brutally and used every means to remove the squatters—from court actions, illegal nighttime demolitions, and personal harassment, through full-on paramilitary assaults with helicopters, armed riot police and, in 1995 on 13th Street, a tank.

In an astounding turnaround and an unlikely alliance with the city's Housing and Preservation Department and the Giuliani and Bloomberg administrations, August 2002 saw eleven of the remaining twelve squats sign a deal to become low-income cooperatives. With the help of the Urban Homesteading Assistance Board, a local nonprofit, the squatters have worked toward financing and legally owning their buildings. I am one of those squatters, and this is the story of one squat.

The tenement house at 292 East 3rd Street on the Lower East Side was built in the last decade of the nineteenth century. By the last decade of the twentieth century it was at the heart of a fight to preserve this neighborhood's history and its build-ings—and to use our ideas and hard labor to realize dreams and make the land our own. This building is called Bullet Space, named irreverently after a brand of heroin that was prevalent, and constantly advertised in sing-song calls, on the block.

The late seventies and early eighties were years of destruction for the Lower East

Maggie Wrigley at home. (Photo by Maggie Wrigley)

Side. As in the infamous South Bronx, landlords abandoned buildings and their tenants in massive numbers through nonpayment of taxes and dereliction of repairs. The city seized these damaged homes only to abandon them, evicting tenants and condemning buildings for lack of the simple repairs they refused to make, like broken front doors, smashed windows, and leaking roofs. Plumbing was ripped out entirely and sold for scrap. Arson was common. At the same time the city was sealing and warehousing these buildings, a housing crisis was growing in New York. Rents escalated and the homeless population grew swiftly on the city streets. Buildings were being sealed and demolished at a furious rate despite the obvious housing needs. It became a neighborhood of junkies, gangs, yuppies, crackheads, poets, squatters, and punks.

On January 30, 1986, a group of squatters moved in through the back of the building and laid claim to 292 East 3rd Street as their home. This was the start of the squat known originally as 6 O'Clock, named for an artists' collective from the neighborhood, and soon to be known as Bullet Space.

For over a century this five-story tenement housed immigrants and their families chasing the American dream in changing waves of ethnic populations, through the early Eastern Europeans, the South-to-city-bound blacks, to the Puerto Rican and other Caribbean islanders of later years. Like so many on the Lower East Side, the building fell prey to abandonment and neglect in the seventies.

Previous tenants of 292 suffered under the ownership of Henry J. Shapolsky, a slumlord hiding behind multiple realty company names. One title to 292 was in the name of Ministers and Missionaries Benefit Board of American Baptist Convention (the lord works in mysterious ways). Shapolsky's holdings were concentrated in Harlem and the Lower East Side. In this city with a history of pay-off scandals, Shapolsky had been indicted for bribery in 1958 and convicted of rent gouging in 1959. Yet the city continued to give him pretty much free rein—a forty-eight-hour seizure and demolition action on 292, prompted by violations and debt, was once stayed by a $15 payment towards monies owed. The landlord kept the building.

But still Shapolsky and his partners up and left. The building was seized by the city for nonpayment of taxes but, rather than being repaired for housing, it was boarded up and made uninhabitable. Holes were cut into the boiler, plumbing ripped out and sold for scrap, floors pulled up, and window frames destroyed—the city as vandal. The damaged roof poured water into its insides and rotted its beams. The only occupants were rats, fleas, and sometimes the junkies or homeless of a derelict neighborhood. So much for the American dream.

With a sledgehammer (hidden in a guitar case) to break through the cinderblocks, a small group of squatters opened the house that January of 1986 and worked for weeks by candlelight and flashlight, clearing the floors of debris and rubble. Six people moved into this building with no front door, power, heat, or water, and a roof leak flooding every floor. There was, however, a hydrant outside the front door and a reasonably solid interior. They moved in, artists with an anarchic streak, to make use of one of so many empty buildings, vacant in the face of the great need for housing and the city's inaction to help the homeless and displaced local people.

"It was our choice—our political choice—to do what we were doing," says Andrew Castrucci, an artist who lives at Bullet with his wife, painter Alexandra Rojas, "but everyone had their own reasons. The neighborhood was in transition, and with the housing situation some people had no choice. We were self-help—and we built a community out of it. Historically, the Lower East Side was always a magnet for political and cultural action. We were part of that tradition. We were the dropouts of society, or we were kicked out of society. Twenty years later, we have a victory."

In June 1986 the squatters had installed a front door, in July a toilet in the basement connected to a sewage line. "I remember when we hooked up one light bulb," Castrucci says. "It was so beautiful to turn on the light."

Group work cleared rubble and garbage from the building that would have filled more than twelve dumpsters. But a dumpster rented for $400, so we carried it out bucket by bucket. The backyard was ten feet deep in rubble from the house.

Work sealed the roof in September; no more living with water running into your room and onto your bed. In October we built a bathroom with water pump, bath, and toilet. We rotated the monthly super's duties, which included keeping a dozen buckets filled from the hydrant outside for flushing. The bitter cold of a New York winter meant we often had to crack through an ice layer to pour the water.

By the fall of 1986 the building was secured—locks, doors, and windows. Blackout curtains disguised pirated electricity. Welders built stoves from discarded metal, and we scavenged factory pallets for firewood.

Recycling was the heart of our renovation of 292. Most materials—wood, windows, pipes, metal—were found on the street, in dumpsters, discarded. A building supply company donated its damaged sheetrock to fireproof walls and ceilings. Four of us spent three days in jail for the "crime" of taking windows from a demolition site. Better they be trashed than reused? It's like being arrested for stealing trash from a garbage pile.

Rolando Politi calls himself a "waste recovery and salvation" artist. "I was involved in the squatter movement for twenty-one years before I came to Bullet," he says. His glass mosaics of recycled bottles glow above the doorway at 292 and other squats. "It has inspired and helped me put ideas into practice, and it proves that in a situation of need, it's good to take a chance and not leave the abandoned to a rotten urban neighborhood. We achieved a groundbreaking action by taking unclaimed property and holding on. We proved it was possible to override the system, in a way. We stayed long enough, against a lot of odds. It should inspire other movements—and it has."

In a loosely organized grassroots action, squatters occupied and began to fix dozens of buildings in this derelict neighborhood. The buildings were often named

Artists Alexandra Rojas and Andrew Castrucci in the office of their live/work space. (Photo by Maggie Wrigley)

Gillian Rogers and Griff. The wood-burning stove will be replaced
by a boiler. (Photo by Maggie Wrigley)

after their situations, or aspirations—Serenity House, Glass House, Dos Blockos, C Squat, Rainbow Co-op, Umbrella House (for the system of tarps and buckets protecting residents from leaks). Carpenters and plumbers, electricians and laborers used their skills and taught others to repair and renovate. We cleared adjoining lots and planted community gardens. Lawyers, including civil rights activists William Kunstler and Ron Kuby, volunteered their services to fight the city's eviction processes. The city fought us tooth and nail, not to mention tank and gun.

We tried at many meetings to talk with the community board, to become a recognized homesteading group, but were ignored and reviled as it parceled out the properties of the neighborhood to developers. Our often theatrical and anarchic methods of protest did not endear us to these groups competing for the same dwindling stock of city-owned housing. We opposed developers whose deals included a "low-income" expiration date, say twenty years, when the buildings would revert to market value and the rents would no longer be protected. We staged loud protests, literally drums and whistles, when they would not let us speak. Puppets aped the power figures of the city and the community board, and we held rowdy street demonstrations and marches to protest at the offices of these development groups.

We fought the city's eviction attempts in court and won on creative and practical grounds. When the city said it had rung our doorbell, we brought our "No Bell—Whistle 3 Times" sign; when it said it had posted notices on our apartment doors, we showed the photos of our apartments—with no doors.

Many of the squatter buildings fell to the same predators of gentrification that were destroying the neighborhood—sale to developers and local "nonprofit" groups, police evictions, fires that were allowed to burn the buildings down. Literal battles were fought in the street with cops doing the landlords' dirty work.

The police riot in Tompkins Square Park on August 6, 1988, was the culmination of opposition to these brutal conditions in the community of the Lower East Side—homelessness, ever-increasing rents, inaction by the city government, and police brutality. Squatters, along with our neighbors and the beleaguered homeless who slept in the park, protested—to oppose the park curfew, city neglect of the area, and oppressive police presence. There was a horrible ferocity to the city's response to this partly organized, partly spontaneous people's statement— that perhaps we should take to the streets more and again to make ourselves heard. An uncontrolled army of cops (with badges covered) beat protesters and passers-by alike and tried to destroy cameras recording their actions. The result was six arrests (including Castrucci, with a cracked elbow) but over sixty (investigated) police brutality complaints. The city's officials, police department, and community boards were forced to reassign department heads and appear in court.

Three squats on Thirteenth Street were evicted, following sale to developers, in 1995 in a days-long showdown with hundreds of police in riot gear and an armored vehicle. In 1999 a similar confrontation at Dos Blockos on 9th Street ended after Emergency Services workers drilled through the brick walls and removed residents who had chained themselves to the fire escape. We were some of the hundreds of supporters on the street but were unable to stop the evictions.

We kept working on our building. Floors were raised and straightened (as much as possible in these notoriously crooked old tenements). Windows were replaced. Tree trunks from upstate became columns in the lobby and apartments. We cleaned and lined the old chimneys and, like the old days, burned wood stoves against the cold. Brick by brick, crumbling masonry inside and out was repaired or replaced. We sheetrocked and insulated walls and ceilings. We connected the water from the street and built plumbing for every apartment, from the ground up. Power lines were connected, electricals installed. Skilled workers from different buildings pooled skills and taught each other. An emergency in any building activated the "eviction watch" and brought workers and supporters to help. After a fire, squatters from other buildings rode up on their bicycles with tools, replacement windows, and ceiling beams that were in place by nightfall.

John Farris is a poet and writer who came to Bullet after he and the longtime troupe Living Theater were evicted from a nearby storefront. "Being an unsuccessful writer, and having lost much of the use of my legs, I was without a place to live," he says. A story he wrote for a Bullet publication brought him to the house as a space opened up. "I have a place to live because of that story," he says. "But when I came here the situation was very confrontational with the police. I am not an anarchist, but I question the state and question authority. Now we are getting the building, the stress level is way down. I have done quite a bit of work since I have been here, and have been published quite a lot." Farris's poems have been exhibited at Bullet and other gallery shows, and his work is published regularly in the Lower East Side-based magazine *A Gathering of the Tribes* and other anthologies. But daily hardships are paramount in a New York City winter. "Now," he says, "the only enemy is income—and the weather."

Other residents of the building are sculptor Johanna Bartelt, painters and playwrights Regina Bartkoff and Charles Schick with actor-daughter Hannah, and the musicians Ali Rogers and husband Griff, with her daughter Gillian, now ten. Former residents include the painters Thom Corn, Al Blue, Sebastian Schroeder, and Andrea Neumann and the writer Jonathan Leake.

Bullet was an artists' house from the beginning. The gallery at Bullet Space was created in December 1987. People in the building needed an outlet for their creative energy and wanted a place to present their social, artistic, and political views. Bullet became a multi-media art and performance space, a "battlefield of ideas" for residents, associated artists, musicians, and people of the local community. The first show and performances were in January 1988.

Multi-media art exhibits and installations, theater productions, dance, fire

Poet and writer John Farris at home. (Photo by Maggie Wrigley)

Rolando Politi uses recycled materials to create masks and costumes
for his activist group performances. (Photo by Maggie Wrigley)

eaters, readings, and musical performances have graced the gallery and the backyard stage. A print shop was built. *Your House Is Mine*, an artists' book and poster project organized and edited by Andrew Castrucci and Nadia Coen, was printed and bound in a "factory" in the house over four years and is now in the collections of the New York Public Library and museums around the world. The book contains works by a hundred artists and writers, many from the neighborhood, some who were or had been homeless, or living with AIDS. The posters—"An Act of Resistance"—were hung in huge swaths across abandoned buildings of the neighborhood in colorful political outrage. The original printing setup was powered by the house industrial vacuum cleaner, the pages hung to dry on wires all over the house.

Artists such as David Wojnarowich, Richard Hell, Stefan Eins, Martin Wong, Darius James, and Bimbo Rivas and other Nuyorican poets have performed, shown, or worked with Bullet, as have the graffiti artists Lee, Lady Pink, and A-One. A production of *Medea*, adapted by Schick and Bartkoff, had two runs. A pirate radio station, Steal This Radio, evaded the FCC and broadcast for a time from the space, featuring musical, community, and political programs, some run by local teenagers, and live performances by musicians from all over the world.

The sale of the building for conversion to ownership by the squatters has aroused conflict with some neighbors, especially new renters who are paying huge rents in a gentrified area. Real estate is incredibly expensive here now, and some renters pay $2,000 a month for cubicle-sized apartments with little light. "People are jealous," said Farris, "but they didn't want to be here before." We hope to keep our rents down to about $400 for 500 square feet. We are proving that housing can be created without unnecessary expense, through recycling and sweat equity.

Our deal with the city, however, contains a gift to the city. These buildings will be low-income forever—no resale value ever at market prices, no speculation, no expiration on the rent protection. These are the last buildings in the neighborhood to be able to do this: permanent affordable housing for the people of this city. It is why we squatted in the beginning. Our new challenges are bureaucratic and practical—the paperwork for a mortgage, the cost of renovation up to code, and the plans for installing a boiler and radiators, laying gas lines for kitchens, and rebuilding the stairs. Sweat equity to keep it affordable means we have many workdays to go.

The squat at 292 has housed people from the streets, shelters, neighborhood, and from overseas. Hundreds have exhibited and performed here. Many more have contributed their work, ideas, and spirit. They have a space, which, but for our work, would never have existed. This building shelters and nurtures many lives and dreams.

• • •

This story first appeared in the September/October 2003 edition of *DESIGNER/builder* magazine.

BULLET SPACE

Wentworth Gardens women residents receiving the American Planning Association's Award for Social Advocacy. (Photo by Roberta Feldman, courtesy of Roberta Feldman and Susan Stall)

KINGSLEY HAMMETT

LET US NOW PRAISE THE WOMEN OF WENTWORTH

IT'S NOT EASY BEING POOR IN AMERICA. IT'S EVEN HARDER IF YOU are a black woman living in dilapidated public housing in the segregated South Side of Chicago. Chances are a combination of a leaking roof, crumbling exterior brick, drafty windows, and faulty plumbing leaves your family living amid mold and mildew. The paint peeling off the walls and woodwork is likely lead based and poisoning your children and grandchildren. The building probably harbors packs of rats and feral cats. It's quite likely the cracked and broken pipes that radiate out from a central heating plant spit streams of steam from the ground between buildings. And there are few parks and little playground equipment to allow your family to enjoy the outdoors.

In 1949 the federal government endorsed a policy that guaranteed every American a safe and decent place to live. But in the last fifty-five years it has never come forward with adequate funds to build nearly enough subsidized housing for those who need it, not to mention enough for management or maintenance. The sad irony is that the federal government appears to resent the needs of the poor while it constantly showers benefits and tax breaks on the wealthy.

The conditions suffered by public housing residents have infuriated University of Illinois at Chicago (UIC) architecture professor Roberta Feldman who has been working with the women of Wentworth Gardens for the last ten years. They have made such progress in helping to plan and direct the future of their public housing development that Feldman nominated the group for a social advocacy award from the American Planning Association.

"I got involved because I was just outraged that in our country we don't have the will to assure that all Americans have safe and decent homes, clothing, food, and medical care," says Feldman, co-founder of the UIC City Design Center. "I worked with the public housing women of Wentworth Gardens to assist them in saving their homes from the wrecking ball."

In the end Feldman views public housing tenants very differently from the stereotype. She sees women who are creative, intelligent, persistent, ingenious, and resourceful—in short, amazing. But despite their efforts, at the end of the day, when the tenants have struggled to survive and sustain their human dignity, the challenge is no less than the day before. This makes Feldman even angrier.

"They shouldn't have to do all this work," she says. "They have a right, just as I do, to take for granted that there will be food on the table, a decent roof over their head, a safe school for their kids, and available medical care so they can go on with their lives and do other productive, wonderful things. But they have to put all of their energies into surviving because in this country we simply don't believe these people deserve basic rights."

Feldman put her experiences together in a book, co-authored with Northeastern Illinois University professor Susan Stall, titled *The Dignity of Resistance: Women Residents' Activism in Chicago Public Housing*. They wanted to burst the image of the lazy, indolent, if not pathological welfare queen; to celebrate the resolve of the women of Wentworth Gardens; and to paint them accurately as amazing individuals doing remarkable things with a paucity of resources. As far as the authors are concerned, the way society brands such women is nothing short of an act of violence.

"Susan and I set out to make their efforts visible," Feldman says. "But at the end of telling the whole story we felt that society still will not recognize what these women are doing and will not recognize the racism, the sexism, and the classism that has produced and maintains poverty."

Contrary to popular myth, the women of Wentworth Gardens and the thousands like them in public housing everywhere don't choose to be poor and don't like to live in substandard housing, Feldman says. The fact is that public housing, a poorly conceptualized program that was underfunded from day one, made it impossible for the government to build, operate, and maintain enough units. Then it located the ones it did build—at least in Chicago and many other cities—so as to segregate minority families. By the 1960s the condition of public housing began a precipitous slide, fueled by a lack of federal funding for building maintenance and cutbacks in social services and youth activities for low-income tenants, things accepted as given in middle-class apartment complexes. After another twenty years of neglect, Chicago's public housing was in an abysmal state of affairs. Many of the developments had had no repairs whatsoever, leaving a truly dangerous situation. As the federal government dramatically decreased its funding for public housing, as building maintenance and energy costs rose, as playground equipment aged, as field houses were closed, and as youth programming services were terminated, the environment became unlivable.

Meeting of resident leaders. (Photo by Diana Solis, courtesy of Roberta Feldman and Susan Stall)

Back in the 1980s Feldman attended a conference of a coalition of public housing activists to discuss the issues around how public housing tenants collectively might be able to do something about the condition of their homes. They hoped that if all of the organizations—both formal and informal—got together across the public housing spectrum, they might have more power to pressure for funding to renovate their buildings, provide social services, and secure better management.

To demonstrate what their homes meant to public housing residents, Feldman compiled a photo documentary accompanied by the words of the tenants. By then the women of Wentworth had heard the federal government was going to tear down a lot of public housing. So part of the initial battle was to change public perception that all public housing residents wanted to run and get out of their deteriorating units. Instead, Feldman could see that these women were very attached to their homes.

"After the conference I got a call from a woman in Wentworth Gardens to come and help them," she says. "They were very concerned that their development—along with many others—was going to be torn down. They also had heard that they could take part in a federal program to become resident managers. They chose to participate not because they wanted to become resident managers, but because they thought it was a way to save their homes and community."

Mistrustful of the Chicago Housing Authority's report on the condition of their building, the women of Wentworth Gardens asked Feldman to conduct an

Resident-run convenience store. (Photo by Jack Naughton, courtesy of Roberta Feldman and Susan Stall)

independent architecture/engineering survey. They wanted to make sure that if they were going to assume management responsibility they understood what condition the physical plant was in. And they wanted to know that they would have an adequate budget for maintenance to deal with the building that at the time had been cited for 1,000 building violations.

"Any other building owner in the city would have been required to correct them," Feldman says of the code violations. "But the Chicago Housing Authority was never pressed. And this was in just one small 422-unit building. So you can imagine what it was like in the larger developments."

With colleagues from UIC, she did the survey and recommended they not take on the heating plant, which would have required millions of dollars to fix. And the women used this knowledge in their negotiations with the housing authority. "That was one of the things that was amazing about these women," Feldman says. "They were always on the lookout for technical assistance, and they were very effective in finding people to help. They kept me busy constantly, which is part of their remarkable organizing skills."

Feldman wanted to make their story public to show that the very damaging stereotype of public housing residents is the antithesis of the reality. "What I saw was that the residents were not lazy, not childlike, and certainly were not vandals and criminals," she says. "In fact, they were intelligent, creative, caring, and more energetic than I could imagine myself ever being. And they clearly were concerned about their community in ways I haven't experienced in my own middle class community."

Feldman was amazed at the number of strategies the women used to achieve their goals and the relentless way in which they pressed their case. They met, whether informally in a backyard or in the local advisory council's office, to discuss current problems and to develop ways to deal with them. They wrote grants to get money to pay for improvements in youth and social services. They badgered higher management at the housing authority for whatever they needed and recently secured $1 million to renovate and reopen the field house. They visited local and state politicians. They rented buses and took groups of residents to public meetings at city hall and got up to the mike and asked for renovation monies. Whenever they met a professional who had a skill they needed, they would immediately ask for help. And they maintained those relationships so they could call for help when they needed to.

Their success has been remarkable. When the Chicago Housing Authority closed the laundromat, the women managed to pressure the on-site manager to get some funds to open a volunteer laundromat that's still there, forty years later. When the retail stores abandoned the community and when the White Sox stadium was built and destroyed the commercial street and people had to go two miles to get their groceries, they opened up a volunteer-run convenience store in the basement. They have organized an amazing array of youth recreation and educational programming, from taking trips to museums to tutoring to getting play equipment for their children. They have a free food program, where volunteer residents cook for the elderly and infirm. One of the women—out of her own pocket—cooks rice and beans and serves simple lunches and dinners to about thirty hungry kids. She also started a resident-led spiritual development center that has become so popular it has drawn people from outside the housing development. And when the field house was closed the women fought with the management for two years to allow them to reopen it for a pre-school program equipped with things they brought from home until they could get the Chicago Park District to run programs in the field house again.

"This is all done by volunteers," Feldman says. "These women are spending twelve hours a day doing this work. And in many cases they are working full-time or raising grandchildren while their daughters work, as well."

Feldman devoted so much of her time to the women of Wentworth Gardens because she believed people needed a say in planning the future of their own housing. She is happy they have succeeded in saving their development from destruction and that the housing authority is renovating their housing and providing the social services they can't afford to purchase on their own. But her experience taught her that participation in and of itself is not the answer to solving what she believes is a national housing crisis. There simply is not enough affordable housing, even for the working poor, let alone for the very poor. While the estimated

Children dancing at a resident-organized community-wide celebration.
(Photo by Roberta Feldman, courtesy of Roberta Feldman and Susan Stall)

need is for 50 million new units, the federal government is tearing down many of the 3.5 million units it built over the last fifty years.

"I see these women working effectively," she says. "Their participation skills are honed and creative. But participation alone is not going to solve the housing crisis. When we tear down public housing, we're not just tearing down decrepit buildings. People are attached to their homes and their communities. These communities are necessary for their survival and we're breaking them up."

The current federal government's policy is to tear down public housing and turn the land over to the private market for redevelopment as mixed-income housing. Yet this policy will replace only 14 percent of the pubic housing units that are eliminated.

"Today in Chicago," she says, "a combination of federal and city housing programs are effectively sweeping out the poor, and low-income residents are being dispersed to the fringes of the city equipped with no more than a rental voucher that will pay only for housing conditions as terrible as those they've left. This is not the answer for providing the safe and decent housing we all need."

• • •

This story first appeared in the May/June 2005 edition of *DESIGNER/builder* magazine.

Doug Young. (Photo by Francisco Ferreira)

JERILOU HAMMETT AND KINGSLEY HAMMETT

DOUG YOUNG

A CRITICAL URBANIST LOOKS AT THE GLOBAL CITY

*In 1975 Doug Young fulfilled a boyhood dream and graduated from the University
of Toronto with a bachelor's degree in architecture. In those days the program,
born in the 1960s, was open ended, student centered, and very exciting, something
hard to imagine at big institutions today. But his first day at his first job was one of
the most depressing days of his life and was nothing like what he imagined architecture to be. A few years later he drifted away from architecture and into urban
planning, first for the city of Toronto, then for a nonprofit housing organization,
and finally as a teacher.*

*Today Young teaches urban studies and planning at York University, is finish-
ing his PhD, and is working at the City Institute, a recently established research
center at York where people in all the different departments doing urban-related
studies can connect with each other. He's also a member of Planning Action, a radical group of architects, planners, and concerned citizens that believes that planning
has more to do with the retention and preservation of traditional neighborhoods
(and their residents) than with rubber-stamping expensive development projects. In
a conversation from his base at York University, Young shared with Jerilou and
Kingsley Hammett the journey he has taken from neophyte architect to radical planner and critical urbanist.*

DESIGNER/BUILDER: How did your disillusionment with traditional architecture
unfold?
DOUG YOUNG: The first day on the job I was given a plan for a piece of property out
in the suburbs and was told I had a free hand to lay out a development. I came up
with what I thought was a very clever arrangement of streets with a mix of houses
for wealthy people and houses for poor people. At the end of the day I showed it

to my boss, who said very nicely, "This is not how development takes place." Mixing housing for different income groups was not going to happen and the street plan was too unusual. There was a template to follow that I wasn't aware of and if you were going to do that kind of work you had to follow the template. I remember going home absolutely devastated. All those years I had dreamed of being an architect and it all came down to satisfying some market idea of what housing should be like. As I worked for other architects I became increasingly disenchanted.

I remember being struck as an undergraduate by the remarks a guest lecturer in architecture once made. He said of all the graduates of architecture programs about one-third of them go on to really embrace architecture and have their own practices. One-third go on to something else related, like maybe planning. And one-third become fodder in giant offices. I felt like part of the fodder, given tiny, boring, minute tasks. I worked for small offices with neurotic relationships among the staff and the boss. I found it very unpleasant. Some projects were more interesting than others. One firm did social housing, and that was kind of fun, except as the junior I think the most exciting thing I was given was to come up with some decorative brickwork for this apartment building.

I was getting sick of what appeared to me to be the role of architects in facilitating how cities got built and what they looked like. I have an architect friend who worked for a practice where the partner once asked him to come into his office and said, "I really want you to spend a long time designing this big building. I want you to spend a whole day on it." And I think that's pretty typical. It's just product.

So I left the last firm that I worked for and did a bit of freelance work with a friend. Six months later I was hired by the City of Toronto planning department to be a kind of architectural support to the other people who were trained as planners. It had dawned on them that here were planners reviewing projects and architectural drawings and they had no idea how to even read a drawing, making it very difficult to comment and negotiate. I was lucky in that it was 1979, the tail end of the most progressive era in municipal planning in Toronto that had been instituted in the early 1970s. The city was very much into having neighborhood satellite offices away from city hall and citizens involved in the planning process. In the city that was then about 700,000 people, at one point there were thirteen satellite planning offices outside of city hall. That was one office for every 50,000 to 60,000 people. When I arrived there were five. Now, in the city, which is about 2.6 million, there are a total of four. In the early days, they were all engaged in coming up with new official neighborhood plans, and they truly believed they should be out there talking to people who lived in those districts and having them be almost equal partners in determining what was good planning.

I was also lucky in that I became attached to this small group of very interesting people who were pretty much all politically on the left. That was part of the era as well. This new batch of planners had come out of the universities in the early 1970s having been exposed as students to what was a neo-Marxist kind of radical critique of traditional methods and ideas about planning.

DESIGNER/BUILDER: Can you talk about what this philosophy looked like, this critique?

DOUG YOUNG: Planning had been considered a rational science where planning experts knew everything about everything in a city and made wise decisions. Beginning in the late 1960s and early 1970s, some planning activists and theorists began to critique this view. People in the streets in the 1960s in the United States and Canada knew that that approach to planning had not delivered the good city it had promised. There still were lots of problems. People in their neighborhoods and some planners started to understand that planning is not a science. It is political; it is contested. And there are different ways of knowing a city and different ways of thinking about planning.

So I went to work with this group of planners. It was very exciting and I had fun. I thought what I was doing was good work. I was working in the public sector for the benefit of the people of Toronto. I thought I could help produce a better city. But even though we saw ourselves as working with the people and for the people, we still were technocrats who just gave professional expert advice to politicians who would decide on things. I remember one councilor called those of us who would be working in his part of the city down to his office and said, "I want to make it very clear. This is my ward. I don't want any of you to think that you're some kind of advocate planner stirring things up out there. This is my part of the city, and what happens here will be what I want to happen here." Another time I went to a public meeting with a councilor who, as we walked in, turned to me and asked, "What do I think about this project?"

So I became increasingly frustrated with my inability to actually effect any kind of real change. I would produce reports that went nowhere, or I would give advice to developers. A developer would come in with a proposal. I would look at the drawings and say, "I think you should make these changes." He would go away and do them, and then I thought, okay, what I've really just done is made it easier for this guy to sell these apartments or to rent this space. I've just helped him make more money. I became really troubled again by this role of merely being a support to private-sector development. And even though I was now operating from the public sector, I was just reacting to these developments that came in through the door, but couldn't on my own initiate what I thought would be something good for the city. So I decided in 1984 to take some time out. I went to England to study planning, thinking I really wanted a deeper, theoretical understanding of what planning's role is or could be in a capitalist society.

DESIGNER/BUILDER: Why did you go to England?

DOUG YOUNG: I was really eager to have an experience outside of Canada. It was a choice between MIT and the Architectural Association (AA) in London. I decided to go to another continent. The AA was founded in the 1840s in the spirit of independent thinking. It's generally known as an important school of architecture, and at the time it also had a very small graduate planning program. It was taught entirely by extremely radical critics of planning and critics of capitalism. It was a brilliant, wonderful experience.

DESIGNER/BUILDER: What did you come away with?

DOUG YOUNG: A very clear, radicalized understanding of the role of planning in a capitalist society. I saw that the state's role is to assist in accumulation and legitimation to help capitalists continue to thrive. It does things like establish a legal system and a banking system so that the capitalist system in general doesn't dissolve into total chaos. It enforces contracts and it sets rules about banking, etc. It also gets involved in planning cities where capitalists operate. A Marxist would say this is a system that is inherently unequal, coercive, and hierarchical. It's a system that treats a lot of people very poorly. And so planning, in supporting this system, also treats people very differently; it assists in the enrichment of some people and the impoverishment of others.

The legitimation function of government is to make people think that even though the system is inherently unequal in the distribution of benefits across society, it's not such a bad life after all and maybe one day they, too, will be able to move out to the suburbs to a new house. Government occasionally makes concessions to poor and working-class people. It will open a daycare center in a poor neighborhood or call public meetings to discuss planning proposals, giving people the illusion that their voice matters in the planning process.

DESIGNER/BUILDER: What did you do after you got your planning degree?

DOUG YOUNG: When I came back, I made the mistake of going back to my old job. I'd taken a leave of absence rather than quitting, because I think I was just afraid. But I was even more frustrated now because I was this radicalized planner. Yet how could I speak those words of a radical planning critique within the bureaucracy of a huge planning department? It was very difficult. I more or less kept it all inside me. But when I reviewed a planning application, I was very explicit in my own mind about who would win and who would lose, who was going to benefit if this was approved, and how could we possibly change this to benefit different people or more people?

DESIGNER/BUILDER: Were you able to make a difference?

DOUG YOUNG: In one neighborhood I worked on an issue where builders had illegally created tiny apartment units that were known locally as bachelorettes. A studio apartment in Toronto is called a bachelor apartment and these were even smaller. Typically somebody got a building permit to put an addition onto an old house and create a rooming house with maybe thirty rooms. In a rooming house you could either have a bathroom or a kitchen attached to your room, but not both. They would generally show drawings with the bathroom and then sneak in a little kitchen. There were also questions of bribes. The result was a neighborhood with many buildings comprised of 150-, 200-square-foot apartment units, with no parking, with no amenity space within the building for tenants, etc. Somehow the situation had to be legalized, but I felt that whatever we did we should not punish the tenants, who could not afford to live anywhere else. My view was there are many people in our society who cannot afford even the cheapest product that is legally produced on the housing market. Either they get help from government, live in illegally created substandard housing, or live on the street. It's not their fault. So I tried to develop a policy that would guarantee at least a minimum standard of quality housing but do minimum damage to the living situation of the tenants.

We decided to identify those units that were below the Ontario Building Code, which I think for a studio apartment is 275 square feet. When people actually moved out and units became vacant, we then could combine units to create bigger ones that met the standards. In this way we would gradually upgrade the housing, we would not evict anyone, and we would minimize the upward creep of the rental costs by keeping units very small. In the end we would get legalized housing of at least minimum standard with as few people as possible de-housed. I felt good about that.

But I came to realize I was a tiny bureaucrat in this huge organization. My day-to-day power was to decide which file in my in-basket would go to the top. If an ordinary citizen came in to see me to talk about how to put an addition of one room on the back of his house, I could give him a lot of my time and be very helpful. I realized that one power I had was knowledge of the system. I could actually read the zoning bylaws and understand them, make them comprehensible to an ordinary person, and help him get through the system.

But I also realized that this was no way to have any impact on the city in which I live. So I contacted a nonprofit organization called the Cooperative Housing Federation of Toronto (CHFT), which in those days developed nonprofit housing co-ops and also provided support services to those they had helped build as well as others. I just called them and said, "I would like to work for you people."

I quit my job as a city planner in 1989 and went to work as a project manager at CHFT. They somehow thought, "Oh great! We have a planner. He'll cut through all the red tape in the planning process that we have to go through with all of our projects." The late 1980s was a period of really generous financial support from the province and from the federal government for nonprofit housing. It was very stressful work because I had to deal with private-sector builders, private-sector banks, and bureaucrats in the provincial Ministry of Housing. But at the end of the process, I saw people move into their affordable housing units, and it was wonderful. It brought together my interests in planning, architecture, housing, and public policy. It had been a long journey from that first day on the job as an architect, but I reached a point where I was pretty happy with what I was doing.

Over a period of seven years I was responsible for something like 1,000 units of nonprofit housing being developed. In seven years as a planner, what did I produce? A lot of reports. In five years on the job as an architect, what did I produce? Some buildings that I'm not really thrilled to think that I had a hand in. In seven years with CHFT I produced housing for probably 2,500 people, housing that will probably last a hundred years. So it's like 250,000 person years of housing. And I'm really happy about that, not in any way to brag about it, but just in terms of having made or helped create material impacts on the lives of ordinary people.

But in 1995 a radically right-wing provincial government was elected in Ontario. Within a week they announced they were canceling all funding for new social housing construction. Subsidized housing so contravened their ideology that the private market should provide housing and that it's the individual's responsibility to take care of themselves, to house themselves. They should not look to government. It was not government's business to provide housing. So a year later I was out of a job.

Today I see an absolute crisis in housing affordability in Ontario. Twenty years ago, homelessness was not an enormous problem. Now you kind of step over homeless people. I live in a very middle-class neighborhood in the center of the city, and adjacent to it is a very wealthy neighborhood. My apartment building looks onto some very nice bits of parkland with some very dense shrubbery. There are many homeless people who live there. I had no idea until I moved into this neighborhood. It's very interesting. Middle-class people leave my building heading off to the subway station in the morning, and then you see the homeless people moving through the neighborhood. I started recognizing the homeless people as my neighbors. I would see them shaving in the men's room of the food court under the office building where I take the subway. It's just extraordinary the social damage that eight years of radical right-wing government has done in this province—the damage it did to the city in terms of levels of poverty, people sleeping in the street, people begging.

DESIGNER/BUILDER: What is your critique of Toronto as a new global city?

DOUG YOUNG: While Toronto is going after new-economy knowledge workers, what is it doing about the old-economy factory workers, of whom there still are tens of thousands? Aren't they important to the city of Toronto? Do we really think all we need to do is create some glamour zones downtown, and that's doing a good job of making a good city? What about the neighborhoods where most people live? Don't they deserve good planning? Don't they deserve investment in public resources? Don't they deserve good public transit? Don't they deserve beautiful parks, libraries, and schools?

In terms of the new kind of approach to planning, I think it goes back several decades and tries to de-democratize the planning process. It now is virtually impossible for an ordinary person to participate meaningfully in a public planning debate. The new discourse is all about the idea of beauty and creating beautiful places. Gone are such things as density or height limits. The idea is all we should care about is design and whether or not a building "fits." If a world-famous architect stands up at a public meeting and says, "I believe that my proposal for a seventy-five-story condominium is a beautiful one that fits perfectly with this neighborhood," how does an ordinary non-expert resident of that neighborhood challenge the opinion of the expert architect? It's impossible. It becomes "he said, she said," or "in my opinion and in your opinion," and the whole discourse is geared to being globally attractive and globally successful. It's geared toward, "We need buildings by Daniel Libeskind and Frank Gehry and any of these internationally famous architects." How can an ordinary person, living in a very ordinary house, stand up and challenge Daniel Libeskind and say, "I think your building is ugly?" Who is going to be believed? I think this has just completely gutted any kind of democratic process.

I tried to get involved in a development proposal in the neighborhood where I was living until about six months ago. I spoke against it at the public meeting and realized as I was speaking that I couldn't actually make an argument that would be recognized as a solid planning argument against this building. Under earlier rules I could have. I could have said, "There is a neighborhood plan that was produced twenty years ago, after extensive consultation with the neighborhood that determined that a building shouldn't be taller than six stories or have a density higher than three times lot area. And this proposal is for a twenty-two-story building with a density of nine." And I asked, "What is the planning rationale for quadrupling the height and tripling the density?" But at the same time I was asking those questions I realized under the new rules it doesn't matter anymore. You do not have to justify the density or the height. You just have to make, as the architect and developer made, an aesthetic argument about this being a future landmark and a gateway to the neighborhood, and that it supported the city's policy of intensification, which is pitched as being how you create a sustainable city. It's argued that you have a black-and-white choice: you either accept hyper-intensification in the city or you produce an unsustainable region of urban sprawl. There's no nuance to that argument. There's no gray area in between.

DESIGNER/BUILDER: And there's no proof of that.

DOUG YOUNG: No, there's no proof, but so far it's been very successful for developers and for politicians and planners who support these views. There is an unbelievable wave of intensification in the form of new condominiums being built in the city.

DESIGNER/BUILDER: Do you think these politicians buy it on some kind of rational basis or because their pockets are being filled with campaign donations or whatever it's called in Canada?

DOUG YOUNG: I think it's a mixture. I think the question of the donation applies, in fact, more in the outer suburban municipalities. A professor at York University did a study of one municipality. He went through all of the donations and it was remarkable how many politicians in the outer suburbs are entirely bankrolled by the development industry. I think in the central city it's more a belief in the growth machine. It's a belief that this is good for the city, that investment is good, development is good. In one sense nothing has changed. It's the same kind of boosterist belief that we need development and without development we have a crisis. But now it's seen in a global context where we're competing with Brussels, we're competing with Chicago, we're competing with Hong Kong. We need as many people living here as possible. We need wealthy people. We need highly educated people. And we've got to give them a glamorous, pizzazzy city of glamorous condos and fancy shopping and world-class cultural facilities or they won't come here. And if they don't come here, we're a failure as a city. That's driving planning work at the moment. Although they still go through the motions of public meetings, etc. I think that kind of democratic, neighborhood-based approach to planning has been gutted and replaced by a belief that there is a global economic imperative and we have to comply with it or we die as a city.

DESIGNER/BUILDER: Meanwhile, prices go up, services get cut back, the city faces constant financial crisis, and it cannot afford any of the amenities that its people need.

DOUG YOUNG: Absolutely. But it's so contradictory because on the other hand, there are signs of extraordinary wealth and glamour. It speaks to the unevenness inherent in capitalist development where, as the city gets wealthier, it also gets poorer. There are more millionaires than ever before. In Toronto, you can read in the same edition of the local newspaper that more houses were sold at prices over a million dollars last year than ever before. Then turn the page, and it talks about how more people are sleeping in the streets. This region is growing at an extraordinarily fast rate and the problems are at the point where they're almost strangling it.

Transportation is impossible. You would think that the people in the far-out suburbs who drive everywhere would demand more freeway speed belts. You would think that truckers, who carry everything that we use in our daily lives, who are stuck in traffic jams all day long, would demand some action. It takes me an hour, using public transit, to travel about ten miles from downtown to my university. You'd think that we would have the power to demand better transit. You would think that if a region wants to be globally competitive, it would understand that it's got to move people around from home to work and back again and allow trucks to move freely. You would think that government would actually open its checkbook. But there is such a political culture here of not raising taxes and of wanting to spend as little money as possible that apparently senior government is prepared to let six million people choke on their traffic.

We have nowhere to put our garbage, and presently it's shipped to Michigan. Hundreds of trucks go down the freeway every day carrying Toronto's crap to a landfill site outside of Detroit. But Michigan has recently announced that it's going to stop that a couple years from now. That's a big issue. We have very serious air pollution problems. In summer it's unbelievably bad. We have a crisis in affordability of housing. You read articles that trumpet how much the cost of housing went up last year. That's great if you're a developer or a landlord or you already own your own house. But there are 70,000 households waiting for subsidized housing just in the city of Toronto.

Many people have written about the global city and the dual economy. In the financial district we have a huge core of giant office towers and the headquarters of Canadian banks. Then there's an army of thousands of minimum-wage workers, many of them probably illegal, scurrying around delivering things and cleaning offices and living in crappy basement apartments and not able to take their kids to the dentist. Between 1995 and 2003 there was a radical right-wing provincial government that slashed welfare rates by 20 percent, de-listed services from public health care, and stopped building any more nonprofit housing. They also decided they would cut all financial support to local public transit systems.

DESIGNER/BUILDER: Does Toronto impose impact fees?
DOUG YOUNG: Yes. But then the argument is if we set ours too high, development will go to the suburbs. There's a local competition for investment and people between the city of Toronto with about 2.6 million people and the outer suburban municipalities where about 3 million people live.

There's also something called Section 37 benefits. In the Official Plan, there's a section that says if you approve a development that in some way exceeds the zoning bylaws, you can make up for it with a cash contribution that would then be spent on some kind of public facility in the neighborhood. But the counterargument is that's just a sort of checkbook planning where a developer comes in and says okay, how much do you want? It takes the onus off of government from having any responsibility for building those social services, those libraries, and those improved parks.

DESIGNER/BUILDER: Do they actually ever get built, or does that money just go down the rat hole?

DOUG YOUNG: No, they get built, but it seems not to be a good way of making a good city. I went to the opening of an addition to a wonderful community center downtown that does wonderful work and has fabulous programs. But the city councilor, cutting the ribbon to this addition, said, "Isn't it wonderful that your future neighbors have paid for this addition in the form of the contributions that the developers made in exchange for permission to build all of these high-rise condo towers." And I thought there's a problem here. We should be getting this addition without having to accept this incredible hyper-intensification of the center of the city.

DESIGNER/BUILDER: How is planning viewed today?

DOUG YOUNG: There is a general belief that government should step back and allow the market more freedom. In the 1950s, 1960s, and into the early 1970s, while working within the context of a capitalist society, government saw that it could have an active role in producing good cities and good nations and that it should support individuals in terms of social welfare who could then go out into the market and buy a house or buy a car or buy clothing or whatever.

I think since the 1970s, there's been a global shift away from that to this fear that if you over-regulate investment will go somewhere else. Production is so global and so flexible that companies will, if they don't like your regulations, just pick up and move somewhere else. If you look at planning department websites for cities around the world they all have the same language. It's this fear of footloose capital: if you have too rigid or too demanding planning regulations, investors will go and build a shopping mall in another city, in another country, on another continent.

Toronto is completely caught up in the whole discourse of global economic competitiveness and sees itself competing for investment with every major American urban region and every major region around the world. The discourse is: we need to attract new-economy knowledge workers who can relocate to anywhere in the world, so we have to produce an exciting and attractive city for them. In the past, government saw that it had an interventionist role to play in producing a good city. Now, in terms of planning, the role is to completely loosen up regulations to make it easier than ever to build a glamorous, fifty-story condo tower or an office building, to draft a new official plan that encourages more development than ever, and to cloak it all under the guise of creating a sustainable and green city.

Designer/Builder: What impact has this had on existing neighborhoods?
Doug Young: Right now we have a different provincial government that is somewhat less conservative. There is a program called the Neighborhood Action Plan where the municipal and federal governments are channeling investment, however small, into thirteen neighborhoods (out of a total of 140) that have been identified as priority neighborhoods. But the damage is very difficult to undo.

As part of the new entrepreneurial approach, the school board made individual schools compete for money. In one of these priority neighborhoods that I have studied one of the schools was selected to serve as a model. That school received extra money, which means it can restart a music program that it used to have but had to cancel. This is now seen as an extraordinarily generous donation, or rather, not a donation but an investment in this neighborhood school. But you could also argue, why doesn't every school have sufficient money to fund a music program?

It's a very clever strategy that you pick thirteen neighborhoods and you—meaning government—channel money toward them, piddly little amounts of money compared to what would have been spent there thirty or forty years ago in terms of social services. The government can then say, "See, we care." And then private corporations, if they want to appear to be socially responsible, can announce that they are making an investment in one of the priority neighborhoods. And they get a lot of press out of it. This begs the question, what about the other 127 neighborhoods? They're absolute losers. In this new approach, the thirteen "loser" neighborhoods become the winners, because they're getting the attention and the money, however small it is. All other neighborhoods are left to struggle on their own with their crappy schools, their crappy libraries, their crappy bus service. The school that got the extra money, I'm sure, should be really happy. But somehow that school, and all other schools, and all other community groups have to go public and political and argue that every school deserves that level of funding, not just one model school in one of the thirteen targeted neighborhoods. All 500 schools deserve that money.

DESIGNER/BUILDER: Didn't that money go to tax cuts?

DOUG YOUNG: Exactly. The systemic problem is the cuts that were made to education funding ten years ago in this province when our taxes were cut something like 20 or 30 percent. At the same time that education funding was cut, transit funding was cut, welfare funding was cut, and services were de-listed from public health care. I think the question is, and it's a question that was asked by those first radical planners in the late 1960s: if you want to create a city or a society of social and environmental justice, is planning the way to do it? Maybe planning isn't. Maybe it's broader-based political activity, which some planners will want to join. Maybe planning isn't the way to a socially and environmentally just and democratic city. I don't think it is. I think planning is institutionally incapable of being radical or progressive. It can be kind of reformist. Maybe, under pressure, tweak this or tweak that. If all the planning rules and the planning policies have been rigged in favor of development, there's very little room for an individual radical or progressive or democratic planner to do anything. I'm very pessimistic about planning as an institution or state-regulated process to achieve what I would consider a good city. I think it has to come through broader social movements and political action. Planners can take part in that. Planners can form groups like Planning Action in Toronto. What's interesting in terms of framing Toronto as a case study is that this is the city that used to be looked to in the 1970s as a model of good planning, good governance, good transit, etc. I don't think anyone looks to Toronto as a model of anything good any more.

• • •

This story first appeared in the January/February 2007 edition of *DESIGNER/builder* magazine.

Tom Klem installing a sign and speaking to the press at the Gowanus Houses at Baltic and Hoyt Streets in Brooklyn where Nicholas Heyward Jr. was killed while playing with a plastic toy gun. A second copy of this sign was placed at the Criminal Court Building on Centre Street in Manhattan. This sign addresses the issue of police brutality and the deaths of three victims by police officers. (Photo by Adam DeCroix, courtesy of RepoHistory)

KINGSLEY HAMMETT

WHOSE HISTORY IS IT, ANYWAY?

HISTORY, THEY SAY, IS WRITTEN BY THE VICTORS. SO IT IS HARDLY
surprising that historical markers generally document the sites of power and privilege while the rest gets easily forgotten. An attempt to correct this chronic imbal-
ance was made fifteen years ago in New York City by an imaginative organization
called RepoHistory, which sought to mark sites and tell stories of significant but
ignored events and individuals.

"We wanted to focus on the untold histories of lower Manhattan, to 'repossess
forgotten history,' to reclaim the past, and to represent it in a multi-layered, living
narrative that would tell the stories of race, class, gender, and sexuality among the
marginalized and disenfranchised," says Tom Klem, one of the group's founding
members. "The powerful write history, and they eliminate the items they don't
want remembered. RepoHistory was there to put back those histories."

RepoHistory was a reaction to what its members considered the premature
declaration of the death of political activism. By the late 1980s, groups like
PADD, Political Art for Documentation and Distribution, were gone. Artists for
Nuclear Disarmament no longer existed. Artists Call had ended. But a diverse collective of New York City artists, actors, writers, filmmakers, historians, and educators refused to accept that verdict. They got together to form a reading group
and to discuss ideas. Out of those discussions came the idea for some kind of
unusual project or action to commemorate the 500th anniversary of the arrival of
Christopher Columbus.

"At first we didn't know what we were going to use," says Tom Klem, a sculptor who had experience with public art. They initially considered using kiosks or
some kind of guerrilla action to publicize their message. "We talked of plopping
down a kiosk that said everything we wanted to say. But then it would last only

Placed in front of the New York Stock Exchange, this sign challenges the myths of the free-market economy and that stockbrokers jumped out of windows along Wall Street after the 1929 stock market crash. The sign documents that government regulation and fraud led to market crashes and depressions at the turn of the twentieth century, in the 1920s, and in the 1980s. (Photo by Tom Klem, courtesy of RepoHistory)

a day or two before being destroyed. Finding any space in New York City to do public art is difficult."

After a year of long, arduous discussions they decided to make their statement within some official city structure, and came up with the idea for the The Lower Manhattan Sign Project. They identified thirty-six sites whose stories they wanted to tell. They knew that to say something profound about race or class, they would have to engage the public in a dialog, so they designed a series of signs that had multiple readings. On one side were a provocative visual image and a couple of identifying words. On the other was a text block about the important but forgotten individual or moment along with a quick series of questions, such as "Whose history is remembered? Is history truth or desire? Is history progress or power? Who makes use of history? What does this place mean to you?" They sought to provoke among pedestrians alternative considerations of the meaning of history and who and what deserves to be remembered.

Since Klem had had a good deal of experience working on placing art in public places, it was decided that he would approach city officials to explore a project that met city guidelines. He turned to the city's Department of Transportation, which has jurisdiction over a range of public spaces, traffic islands, and light poles—anything that was not private property or controlled by the city's parks department.

"Frank Addeo is one of the unsung heroes of public art in New York City," says Klem of the city official who at that time was the assistant to the DOT commissioner and who Klem was happy to discover was not judgmental about the political content of what he and his cohorts had in mind so long as it wasn't libelous. "He embraced the findings of a study that showed that tourists came to New York to see art, took that idea much further, and put people like Richard Serra out on public plazas."

Klem and his group learned they could get a permit for six months and then get a six-month extension, after which the art would have to come down. So they raised some money from the Warhol and Puffin foundations, secured the necessary approvals, and put together their sign project.

RepoHistory's signs marked a variety of sites in honor of women, workers,

This is the first of nine signs marking underrepresented sites of gay and lesbian history that were created to celebrate the twentieth anniversary of the Stonewall riots in New York City. (Photo by Jim Costanzo, courtesy of RepoHistory)

slaves, and immigrants. They recalled labor struggles and subway fires. And they identified the sites of the city's original Chinatown, its first alms house, and the debtors' jail.

Three signs marked the location of the Great Negro Revolt of 1741, when, in the aftermath of a fire that destroyed nearby Fort George, thirty-four people, mostly black men, were executed for conspiring to overthrow the ruling white society. The signs tell the story of the "plot" and the inquisition that followed, and explore the social conditions that, today as in 1741, allow for this type of racial witch hunt to occur.

One sign memorialized Jacob Leisler, who in 1689, as leader of the local militia of New York, seized nearby Fort James, overthrew the colonial governor, and established a popular government that ruled the colony for two years. When he was executed by the reinstated elite, no carpenter would furnish a ladder for the gallows.

And a sign marking the Meal and Slave Market stated that in 1746, nearly one in every five New Yorkers was black and that New York City was the country's second-largest urban slave center. The text recalled the vital role that enslaved Africans played in the city's social and economic growth from the early 1600s until the state abolished slavery in 1827.

"We were hoping the visuals and questions would be the quick read that would interest pedestrians enough to pause and read the full text," Klem says. "And the response was tremendous: a full page in *Newsday*, three pieces in the *New York Times*, walking tours set up by others who took people to the sites."

The group spent about $10,000 to make five copies of each sign so a replacement would be available in the event a particular sign was destroyed or stolen. A popular one that disappeared repeatedly from its location on William Street near Fulton was the sign recalling the Washington Irving story that the name "Gotham" came from a village in England where the residents feigned insanity to avoid paying taxes.

"We were surprised by the success of this project," he says.

Two years later RepoHistory moved on to do a show called "Queer Spaces" to coincide with the anniversary of the police raid on the homosexual hangout known as the Stonewall Tavern and to mark sites of importance to the gay community that were far less known. They mounted a sign at City Hall Park to commemorate the passage of the city's antidiscrimination legislation, one to mark the first demonstration by gay men and women in New York City, one dedicated to the first demonstration of ACT UP, the anti-AIDS advocacy organization, another at the site of the death of a transvestite, and many more.

Their last project in New York was called "Civil Disturbances: Battles for Justice in New York City." It highlighted landmarks in public law. Here they

Mrs. Sara Lena Echols MALONE

raised
her family
on
267 Pine Place
Apt. #3 in the
early thirties.

This sign marks the home and history of the Malone family in the segregated community of Buttermilk Bottom in downtown Atlanta in the 1930s. When discussing working on this project, James Malone took this worn but loved picture out of his wallet at an early meeting for the project. Artist Tom Klem had searched but could find no photographs in Atlanta's city archives of those who lived in this community. This image became the face of the project. (Photo by Tom Klem, courtesy of RepoHistory)

marked sites related to cases that made domestic violence a police priority, the first AIDS discrimination lawsuit, the fight to save public hospitals, and cases concerning fair housing, welfare rights, handicapped access, and the illegal demolition of single-room-occupancy hotels, among others.

"The day of our opening we were denied our permits," Klem says of the project that was sponsored by New York Lawyers for the Public Interest. "There we were on the steps of the state courthouse with the *New York Times* and National Public Radio. It became a wonderful story for us, and there was a battle over which law firm would represent us against the city."

Three months after the denial, RepoHistory was granted its permit. But the case prompted the city to change its permitting process, and the group lost its ability to put signs up in Manhattan. Their primary offense, it turned out, was that many of the signs read "So-and-so vs. Giuliani," and the city did not like being criticized in such a public way.

"This happened at the height of the art/religious controversy at the Brooklyn Museum," Klem says of a show that so offended the mayor that he threatened to close the museum, "and when Giuliani was busting gypsy cab drivers, kicking food vendors out of midtown, and changing the traffic patterns so you couldn't walk across certain streets, all because they were an annoyance to him. He had run out of good things to do and started picking on artists."

In the meantime RepoHistory had been invited down to Atlanta to do a project for the Atlanta Arts Festival where they reclaimed the history of Buttermilk Bottom, a forgotten inner-city African-American neighborhood. Once located two blocks from the Fox Theater where *Gone With the Wind* had its premiere, it had been leveled in the early 1970s. RepoHistory mounted signs that told the stories of the people who had once lived there without benefit of electricity, sewers, or phones, people who had been promised new housing but had received none, people whose homes had been replaced by shopping malls, office buildings, and a civic center.

"We went into that civic center's gigantic parking lot and stenciled onto the asphalt the outline of the streets, buildings, stores, churches, and homes of the people who had been there before," Klem says. "We put up signs around the border of this community so people knew when they were driving through what had been Buttermilk Bottom, and we put up specific signs about histories of different individuals and places."

They encountered a significant dead end when they went to the city archives and found nothing about Buttermilk Bottom. There were no photographs of what it had looked like. The community had no face. It had gone unrecorded in the archives of Atlanta, considered by the establishment to have been nothing more than a crime-ridden slum best forgotten.

"But the Sanborn insurance maps showed us what had been there," he says. "We could see all the churches, the houses, and the public school."

They also pulled what photographs they could out of people's attics, interviewed former residents and their descendants, took oral histories, and made a film they showed at the opening of the festival. And then they held a reunion of former residents at the civic center.

"The beauty of all this is that they then formed a Buttermilk Bottom association, and every year they come back and talk about it," Klem says. "One of the things RepoHistory wanted to do was act as a catalyst and not be the final story.

Rather than substitute our version for the official version, or make a sign that would be permanent forever, we wanted to start a dialog. We also sought to get publicity, not for us, but to get the information out into the newspapers so people could read about it. That's how we got the story of New York's slave market into the *Washington Times*."

The principals of RepoHistory have since moved on to important positions in their respective fields, including Klem, who is now working to create street markers for a New York program called Place Matters. They knew it wouldn't be possible to keep their collective together forever. So they have archived all their materials—research, signs, maps—and donated them to the Downtown Art Collection at Fales Library at New York University, making them available for students of New York history for years to come.

Soon after Klem's group did its first Lower Manhattan Sign Project, American Express came along and spent $10,000 per sign to permanently mark a number of common history book places, like where Thomas Edison demonstrated the first commercial use of electricity by lighting up a city block (with all reference to unofficial history edited out). "So I think we shook things up a bit," he says.

• • •

This story first appeared in the May/June 2004 edition of *DESIGNER/builder* magazine.

Volunteers and patrons on the food service line. (Photo by James Whittier Parker)

KINGSLEY HAMMETT

PUTTING A FACE ON HUNGER

ACCORDING TO THE LATEST CENSUS, BASED ON HOUSEHOLD INCOME, Trenton, New Jersey, is the capital of the richest state in the richest country in the world. Its population peaked at 135,000 in the 1950s, and its factories once turned out miles of wire rope to build the Brooklyn Bridge and enough porcelain to proclaim itself the toilet capital of the world.

But like other once-proud industrial giants, Trenton lost population to the suburbs after World War II and manufacturing fled to the Southern states for cheaper, nonunion labor. Today the city's population is down to 85,000 and dropping. And once the government workers have gone home after 5 p.m., the streets are virtually empty. It is a sad irony that the current growth industries are jails and soup kitchens. The largest soup kitchen in the capital city is the Trenton Area Soup Kitchen (TASK), which serves more than 3,000 meals a week, approximately one-third of them to poor people working at jobs that do not pay a living wage.

After the devastation of the Great Depression, it was taken for granted that we had put in place laws and policies—the right to unionize, minimum wages, and Social Security, to name a few—that would prevent us from having to go back to bread lines and soup kitchens. But after World War II the union movement lost ground, first to the nonunion South, then Mexico, and now China and Bangladesh. The mentally ill have been deinstitutionalized and put out on their own. The minimum wage has not risen in buying power since 1968. And by the late 1970s cities like Trenton began to see the development of a permanent underclass living on the streets in dire poverty. Founded to deal with the growing need were a number of nonprofit social service organizations like TASK.

At first glance, TASK director Peter Wise seems an unlikely candidate to be running a soup kitchen. He has a degree in physics and spent a long career in the

Peter Wise in the dining room during a busy meal. (Photo by Jaime Parker)

aerospace industry making weather, communications, and scientific satellites as well as components for moon missions while living in the neat and tidy eighteenth-century village of Cranbury. Twenty years ago, in the middle of his career, a friend invited him to come down to Trenton to volunteer at a Saturday soup kitchen known as Loaves and Fishes, which was run out of a church.

"I'm a white guy from the suburbs," he says. "What am I doing Saturday morning? I'm mowing the grass, playing tennis, whatever. But this friend twisted my arm, so I went."

In that environment he saw, heard, and smelled things he had never seen, heard, or smelled before. He was in a room filled with street people and he was depressed and turned off.

"We rode back to Cranbury, I had done my friend the favor, I'd been there, done that—that was it," he says. "I do not know what happened in the next couple of weeks, but I did not have what I call a 'Shazam moment,' or what in theological terms might be called an epiphany. I did not even have what's sometimes called the small still voice in the night, the whisper in the ear. Or if I did, I didn't hear it."

Nevertheless, a couple of weeks later he found himself back in Trenton at Loaves and Fishes. This time he saw that these people were basically no different from him. "Once I was able to see behind the façade, it made all the difference," Wise says. "I am grateful that I have never lost that feeling twenty years later."

Wise became a regular volunteer at the Saturday soup kitchen until 1998 when Lockheed Martin decided to close the plant where he worked outside Princeton. The company made him a generous offer to move to California, but the family decided to stay in New Jersey. At the same time he heard that TASK was searching for a new director, and Wise was chosen for the position.

The Trenton Area Soup Kitchen is a nonreligious, nonsectarian, nonprofit organization founded in 1982 with a three-pronged mission statement. Its first objective is to provide food service, as its name implies. It has a 7,000-square-foot facility with fifteen tables that seat eight, and it serves up to 400 people twice a day.

The second objective is advocacy and outreach, to testify at statehouse hearings, to provide information to reporters and legislators, to educate the public about the soup kitchen and the work it does, and to solicit donations.

The third objective is what sets TASK apart from the typical soup kitchen. Beyond simply providing a free meal, it seeks to help its patrons by addressing the root causes of their problems. To that end it has fifty-five volunteer tutors who provide basic literacy and GED preparation to some eighty adults. It provides computer skills training, Internet job search, résumé preparation, and use of e-mail, fax, phones, and postal and UPS delivery for those without a permanent address. From 9 to 11 in the morning, the dining room becomes a school. From 11 to 1 it's a dining room again. From 2 to 4 it's back to a school, and from 4 to 6 it's used to serve the evening meal.

There is one full-time social worker on site (with plans to add another) and the door is open to all other social service practitioners who want to come to the soup kitchen to meet with their clients. On any given day there will be mental health practitioners, nurse practitioners, addiction and HIV/AIDS specialists, and pro bono lawyers. They're given a table, use of the PA system, access to a copy machine, and a private room if necessary. "If you want to provide your service, come to the soup kitchen," Wise says. "This is where the people are."

His goal is to help lift people up so they can get a job and take care of themselves. But there are those, like the elderly, for whom that paradigm is not going to work. In those cases he simply hopes to make their lives a little easier. Crossover programs that address the needs of all include supplying clothing, giving out hygiene bags filled with items that cannot be purchased with food stamps, and providing an artistic outlet for those who want to assert themselves creatively.

Several years ago, one of the volunteers, a psychologist from Princeton, began a once-a-week art program called Arts and Ideas. Many patrons living difficult lives had a need to express themselves and took up painting, drawing, or photography. It became such an active group they began to exhibit and sell their work. It evolved into an artists' co-op that has since spun off from the soup kitchen into its own organization that meets in a back room at the facility every Tuesday. And the walls of the soup kitchen are covered with the members' artwork.

"It's a win-win situation," Wise says. "We have some patrons who are illiterate and inarticulate. So it offers another option for people to express themselves. I am in awe of what's hanging on the walls outside my office and the people who come in here are blown away by this artwork. It makes an institutional room feel light, airy, and very colorful and it makes the patrons feel better about themselves."

TASK provides its services through an open-door, no-conditions, and no-questions-asked policy. Wise offers one added benefit to those who by their demeanor, their uniforms, their tool belt, or their paint-spattered clothes are clearly working. He asks that they bring some note or other evidence from their employer so when they come for lunch he logs them in, gives them a worker's pass, and they take their place at the head of the serving line.

"It's an express service," Wise says. "Ninety-five percent of the people who come here are pedestrian. If they have walked twenty-minutes from their job to get here and need to walk twenty minutes back and I keep them waiting to get served, they'll lose their job."

Most people's reaction to that policy is "Great!" But on second thought, how insane is it that Wise has to give express service to people who are working but still in need of a free meal? The simple answer is that the living-wage jobs once available in manufacturing, which required neither a college nor a high school education, are gone. In their place is a service economy with wages too low to afford transportation or lunch and still have enough to pay the rent.

Two-thirds of his clients, many who were put off welfare and into WorkFirst New Jersey, don't have jobs because they have multiple barriers to employment, including insufficient education or training, mental illness, physical disabilities, or addictions. There's also been a great influx of Central American immigrants who are further hobbled by their illegal status and inability to communicate in English. Many of them become victims of substance abuse and violence, and how to absorb them into the general population has become a huge public policy challenge.

Serving as director of the soup kitchen is teaching Wise lessons he never could have learned in aerospace. "One is to take care of yourself in order to take care of others," he says. "And it's something you never stop learning. Like recovery, you're always in it. You learn to dip-stick where you are emotionally."

The other major lesson is the fallibility and vulnerability of our systems. When he was first working in Aerospace America he assumed Government America was taking care of the less fortunate, that we certainly didn't have people living in such desperate conditions in this country, that we were a progressive society far beyond the "You're on your own, Jack" mentality.

"Now I realize how fragile and inadequate those systems are," he says, "and how much of our politics and policy making are dysfunctional. I was probably very naive to think that it was all rational and everyone has the best interests of the

Adult education students at work. (Photo by James Whittier Parker)

poor at heart. It's not that way at all."

There is something in the American psyche, Wise believes, that starts with a sense of free choice, rugged individuality, and personal responsibility for your own fate that if unrestrained can become a lack of empathy for the plight of others. He has come to realize that America's being The Land of [Equal] Opportunity is a myth. Take the ten-year-old child, he says, who comes home from school to three families jammed into a two-room apartment without electricity. How can that child be expected to compete with a student who comes home to a computer in his private bedroom?

"It's not a level playing field," he says. "Anything is possible in America. But let's be real about the challenges that some kids and families face. Whether the problems are the result of bad personal decisions or flaws in the system, particularly in this, the wealthiest state in the country, we can and we should do better. We cannot be healthy—economically, physically, socially, spiritually—in the greater Princeton/Trenton region if in the center of it we have the kind of poverty that we see in the state capital."

We have to address the root causes of poverty, Wise says, and advocate for sensible programs and policies, while developing a narrative that speaks to people where they are. "I'm serving people whose grandparents and great-grandparents were slaves," he says. "How does that get handed down? I think there may be undercurrents of justified rage."

The most important element TASK has in its tool box, Wise says, is a smile. "It is the most disarming thing around. Street smarts say avoid eye contact and keep moving. But we turn that on its head. We try to greet everyone with a smile and to let them know that this is a safe space."

Patrons go through the cafeteria line and the first thing they face is a tray of desserts of all kinds. "You get to choose what you want for dessert," he says. "That slows down the line, but people get to choose, and to a person who doesn't have many choices in his life, that's very important."

The problem of a growing underclass is too large to be solved by nonprofit organizations, Wise says. Increasingly, the solutions to these problems are being delegated to the nonprofit sector by the government. "I thought there were words in our founding documents stating the government's role in promoting the common good and the general welfare. Instead of devolving responsibility to the nonprofit sector, we need our government to change policy and craft adequately funded programs to combat poverty. In the final analysis, it really becomes a question of what kind of society and what kind of world we want to live in."

Twice a day, Wise makes the commute from upscale Cranbury with its blue-ribbon schools to the mean streets of the North Ward of Trenton. At one end he sees gracious houses and glorious foliage lining the quaint streets, and at the other boarded-up houses and endless coils of concertina wire protecting the little remaining industrial activity. The fact that he never gets used to either polarity he views as a gift.

"It's a jarring thing," he admits, "but it helps to keep me real. And I am very grateful for that."

• • •

This story first appeared in the May/June 2006 edition of *DESIGNER/builder* magazine.

A young man in his work site in the garbage dump. (Photo by Lily Yeh)

BAREFOOT ARTISTS

For eighteen years, Lily Yeh was the director of The Village of Arts and Humanities, a non-profit organization that she founded in inner-city North Philadelphia devoted to helping those devastated by disinvestment and abandonment. Using creative thinking and action through the arts, The Village transformed both landscapes and lives. It became a model of community revitalization and put art and artists in the center of social change.

By 2001, when The Village was on firm footing, Yeh decided to bring her amazing talents and all that she had learned in North Philadelphia to other parts of the world that are experiencing crushing deprivation and suffering. To that end, she has founded a new organization called Barefoot Artists, which was inspired by the Barefoot Doctors who were sent to the most remote corners of rural China during the Revolution. Her goal is to practice her art in the neediest of communities, to empower people, to bring them the healing power of beauty, and to help create a basis for hope. Her international journey began more than a dozen years ago with a trip to Kenya.

I FIRST WENT TO AFRICA AT THE END OF 1993 ON BEHALF OF THE Lila Wallace Arts International Grant, whose purpose was to send artists as ambassadors to different countries to learn the local culture and to bring innovative ideas. It allowed artists to go to the host country for three to six months. I went to Kenya, and that changed my life. Three months is a long time, and the first month I just traveled and enjoyed the national parks and met people in diplomatic circles. When I showed people my work in North Philadelphia they said, "You must meet Father Alex Zanotelli."

Father Alex had inserted himself into Korogocho, a squatter community outside Nairobi of 100,000 of Kenya's poorest and most destitute people built around a huge dump, which is the only resource they have.

He lived among the poorest people. He lived in the houses they lived in, wore the things they wore, ate the things they ate, and in this way he lived the example of Christ. He organized the people so they didn't just work on an individual scale. He organized them into corporations: the mothers into weaving, the young women into beadwork, the talented artists into a batik workshop, and the drug-addicted and the alcoholics into furniture-making. The most difficult group is the Mukuru, the most despised, the most impoverished, the most oppressed people who go through the trash every day to scratch out their living. And even they have a cottage industry of helping each other recycle and sort in order to make a better living.

Father Alex established a church, called St. John's Catholic Church, in the heart of Korogocho. Every day thousands of people use that church. He created an informal school with maybe 600 to 800 children who cannot go to other schools.

I went to meet him at the church. It was very hard because it's frightening to go into Korogocho. I was more frightened there than in North Philadelphia. It's like going into a labyrinth of narrow streets crowded with people, shops, cooking, animals, open sewers, and piles and piles of trash everywhere. But it's amazing because in that environment there is life; there are people trying to make a living, raising their children. Some of the houses are nailed together and look like rustic art pieces. The streets are built on layers and layers of trash. And the pollution smell is bad. It's amazing because the city of Nairobi is so beautiful. It's 7,000 feet above sea level, beautiful terrain, blue sky, dazzling white clouds, and the air is really sweet.

In one part of me I felt that I really could do something in Korogocho, just what I had done in North Philadelphia. I felt that I could maybe make a difference. But I was frightened of the situation, frightened of getting sick. I was frightened even to go in because it's such a polluted environment. When the wind blows it comes from the bowl of that garbage dump, it blows up in the air, and you can smell the garbage.

So I struggled and struggled, and finally I decided this was just like before I entered North Philadelphia. I was frightened, but I felt that the unfolding of my life depended on this project. I felt there was something I had to understand. And more than anything, I related to Father Alex's example of living with the poor and working with the poor. He lives the Passion of Christ every day, and you see God every day in that kind of work. I felt touched. I felt compelled. And so I mustered enough courage. My son Daniel was traveling with me. He saw my struggle, and he just said, "Mom, that's your project." That really helped me and I went in.

Once I settled in, everything changed. My attitude changed. I opened up. I didn't live in Korogocho. I was hosted by an art center, called Paa Ya Paa. It's the oldest East African art center. It helped me with transportation, securing materials,

A house constructed with recycled materials. (Photo by Lily Yeh)

and making connections with local people. Father Alex also got people to help. And I started the most powerful project I'd ever done in my life!

I needed to find a place to paint because I am a painter. The only place that had solid walls was the courtyard of the church. The church is a very big building. One thousand people can sit in it. But outside it's all just bare cinder blocks, and the courtyard is dirt with small classrooms and an open kitchen. It is right on the edge of the dumpsite, separated by a thin wooden fence. In the heart of the dumpsite is a lake, and from far away it looks nice, green-blue. But it's a stagnant, dead lake, all fouled with algae. I suspect that at one time it was a quarry.

So I said, well, I can paint here, and asked myself what would make sense to paint? I thought painting angels would totally make sense in this churchyard. So I went to Paa Ya Paa, researched the African images they had, and designed a series of angels and a floral theme as a wall mural.

What emerged were the Warrior Angel, the Mama Angel, and the Peace Angel. They're huge, maybe ten, twelve feet high. And angels from Ethiopia—angels with wings, with no bodies. The way to create beauty is by creating things that are beautiful and that brought life to the courtyard.

Father Alex introduced me to the congregation and showed them the designs and the images so they would understand what I would be doing. Once I started it was wonderful, because the children got so excited. Everybody was very curious. We bought a lot of paints, and I tried to get the children involved in whatever way I could—shaking paints, moving things, setting things up, and so forth. I used very bright colors rather than pastel colors. In such a hopeless place, such a bleak place, a place with no beauty, color becomes energy. It energizes the place. When I would put orange, just simple colors, straight from the can onto the wall, it became energy. It became something hopeful, wonderful. Every time I'd paint, the act of painting became the act of performance, because there was always an audience and they were always amazed at what I was doing. I would sketch, draw with charcoals and so forth, and they'd see an angel, a flower, a pattern emerge. I was always surrounded by people watching in amazement.

The place is so dynamic. It's so full of life on the verge of death. Sometimes people get desperate and they jump into the lake. I remember one day painting, and suddenly I could see from the church across the lake there were trucks coming in because somebody had jumped into the lake to commit suicide.

I tried not to drink throughout the day so I wouldn't have to go to the bathroom because the latrine was very difficult. But I had a big bottle of water with me, and one day, as I was painting the Peace Angel holding the dove, a person suddenly stumbled in. He was so thin, so thin. He didn't have anything on him except a little strip of a bathing suit, like a bikini basically. He didn't say a word. He just went to my bottle and drank the whole thing. He just gulped it down. I looked at him when he was drinking and I thought I only saw half of a face. He had a pair of huge eyes, but he was so thin that I could hardly see his chin.

Then he fell to the floor and leaned against the wall. He seemed to go to sleep and I didn't know what to do. I was waiting for somebody to come. Finally Father Alex came with some people. They brought him clothes, but the clothes looked so tattered. There are just no resources. They helped him to put on the clothes. I

Wooden angels in the courtyard of St. John's Catholic Church. (Photo by Lily Yeh)

The Warrior Angel and Mama Angel mural. (Photo by Lily Yeh)

remember the front of the shoes were kind of open. In America you see unwanted shoes thrown up on utility wires. In Kenya people wear whatever they can. Sometimes it's a boot and a sneaker that don't match, and sometimes the front is open like the mouth of a duck. So people got him dressed in something and then took him away. When I saw Father Alex later I asked, "What is wrong with that person?" And he said, "Everything you can think of is wrong with him." I was sure he had AIDS like 60 percent of Kenya's population.

I continued to work, but I was so frightened of being sick I would cover myself completely. I wore long sleeves, long pants, a head scarf, goggles, and even a scarf over my mouth so I wouldn't breathe the air. I felt so bad, because people might think that I was trying to insulate myself from the environment they live in, and I hoped the community would understand. But a child came to my rescue. He looked at me and said, "You must be a ninja painter." Ninjas are Japanese assassins and they're always covered up on the TV. From then on I called myself a ninja painter.

While I was making this painting I also collaborated with a Kenyan sculptor to create seven sculptures of angels made of eucalyptus trees. They are very beautiful. They are like Chinese tomb figurines in an African style. I designed them and he carved them.

I was looking for a home for the angels, and I found the perfect place. At the end of the courtyard, overlooking the big dumpsite and the lake, there was a huge abandoned concrete block. Originally something must have been built on top of it because I saw reinforcing spikes coming out, and I knew it would be the home for the angels. The location was perfect. On the right side were the latrines. And on the left side there was this slab and a stove-like structure where they burned trash every day. I thought that the angels needed to be in a place just like this, with the danger of the filth and of the despised. The smoke from the burning trash became the incense of the angels. So it all fit together.

I went back six times in the next ten years. During my fourth visit I saw fungus growing on the angels due to the dampness. So we sanded them down. And there was some rot at the bottom. I said we should discard the angels and build new ones. But one of the church members, a deacon, said, "No, you cannot do that. We must bring the angels to our school and we'll repair them. Before the angels, three people committed suicide in the lake. But after the angels nobody did." I don't really know how effective the angels were, but this is what he thinks.

Korogocho, even with the dazzling sun every day, is the pit of the world. The garbage is not just from the city, it's dumped from airplanes. One day suddenly there was a lot of excitement and people started running in a certain direction. I said, "What's going on?" And the people with me said that because the airplanes are dumping today at a certain place, they would go there to try to find food. And they can find food. That's when I realized Korogocho's dump is international and is directly connected to the way of life of the rest of the world.

Eventually I had a crew of workers from the community helping me to paint, and the courtyard now has lots of color. And not only on the murals. We painted on the fences, wherever we could touch the surface. When we installed the angels,

Children painting. (Photo by Lily Yeh)

you could feel the joy. And the church planned a very big dedication festival. I felt we needed the people from outside to see how 60 percent of Kenyans live on 1.5 percent of the land. Sixty percent of people in Nairobi live around garbage dumps. There are about a hundred garbage dumps in Nairobi. Korogocho is the third largest, but because of the crime it's the most vicious. These people don't have electricity or water. They don't exist for the government.

I asked my host at Paa Ya Paa to invite all the embassy people to attend the dedication ceremony. I wanted them to see how these people live and to know that the strength and the power and the determination of the community could make something so beautiful in the midst of such garbage and hellishness. We didn't think the American ambassador, Aurelia Brazeal, would come because there was no word from her. But that morning she came herself, mingled with the people, and held the children. It was really amazing. And there were embassy people from Switzerland, Germany, Italy, and so forth. It was like a sudden light coming into this hellhole. There was Father John from Italy, and he couldn't believe the colors. The community had produced a lot of batik, baskets, and all kinds of things. They displayed their creations and their talent. Father Alex wore a beautiful beaded Masai frock. Everybody lined up and we walked from the church into the courtyard and we blessed every single piece of the mural and the sculptures with rice and water and we prayed. We welcomed the guests, had gifts for the guests, and the children sang. It was so beautiful. It was just like a heavenly chorus. And I said, "What do they say?" And the translator replied, "We welcome you, we welcome you, our guests, but when you go please do not forget about us, and please come back and visit us again." Father Alex said it's important that we bear witness so that the people's suffering is not in vain and so they will feel they are not forgotten.

For me personally that changed my life. I felt that together with the community we pushed open the dark, heavy gates of hell and let in sunlight. Father John said to me, "You want to see a miracle? This is the miracle." I felt the power of art and the power of doing things together. And things did change, because after that, the Italian embassy created a cottage industry for cards. I helped Paa Ya Paa get the Rockefeller and the Ford Foundations to do an entrepreneurial program. And we launched a local newspaper that was picked up later by other more professional people. So different things did happen.

That was the first year. It changed my life. But as in North Philadelphia after the first summer, I had fulfilled my promise and had no intention of staying. The same thing happened in Korogocho. I was so happy to go home and return to my normal life. It's more predictable. It is not full of danger. Yet the image of Korogocho came to me every day—Father Alex, the life there, the people singing, the worship. It just haunted me every day and I knew I had to go back. There was just something so profound I needed to be in touch with.

I went back in 1995 with Heidi Warren, a staff member at The Village of Arts and Humanities, and a filmmaker, Glenn Houston, who wanted to do a documentary. Eventually he created a one-hour film about my work at The Village and Korogocho. Every time I went back, I went deeper into the heart of Korogocho, eventually to the dumpsite to work with some of the Mukuru people.

That was the beginning of Barefoot Artists. It has been supported by foundations and private donations. Compared to The Village of Arts and Humanities, it is very modest. It's an organization almost without overhead, although I try to pay local people to help out. Almost every year after my first trip to Kenya I did an international project. I went to Mali. I went to Ivory Coast where I did a project in a tiny village. I did a project in Ghana. And then I did one in Matera, Italy, which is a UNESCO World Preservation Site. Last year five individuals paid their own way to join me on my trip to Rwanda where I'm deeply involved in a project in a refugee resettlement village. I'm also working on projects in China.

My focus is on world culture and working with different peoples, seeing how effective The Village model is in empowering local people in a relatively short period of time. Under that model you honor local talent, embrace and transform the unusable. It's like human ecology. You have the ability to see the potential of all the unusable and the discarded, to cultivate and transform through goodwill, creativity, joy, and togetherness. And then you open up a new space, which I call a democratic space, through art—a new space that is not taken by the existing order, so people can step in on an equal footing. Then you paint the vision for the

Children dancing and singing at the dedication ceremony. (Photo by Lily Yeh)

American Ambassador Aurelia Brazeal and Father Alex Zanotelli with children
during the dedication ceremony. (Photo by Lily Yeh)

people. You give it direction and say what is possible. You let people imagine and describe what they imagine. You articulate that through words and art. You use what they can give. Everybody donates according to their talent and ability.

The artist's role is to take all these seeds and gifts from the people and include them in making something beautiful, based on their understanding, experience, and particular kinds of training. That is The Village model. And then you build hope and strength rather than despair. You can make it small, you can make it big. But it's all-inclusive, it's embrace. And when people have goodwill you do not need to guard your project. That's what makes it very economical. Here is a wonderful way, not disturbing the existing order, but transforming it, from the bottom up, from the lowest, and from the polluted and poisoned. And you stir it up. What you get is the wonder that comes out of the richness of human experience.

• • •

This story first appeared in the November/December 2006 edition of *DESIGNER/builder* magazine.

Beneficiaries provided unskilled labor and produced about 8 million
adobe blocks within three months, which were required for the
construction of 5,000 permanent shelters. Nahrin, Afghanistan.
(Photo courtesy of Shelter for Life International)

KINGSLEY HAMMETT

HOME IS WHERE THE HOUSE IS
REBUILDING COMMUNITIES BY BUILDING HOUSES

ON ANY GIVEN DAY, AT LEAST 100 MILLION PEOPLE WHO HAVE BEEN ripped from their homes and communities by war, poverty, repression, and natural disaster are in need of decent housing. The common response on the part of those who want to help is to send in a solution created elsewhere—everything from plastic sheeting to Red Cross tents to the paper-tube houses of Shigeru Ban. But once refugees are given a temporary structure they still have no cohesive family network, no community, no work, and no hope. Nor have they been empowered to shape their own future.

In stark contrast to this stands the approach taken by Shelter for Life, an organization that believes that shelter is about more than four walls and a roof. It's about social capital, about reestablishing community, and about helping to repair the torn fabric of stable village life.

Shelter for Life comes into a devastated area armed with goodwill and respect for the power of local people. In place of preconceived ideas, prefabricated shelters, and manufactured materials, it relies on local cultural knowledge; local building traditions, methods, and materials; and the ingenuity, resourcefulness, creativity, and hard work of the local people who have lived at the margins as long as time remembers. The organization operates under the understanding that for people who have lost everything the first thing they need as they begin to rebuild their lives is a permanent place to live as a family. More than anything else, a safe and decent starter home is an essential stepping stone to the future.

Founded in 1979 and headquartered in Oshkosh, Wisconsin, Shelter for Life has a lean staff of ten in the home office and about twenty working in the field in Afghanistan, Tajikistan, Iraq, and Sri Lanka. Between 2000 and 2003, it affected the lives of 1,117,340 people by building 12,063 homes; supplying 16,576 home repair kits; building or repairing 585 kilometers of roads, 33 schools, and 2 clinics; and constructing 108 wells and 3,864 latrines.

"People in devastated areas have the same desire we have," says Harry van Burik, Shelter for Life's international program director. "They want to have a future and hope. And once they have a house they become stakeholders in the community."

Van Burik studied architecture at the Delft University of Technology in the Netherlands, a school with a strong emphasis on working in the Third World, where he was influenced by those planning and building in developing countries. After finishing a student project to design a spice factory for a small nonprofit organization in Sri Lanka in 1986–87 and completing a master's thesis on primary health care facilities in Ghana, he did some work in the field in Ghana and Southeast Asia. He then returned to Delft to teach in the school of civil engineering, where doing projects meant more than just researching problems and turning out technical studies. It meant actually going places, working with the people, and leaving something behind—a well, a small structure, something.

"That was the philosophy that changed my life," he says.

Frequently van Burik receives ideas for disaster relief shelters sent in by manufacturing companies that are anxious to sell their products. But since every situation, region, and local tradition is different, he turns them down. Shelter for Life works together with local people to build whatever they are already familiar and comfortable with and seeks wherever possible to make simple improvements to local structures in a cost-effective way.

"A lot of thinking has been put into whatever people have been using for generations and centuries," van Burik says. "We respect that very much. We look at what is locally available and how people live, and together with the people—and I want to emphasize that—we design and build."

Shelter for Life's experience and success in Afghanistan these last few years illustrates how it operates. Afghanistan is one of the most conflict-riddled countries on the globe, a crossroads of invasion since Alexander the Great. In the last two centuries it has been attacked, invaded, and occupied by three of the world's major powers: Britain, the Soviet Union, and the United States. It also has one of the highest concentrations of seismic activity anywhere in the world. Most people live in adobe structures with thick, flat, heavy earthen roofs. When the walls shake the roof beams are dislodged and tons of wood and dirt collapse onto the occupants below. Shelter for Life figured that if it could design a stronger structure that would give people more time to get out of the house in the event of an earthquake, many lives could be saved.

The organization came up with a culturally appropriate design for a small adobe home of two rooms and a corridor to which more rooms can be added as time and resources permit. The adobe brick walls are anchored to the stone

Wooden ring beams are securely anchored to both the wall and the roof support joists to help resist both roof-wall separation and vertical cracking in the walls during seismic activity. The ring beams are also braced at each corner for rigidity. Nahrin, Afghanistan. (Photo courtesy of Shelter for Life International)

foundation with vertical rods and the roof is fastened to the walls with a wooden ring beam with diagonal bracing to further strengthen the corners. Sheets of bamboo or plastic are laid over the roof beams and topped with layers of compacted earth, dry soil, and a combination of mud and straw. In some instances they add a soft, horizontal, shock-absorbing layer of material—generally bamboo—above the door and window lintels so cracks will not run from foundation to roof line.

"We train people on the spot so they know how to use these simple measures," van Burik says, adding that some of the old effective techniques had been forgotten over three generations without a severe earthquake. "I do not care if 10,000 houses are destroyed. But I care if one person is killed. Withstanding seismic forces for a few minutes can make the difference between 10,000 people killed or maybe ten people killed."

In one four-month period in 2002, Shelter for Life assigned two of its staff members to northern Afghanistan after a severe earthquake. They in turn marshaled

Afghan children in front of one of the 5,000 shelters, which provided 30,522 people with permanent, decent, and safe living conditions after a devastating earthquake in March 2002. (Photo courtesy of Shelter for Life International)

thousands of local people to help build 5,000 houses in a vast area of seventy-six villages, sometimes without access roads or water to mix adobe.

"We provide them with dignity and decent, permanent housing built according to their own standards for half the price of a Red Cross winterized tent," van Burik says. All the windows and doors were made by local craftsmen, as were all the wood-, diesel-, and coal-burning stoves they fashioned from rolls of sheet steel. "The Afghan people are very innovative and make everything themselves. When I went there in 1998, all I saw at first was dust and donkeys. Then I looked at the marketplace and saw all kinds of things they made from nothing. From tires they made shoes, from small tin sheets they made wood-fired water-heating systems. And when I gave my drawings for furniture to a local carpenter, within one week I had a completely furnished house. They are very innovative and very eager to work."

Once 75 percent of the houses were completed, a follow-up study showed that more than half were being used for home-based enterprises, like knitting, weaving, carpet making, embroidery, carpentry, baking, and chicken farming.

Shelter for Life helps with more than houses. In the countries where it is currently working it is also building schools, clinics, roads, water and sanitation projects, public facilities, and small factories to make building materials, such as cement blocks and roof tiles.

The organization has always been about more than shelter, van Burik says. "We are all about people and restoring their lives. From there they take ownership. The donor community doesn't always realize this. They often see shelter just as a capital investment. But it is much more than that. I will go so far as to say that our shelter programs build secure and stable societies. What we do is help people rebuild their lives through shelter because rebuilding communities starts with a house."

• • •

This story first appeared in the May/June 2005 edition of *DESIGNER/builder* magazine.

Adam Meister on the roof of his row house on Linden Avenue. (Photo by Daryn Nakhuda)

KINGSLEY HAMMETT

BALTIMORE BLOCK BUILDER
RECLAIMING THE INNER CITY ONE STREET AT A TIME

CAN A SINGLE TWENTY-SEVEN-YEAR-OLD COMPUTER WHIZ STEM
the decline of inner-city Baltimore and turn it around? Probably not. But don't
tell that to Adam Meister. He's on a roll and has made a stand in his native city's
Reservoir Hill section, which he hopes to wrest back from disinvestment and the
poverty, crime, and drugs that followed. Using the organizing tool that comes as
second nature to his generation—the Internet—Meister has managed to recruit
three other pioneers to his block of Linden Avenue, and along the way has developed a model for urban reclamation that has caught the attention of young,
house-hungry risk-takers, both in Baltimore and other rusting cities left behind
as manufacturing has moved offshore.

Jack Kerouac spent time talking, drinking, and dancing in Baltimore's waterfront saloons in the 1940s and '50s, and the gritty urban landscape he described
in his first novel, *The Town and the City*, was deeply blue collar and placed the city in
the top rank of America's industrial centers. And like many such cities around the
middle of the last century, Baltimore looked as though it had a bright future. The
port city was bustling with factories that turned out ships, steel, tin cans, canned
food, and chemicals. It was filled with blocks and blocks of neat brick row houses
noted for the front stoops with three white marble steps proud housewives
washed every day. But the collapse of much of the country's heavy manufacturing
during the last half of the twentieth century, advances in technology, plant clos-
ings, loss of union jobs, interstate highway construction, race riots, and white
flight devastated Baltimore as they did so many other cities during the 1960s and
'70s. By 1984, only 696 manufacturing plants remained, down from a high of
1,738 in the 1950s. Today mile after mile of the inner city has become a wasteland
of empty lots, boarded-up houses, excruciating poverty, and a thriving drug trade.

"If you come through East Baltimore today on the train it is disgraceful," Meister says. "You still see rows and rows of row houses. But they're all empty. It's like a scary, post-nuclear war scene."

At its height in the late 1950s, Baltimore had a population nearing one million people. Today it's down to about 650,000, leaving thousands and thousands of houses standing empty. "You can't take away 350,000 people and have things be normal," he says.

Meister got his first full exposure to inner-city life while attending Washington University in St. Louis, which he calls a Midwestern equivalent of Baltimore. After graduation he came back to his native city to help his father in the family vending machine business, traveling to parts of his home town he had never experienced before.

"Growing up in the suburbs, I totally lost any connection with most parts of the city," he readily admits. "I knew the harbor, the sports stadiums, and some of the bars. But I totally lost any connection with where my relatives came from, areas that are today 100 percent black. People in the suburbs can't tell you shortcuts through Baltimore. They only know where to go on the highway and are quick to warn you, 'When you get off there, don't go right, go left! Never turn right!' So you grow up with these natural barriers in your mind, and you don't even know why."

Meister soon moved to New York City to enlist in the Internet revolution and then on to Silicon Valley. Along the way he was continually baffled when he ran into kids he'd known in Baltimore who had no intention of moving back home. He began to see how this only exacerbated a brain drain on an already exhausted city and robbed Baltimore of much needed entrepreneurs and taxes. By late 2000 he could tell the whole dot-com thing was about to implode. The Silicon Valley company he worked for had no substance behind it. He wanted to start his own business, and there seemed to be little future in one of the highest-cost-of-living centers in the country. Baltimore beckoned.

He came back home, founded an Internet research company, and set out to get others to join him in creating a new high-tech frontier by promoting Baltimore as the perfect start-up incubator, with a low cost of living and little competition. His idea was to start an organization called Start-Up City and raise a $2.5 million entrepreneur's fund to accept business plan ideas from young techies. Those who qualified for a $25,000 grant from the fund would have to pledge to live and invest the money within a six-block radius of a designated area. Which neighborhood that would be remained undecided, but it would be a rough one in need of salvation.

"My approach to raising the money was to use guilt," he says. "I saw so many companies in Baltimore that just pour money down the drain of these charities,

Adam Meister strolling along the 2200 block of Linden Avenue. (Photo by Rochelle Robinson)

but nothing gets fixed. I was thinking about the Ravens, the Orioles, Verizon—companies that completely take advantage of Baltimore. But I was twenty-four, kind of an idealist, and didn't really know how to do that."

Unfortunately, by 2001 the bloom was off the Internet rose, not enough people picked up on the plan, and the details became buried on Meister's website. What took its place was another start-up idea centered on housing. He imagined gathering together a group of urban pioneers committed to reclaiming a designated block of blighted inner-city houses. And the neighborhood that drew his attention was Reservoir Hill, the same one you'd wind up in if you made the dangerous mistake of turning right off the highway and not left!

"But I did just that one day," he says, where he found a neighborhood of seven parallel north-south streets bound on the east and west by solid blocks that framed a rotten core. "There is some badness in there: houses totally falling apart, empty houses on every block, very aggressive dudes that come up to your car immediately to try and sell you drugs. And on one block I didn't think there was anyone living there at all."

He immediately changed Start-Up City to Buy-A-Block and put it out on the Internet, and the response was very positive. No $2.5 million fund, no complexity, no asking anybody for anything; just individuals doing it together. Ten people showed up for an initial meeting in his apartment around the middle of 2002, one of whom appeared to be an undercover real estate promoter.

"He was a sketchy dude," Meister remembers, "suggesting other areas and trying to see what we were about."

But Meister didn't have enough people or a firm enough plan on how to proceed. Later in the summer he hosted a second, larger meeting at the library, but again there emerged no clear plan of attack on how to begin. Meanwhile, rumors were swirling that the neighborhood in question was about to burst with development, that prices would shoot up, that the moment had passed, that the street Meister had in mind was about to be taken over by the government, that they wouldn't be able to get any of the houses they wanted, much less a whole block of them. But in November 2002 his marketing hit pay dirt when the *City Paper*, Baltimore's alternative weekly, did a story on Meister, his idea, and the group. Overnight his e-mail list swelled from thirty interested prospects to 100, some of whom wanted to meet with him immediately. He called another, larger meeting at another, larger library, and forty people showed up with about forty different ideas on how to get started.

"The meeting went haywire," he says, and he swore off any more big meetings. A few of the folks Meister got to know a little better gathered later, and by January 2003 this inner circle met to form single-person subcommittees to research and answer basic questions dealing with marketing, finance, and location. Meanwhile, further media mentions swelled his contact list to 300 names, and one of them, Paul Reyes, turned out to be a real estate lawyer who was ready to buy himself a house. "He was older than the rest of us and was a calming influence who said, let's just decide on a block and do it."

It was now May of 2003 and attention turned back to Reservoir Hill, and a series of serendipitous encounters sparked by an article in the *Baltimore Sun* began to point to Linden Avenue. Someone called to say he owned a few mortgages on that street and told Meister to take a look at it. Then he got an e-mail from a merchant mariner named Lenny, who had come to the first meeting a year earlier, and who announced that he had just paid $15,000 for the shell of a house on Linden Avenue.

"Wow!" Meister says. "The first house had already been purchased! That's it. No more playing games. So I made an executive decision and told the rest of the inner circle, hey, this is the block."

Shortly after that Paul the lawyer bought the next house (a gut job for $34,000), Cem and Julie bought the third (a livable unit with a tenant for $140,000), and Meister bought the fourth, a 3,000-square-foot house divided into three apartments with a spectacular rooftop view of the rest of the city that cost him $41,000.

"One of the cool things about our group is that for a couple of days we went over to Paul's house and helped him gut the place for pizza," Meister says. "That's how I envisioned it all along, people who just wanted to do good stuff for Baltimore."

Had the group acted six months before it did, Meister figures it could have beaten a few speculators to the punch. Now there's a shady character from the Bronx who has snapped up a number of houses in the area and listed them for $225,000 each.

"This is not a $225,000-a-house neighborhood," Meister says. "I don't know what drug he's on. He's just trying to pump up the value of Reservoir Hill and make a killing. And now we're starting to see other weird investor dudes."

Where Meister's pioneering can go no one knows. It's hard to tell how many houses can be reclaimed on this specific street.

"I always said it would be nice to have between six and ten people on this block," he says. "But there are other blocks near us with openings. Who cares if we're not on the same block? We're contributing to the neighborhood, we're still helping each other gut, and we can interact with more neighbors that way, too. The name Buy-A-Block is kind of limited. But it's not really Buy-A-Block. I think it's becoming Help-Repopulate-An-Area or something like that, or Sow-The-Seeds. That's really where it's going—just to help Reservoir Hill as a whole."

Meister concedes he isn't the country's first urban homesteader. But he does feel he was the first to launch it all over the Internet, where he met his fellow pioneers, formed bonds with them, and held meetings, all before even selecting a block. "It's using Internet marketing to its maximum," he says, "something I always thought I was good at."

• • •

This story first appeared in the May/June 2004 edition of *DESIGNER/builder* magazine.

106½ East Clay Street before rehabilitation. (Photo courtesy of
Alliance to Conserve Old Richmond Neighborhoods)

KINGSLEY HAMMETT

FROM AN ACORN NEW COMMUNITIES GROW

BY THE LATE 1940s A SERIES OF GOVERNMENTAL POLICIES HAD SET in motion changes that would cause the inevitable isolation of inner-city areas across the country. Banks redlined whole neighborhoods, barring them from future investment. Residents were denied mortgage insurance and home-improvement loans and cut off from vital social services. New highways sliced traditional communities into pieces. At the same time, outlying suburban areas were being developed with new housing, new shopping centers, and new schools, drawing away an emerging white middle class. Decades later cities woke up to find that little was left of their once-vibrant downtowns but crime, drugs, trash, and abandoned buildings.

In many cases the knee-jerk response was to tear down whole square blocks of older structures, clear the site, and float some grand scheme for a gleaming new redevelopment project. But too often the vaunted plans for replacing lost housing stock never materialized and the cancer of decaying neighborhoods was left to spread.

In Richmond, Virginia, the capital of the Confederacy and a city blessed with thousands of Italianate houses from the nineteenth century, the history was painfully familiar but the current response has been different. Thanks to a non-profit organization called ACORN—the Alliance to Conserve Old Richmond Neighborhoods—made up of historic preservationists and contractors who saw potential where others saw despair, efforts are underway to repopulate the largely abandoned inner city, both with suburbanites who have ties to the old neighborhoods and low-income residents ready to put sweat equity into owning their own homes.

Beginning in the mid-1950s, white Richmondites in fear of school desegregation fled the city for the new suburbs and left behind the elderly and poor, most of them black, who had no other place to go. This saddled the city government with a shrinking tax base and an increasing caseload of people in need of special services.

"People didn't want to stay in grandmother's house because the neighborhood was going down," says ACORN director Jenny Knapp. "Grandmother probably died without a will. The house sat there empty. No one felt they had a responsibility to the house because no one person owned it. We could see that pattern over and over and over again."

As time went on, a growing number of beautiful and solidly built brick houses with heart-pine floors, elaborate plaster, and slate roofs fell vacant, triggering all sorts of sociological problems. The physical deterioration reflected badly on the neighborhood, which in turn drove away the few people remaining. By the late nineties, as the city's housing stock got older, more dilapidated, and more depressed, the city manager developed an aggressive plan to use city money to quickly demolish whole neighborhoods in what had become a common reaction to a host of public safety issues. By 1996 a number of houses in the Church Hill area, Richmond's oldest neighborhood, were earmarked for demolition, and orange tape started showing up with alarming frequency on old houses, particularly in the Union Hill section. Three years later, with the demolition imminent, ACORN was born.

"These houses weren't necessarily architecturally or historically significant," Knapp says, "just places where ordinary people lived. But we think that's special and should be saved. Each one of these little communities has a character and a quality, a distinctiveness of its own. It's all part of Richmond history. That's what we want to save. Even modest neighborhoods had fabulous houses worth saving."

ACORN's mission is to act as an information clearinghouse to encourage people to buy and rehabilitate what Richmond has counted as 7,500 vacant, abandoned, or tax-delinquent houses. It neither buys nor sells properties. Instead it hosts workshops and tours aimed at people interested in returning to the inner city. It has launched two new repopulation initiatives: "Live Where You Work" and "Live Where You Worship." The first is designed for city workers who are employed at City Hall in the heart of downtown but live somewhere else. By buying a home in Union Hill, Church Hill, or one of four other historic areas the city now calls "Neighborhoods in Bloom," they can get rid of the car and ride the bus or walk to work.

"That way we don't just attract professional people who want to take advantage of the neighborhood and speculate and try to get rich," Knapp says. "We're very sensitive to that. We've never been interested in gentrification and we never will be. We also think that if you deepen your commitment to your employer you're going to do a better job."

The second program is aimed at Richmondites who attend a church in an old neighborhood but live in the suburbs. Knapp tries to convince them they have an emotional tie to the community and a stake in its future.

106½ East Clay Street after rehabilitation. (Photo courtesy of Alliance to Conserve Old Richmond Neighborhoods)

"We want you to come back and live here," she tells them. "So far we've had a very good response, not from wealthy outsiders but from people inside who already have a stake in the old neighborhood."

Race continues to be a big issue in Richmond, and almost nothing happens there without someone playing the race card, Knapp says. So she tries to demonstrate that prior to the Civil War, people of all races lived side by side in harmony. "It's been done before," she says, "and it should continue to be diverse. Diversity was the hallmark of our early neighborhoods, and that's what we want to see continue to happen."

Now in its third year of operation, ACORN takes prospective homeowners on tours of the historic areas with architectural historians who can cast an old, depressed area in a new light. This helps a potential buyer develop a new understanding of the role a given neighborhood played in Richmond's history, what makes it special, and what sets one neighborhood apart from another. ACORN also holds workshops for those interested in vacant or abandoned properties and provides information on where they can find financing to buy and fix up old houses. There are numerous agencies ready to help individuals of low and moderate

2311 M Street before. (Photo courtesy of Alliance to
Conserve Old Richmond Neighborhoods)

2311 M Street after. (Photo courtesy of Alliance to
Conserve Old Richmond Neighborhoods)

income with down payment assistance or closing costs, Knapp says, but most of them aren't very good at marketing their services and getting out the word on what is available. ACORN is equipped to pull the various threads together and help a person repair his credit, if necessary, so that within six or twelve months he'll be in a position to become a homeowner.

Several thousand people have attended ACORN workshops or tours and the group has set up one database of available vacant houses and another of people who want to buy one. "Our job is matching the houses with the people," Knapp says.

While most of its funding comes from foundation grants, ACORN's biggest ally is the city of Richmond. It has funneled federal funds into improving the six historic neighborhoods, and positive results are beginning to show, particularly in Union Hill, which is home to the city's largest concentration of vacant, abandoned, and tax-delinquent properties. ACORN held a workshop and neighborhood tour of the area and identified every delinquent property within its boundaries. Not long afterward someone who was shopping in that neighborhood called Knapp to report that every property he looked at already had a contract on it. She in turn pushed the city into putting up fifty Union Hill properties for tax sale. Most of them are selling for $10,000 to $15,000 for a shell. But there is evidence of major appreciation. A few years ago an 1840s brick house sold for $2,500. After partial restoration it sold for $25,000. More recently it sold again for $135,000. "And it was a good buy at that price," Knapp says.

New residents formed a neighborhood association in Union Hill. But it's too early to see much new commercial investment yet. "You have to get people to commit to live there first," she says. "It takes a special person to come into a neighborhood that is not established yet."

• • •

This story first appeared in the March/April 2003 edition of *DESIGNER/builder* magazine.

FROM AN ACORN NEW COMMUNITIES GROW

May Day Parade, New York City, 1936. (Photo by John Albok. Courtesy of Tamiment Library, New York University, John Albok Photographs Collection.)

MAGGIE WRIGLEY

RADICAL BUILDERS IN THE BRONX

FOUR GENERATIONS OF FAMILIES, SO FAR, HAVE WRITTEN THEIR histories in this place in the Bronx. Four generations have lived interconnected lives at Amalgamated Houses, a cooperative community that is the proud result and sole surviving originator of a movement that forever changed affordable housing in this country. And as the original residents age and their families have grown, this community continues to find creative solutions to the changing needs of its residents.

It was a vision of utopia, in a city notorious for its tenement slums and crowded immigrant ghettos. In the 1920s, in the north Bronx, four radical collectives began a bold social experiment—building homes and communities that embraced all aspects of a better life for working people—political, economic, artistic, and communal.

Four Bronx cooperatives—the Amalgamated Houses, the Farband Houses, the Sholem Aleichem Cooperative, and the United Workers Cooperative Colony (known as the Allerton Coops)—were built by groups of mostly secular immigrants whose sometimes clashing politics ranged from anarchist to communist to socialist, but who shared the common goal of improving living conditions for their families and hopes of changing society.

These Bronx housing settlements were a reaction against the notorious immigrant slums of the Lower East Side, East Harlem, and Brooklyn. They were created by organizations that were part of the radical labor movement that flourished in New York after the turn of the twentieth century. These unions included the International Ladies' Garment Workers' Union, Amalgamated Clothing Workers of America, the communist-dominated United Workers, and the Zionist National Jewish Workers' Alliance.

Millions of immigrants were coming into the United States, among them two million Yiddish-speaking Jews, many with deep roots in radical politics, most of whom settled in New York City. Italian and Jewish garment workers, and working women, who were alienated from mainstream unions, embraced the socialist, anarchist, and other groups that spoke their languages, unionized their sweat-shops, and staged mass picketing. Subsequent garment workers' strikes in 1909 and 1910 solidified the strength of these labor unions.

These left-wing idealists believed in collective ownership and better lives. With an extraordinary scale of ambition they found large tracts of land available in the north Bronx, by the large, lush Van Cortlandt Park. They pooled their resources and bought the properties, secured mortgages, hired architects, and created affordable apartment houses that they owned and operated cooperatively. Built without direct public funding and based on the principle of limited equity, which barred shareholders from selling their apartments for profit or on the open mar-ket, these co-ops became the largest concentration of nonprofit cooperative hous-ing in the country. This nonprofit, labor-sponsored housing created homes for thousands, connected by subway to the rest of the city, yet with the benefits of open space and courtyards. They became a model for the creation of some 50,000 New York apartments after World War II. Although only Amalgamated Houses still functions with its original cooperative ideals intact, all the buildings still stand.

These visionaries wanted more than just cheap and decent housing—they wanted open space and air and they designed the apartments around courtyards with gardens and fountains. They created cooperative groceries and dairies and one co-op even bought a farm to supply fresh healthy food. Nurseries were open from 7 a.m. to 7 p.m. to provide day care that accommodated working parents. They started restaurants, laundries, and credit unions, schools, libraries, and gymnasiums. They had collective facilities for music, science, arts, and language clubs, literary groups, and religious and social gatherings.

Their vibrant activist communities created newspapers, books and other publications, radical schools and camps, sponsored lectures and concerts, created political campaigns and organizations. They formed the Workman's Circle, a social organization that provided sickness and death benefits. They agitated for tenants' rights and social welfare, ran political candidates for local and state offices, and were anti-fascist, anti-slavery, anti-discrimination—allowing and encouraging African American members. They were factory workers, carpenters, and tailors—but they could also be artists and philosophers, poets and painters. Some famous residents of the Bronx co-ops include the painters Marc Chagall and Abraham Manievich, composer Jacob Schaefer, poets Malka Lee, Isaac Raboy, and Aaron Rapoport, historian Jacob Shatsky, and architect Daniel Libeskind.

The Amalgamated Houses is the only group that survived the Depression with its cooperative ownership structure fully intact, and it has flourished and grown with the changing needs of its original inhabitants and the generations that followed. Amalgamated, built with the support of the Amalgamated Clothing Workers' Union, adapted its financial management during the Depression, both to protect itself from residents "cashing out" (it would return investments in monthly payments, not lump sums, so as to maintain its capital reserve) and to help residents in harsh financial circumstances to stay in their apartments by using their investment to pay rent, on the promise of future repayment when fortunes improved. Management used personal loans to keep the co-op store stocked. The *Jewish Daily Forward* newspaper extended a loan. Tied to the strength of the union, the co-op negotiated with the bank for suspension of interest payments during the Depression years, and a reduction of those rates as they came out of the slump. It cut operating costs to the bone—even built and for a while ran its own energy generating plant. It created flexibility for payments from new cooperators and slowly built back a strong reserve. It was a model of community and cooperation that evolved and strengthened and nurtured generations. The residents have "kept the faith" of nonprofit housing and resisted the temptation to privatize.

Ed Yaker has served as president and chairman of the board at Amalgamated Houses. He was born and raised here. He has a keen sense of the importance of the cooperative's history.

"November 1, 1927, was the day when the first group of 107 cooperators set foot in their apartments," he said. "We survived because Abraham Kazan, the first president, had the vision of a socialist idealist but also the sense of a businessman. He knew if it failed, everyone lost. He demonstrated that it was a viable economic form for the working New Yorker.

"Amalgamated did not fail," Yaker continued, "It grew. It survived the Depression, and it survived World War II. By 1947 it grew to 700 families. It expanded and doubled in size from 1949 to 1951."

A new housing cooperative, Park Reservoir, was created in 1957. For almost fifty years the two cooperatives have shared common management and common activities, and have been a joint community. Their buildings share streets with smaller apartment complexes and single-family homes, creating a comfortable, mixed neighborhood. Amalgamated started with six buildings with 303 units. It prospered and expanded after the war, and has grown to eleven buildings with 1,482 apartments and commercial spaces.

Yaker's family—his mother a milliner from Latvia and his father a furrier and presser from Moldova—moved to Amalgamated from downtown Manhattan in 1941. Many of their friends, also garment and factory workers, were living here. It was a place that allowed them to stay connected to their homelands through culture and politics, yet created a new model for a better environment to raise their children.

"It was a great place to grow up," he said. "There were kids all over the place, lots of friends and no worries. Everyone knew you, and knew you belonged here."

Ed Yaker, who has served as president and chairman of the board of the Amalgamated Houses, was born and raised in the cooperative community. (Photo by Maggie Wrigley)

He loved the time spent at Circle Pine Day Camp, established by cooperators for their children. "We went swimming every day at Tibbetts Brook. We'd play ball, do arts and crafts, ceramics, woodworking."

Political involvement was always a part of life. "My parents had their politics. There was a wide range—all on the progressive part of the spectrum. They were very involved union people." His father stood on picket lines. They belonged to the Workman's Circle—a social bonding group.

There were nurseries and play groups. A print shop put out political pamphlets and magazines. And the cultural was as important as the political. The co-op was designed with working studios—for painters, sculptors, for group classes in ceramics, woodworking, photography, and crafts. The artists who got individual studios taught children's art classes in return for cheap rent.

The grand space of Vladeck Hall, named for B. Charney Vladeck, the editor of the socialist *Forward*, has hosted performances by the theatrical and musical clubs, discussions by philosophical and poets' groups, as well as art exhibits, youth dances, book fairs, weddings, bar and bat mitzvahs, Thanksgiving and other holiday celebrations. Large photographs of such events through the years, and scenes of the gardens and buildings taken by the photographers' club, line the walls of the hall. A piano graces the stage.

Bernie Olshan and his son Aaron are two New York artists who live in and have nurtured artistic careers out of their studios in Amalgamated Houses. Bernie met his wife, who grew up in the co-op, and moved here in 1962. He was an established artist with a period of study in Paris and a number of one-man shows in Manhattan. The educational director, Herman Liebman, found him an affordable studio, on the condition that he teach art classes for co-op children.

"When I was first married, I became part of the community," Bernie said in an interview in his spacious, light-filled studio, full of his large, semi-abstract paintings, the brushes and paints and cloths of his business, and books, sculptures, and drawings.

"It was thrilling to live in a community of people who were close. My wife Lyla lived here since she was a baby. Her parents were original cooperators. We have friends here we have known for most of our lives. We moved into a huge apartment. There was the courtyard with a fountain. We never closed our windows or doors. Everybody was welcome. There was a terrific camaraderie.

"I worked as a cultural arts director at the YMHA for seventeen years, and I painted," Bernie said. "I taught classes here. We set up shows with Manhattan artists and locals. We had lectures, fundraisers, costume balls. Actors and entertainers had café nights; they invited intellectuals and artists and writers and poets. They always had space for culture here. There's always a connection. Poetry and literature and photography and sculpture—it all goes on here."

His son Aaron was on the same path. "From five years old I knew what I wanted to be, from the first moment I saw him do a drawing," he said. He watched his father and hung out with the neighborhood artists. He went to the High School for Music and Art, and as he was preparing to go to college he went to the same Herman Liebman and said, "I don't want to have to paint in my room anymore." The director looked at his work, pronouncing it "very professional" and good enough to deserve a studio. Without it, Aaron says, "I would not have been able to fulfill my dream. It enabled me to develop as an artist. I've had my studio here now for thirty-one years." His studio is overflowing with densely layered paintings and sculptural constructions, and he is involved in the downtown art scene.

Through the tree-lined blocks near Aaron's studio, Ray Martinez was pushing a stroller carrying his son Diego. A graphic designer, he lives in an apartment in the high-rise that Amalgamated built in the late 1960s that has views of the Manhattan skyline. These buildings, with terraces and central air conditioning, were built to give workers the equivalent of modern, even luxurious, apartment living.

Aaron Olshan (left) and his father, Bernie, in Bernie's
painting studio. (Photo by Maggie Wrigley)

"It's a community, when most places are not," Martinez said. "People know
each other and work together for a better place to live." He learned of the housing
opportunity through a friend, another lifelong cooperator.

There's a camaraderie and pride among the residents that speaks of genuine
care and achievement. And as the original cooperators have aged, they have developed what they call a NORC—a Naturally Occurring Retirement Community. It
creates a model for assisted living that lets members stay in their apartments with
full access to medical, social, and health workers—able to remain within the
community where many have lived their whole lives. The weekly bulletins from
the print shop these days detail not rent strikes and activist events so much as
community news and free yoga classes.

Beatrice Simpson, whose family was the first to move into the still-under-
construction Amalgamated, is described by Yaker as "the protector and the love"
of the community.

"I came here in 1927, when I was four years old—and I never left," octoge-
narian Bea said, sitting in her spacious apartment, surrounded by family photographs and art work. Her balcony overlooks miles of the surrounding Bronx
streets, full of trees and gardens.

"We were the first family, and the courtyard was mud, and we had to go up the stairs on boards," Bea said. "We had a beautiful four-room apartment, after living in railroad flats." She and her older sister Sylvia, then seven, would follow the mailman around all twenty-four entrances. "We knew every family, and we would greet all the people moving in—we were the big shots!

"The women immediately formed a women's club," Bea recalls, "where they ended up helping any family in need, helping each other. If somebody had a baby, and had another child, they did the shopping. They acted as if they were one family."

The mothers immediately organized the nursery schools, ran the day camps, held fund-raising bazaars whenever the camp or an activity club had a deficit. "Their whole aim in life was to do for their children what they felt they weren't able to get when they were growing up. The boys went to war, and the mothers— again the Women's Club—would make sure that they visited the families of the boys that were away. Especially if there was anybody wounded or anybody missing in action. It was just amazing, the insight these people had for humanism.

"The Women's Club—I think of them as liberated women. They used to save money and every spring they would take a holiday. They would have a bus. They went to Ausable Chasm, they went to Fort Ticonderoga, they went to Washington, D.C. These were women who never had—they didn't have cars, they didn't have money, but they wanted to experience things in the world. So they would leave us with the fathers and kiss us and the children and the fathers would wave to them. The joy that they would come home with was just tremendous, and it was so fulfilling for them as human beings."

Bea remembers running races at camp while her parents were "off picketing." "We had a wonderful day camp," Bea said. "It was seven dollars a season and they would never ask us for another dollar. We went swimming every day. We had weaving and ceramics, performances, all kinds of cultural classes. Dance classes were twenty-five cents."

She recalls the house bus that took Amalgamated children to school until their parents agitated for and helped build the new P.S. 95. There was such pride in the creation of that school, she said, that to this day—at bar mitzvahs, weddings, anniversary parties, at almost any gathering—the school song is still sung with joy and raucous enthusiasm.

The Depression hit hard, and Bea's father, Israel Lutzin, who started the co-op library, died when she was nine years old. Her mother, Ray, had to raise two daughters.

"It was very hard," Bea said. "But she did whatever she had to do, because she wanted us to have a proper place to live." The family's dry goods store closed, and they struggled to survive on home relief, the welfare of the time, supplemented by Sunday trips to Orchard Street on the Lower East Side to buy goods on order from neighbors. "Over my dead body!" was her mother's response to the city's attempt

Bea Simpson, whose family was the first to move into the Amalgamated Houses in 1927, lives in a spacious apartment that overlooks miles of surrounding Bronx streets full of trees and gardens. (Photo by Maggie Wrigley)

to move them to a cheaper apartment downtown. She negotiated a deal with Amalgamated, using her initial investment to pay the rent and so allowing her to stay and to repay the debt when times got better. "To us, it was the most meaningful and wonderful thing of the cooperative," Bea said. "To know that you were not thrown out of your apartment because you did not have any money to pay your rent. It enabled my mother to bring up her family in the atmosphere that she wanted." This saved other families from losing their homes and prompted the co-op to create a larger reserve fund.

Bea, her sister, and the other cooperators' children grew up together. After knocking around the different playgrounds and hanging on adjacent buildings' fences, she formally met her future husband at a fund-raising dance. Bea Lutzin married Irving Simpson in 1946, after he returned from the war. They had a son and a daughter, and as their family grew they moved to larger apartments and eventually started their own bridal business.

Bea treasures the achievements of their cooperative dream and the kinship that endures. "To see the progress, and the way things worked out, is wonderful," she said. "When there was trouble, everybody was there to help. When there was joy, everybody was there with a smile to share the joy with us.

"All my friends and my support system are here. There is community, if you want it. There's a nurse and a social worker on duty to help the aging people. There's music, poetry, always something on a Thursday or a Tuesday. There's lunch at the synagogue for seniors. I go whenever I can, or want to. There's always a party—for Valentine's Day, Mother's Day, Thanksgiving, any excuse. They will take you for a walk or to see the doctor. They will pick up your meds, your groceries, your mail. They speak English and Spanish. And it's free! Where do you get this?

"I went into the hospital. It seemed like a thousand people wanted to bring me my soup and chicken. It's wonderful."

A flyer is distributed weekly to keep the residents apprised of the discussion groups, the nursery school bazaars, when the trainer is coming to the fitness center, the children's art classes, the pharmacist's visit for medical advice, the theater club, the painting exhibits. As the population ages, transforms, and welcomes new generations, these people are sustaining and re-creating their rich culture and community.

"The original cooperators came out of an ideal, a social movement, and although there were a lot of radical political factions, they all came together on the issue of a co-op as a way to build and own homes. It was a unique idea for working people," Ed Yaker said.

"Our values are of democratic governance, shared responsibility, constant education, mutual respect." It's cooperation for service, not for profit, Yaker said —of what he called "growing up Amalgie."

• • •

This story first appeared in the November/December 2006 edition of *DESIGNER/builder* magazine.

RADICAL BUILDERS IN THE BRONX

205

Demonstrators protest the delay of construction of the Ida B. Wells housing project on Chicago's South Side in 1936. Delays frustrated African Americans who were promised public housing projects would be built predominantly for them. The South Side complex opened in 1941. (Photo by R. Koshuk, courtesy of the Chicago Housing Authority)

KINGSLEY HAMMETT

CHICAGO MUSEUM TO FEATURE
THE HISTORY OF PUBLIC HOUSING

VOLTAIRE ONCE NOTED THAT "THERE IS NO HISTORY, ONLY FICTIONS of varying degrees of plausibility." One of the great fictions of the American story is that public housing has been a complete failure and that the blame for this fiasco lies with public housing residents, the very people it was created to serve. These residents have been so relentlessly stigmatized and demonized, this negative image so seared into the nation's consciousness, that the very concept of providing housing to those in need has been thoroughly discredited in the public mind.

Closer to the truth is that it has been decades of inadequate funding, abysmal maintenance, poor management, a total lack of security, and the absence of political will that has left much of the country's public housing stock unlivable.

Public housing has in the past been and remains one of the most important elements in the health of this or any nation by providing shelter, community, and the social capital of relationships vital to the survival of millions of poor and working-class people who struggle to gain a foothold in capitalist economies that concentrate their resources on those at the top.

To demonstrate the value and importance of what public housing has been able to accomplish, a group of Chicagoans is working to launch the country's first National Public Housing Museum. The goal is to disprove the current notion that public housing was a failure: We tried that and it didn't work.

"At the beginning residents of public housing all felt like family," says Deverra Beverly, president of the ABLA developments' local advisory council and founding chairwoman of the National Public Housing Museum. "Everybody and everybody's mother knew everybody. It was just a beautiful place to live. We had gardens and flowers and when I grew up there was no perception that public housing residents were different. You could go anywhere you wanted in the city and you weren't stigmatized because you lived in the projects. It was racially integrated and many of the residents were interns at Cook County Hospital, living there because they didn't have any money. Doctors, lawyers, airline pilots, musicians, teachers all came out of public housing. It was just a community everyone wanted to live in."

Ten years ago, in a conversation with her friend Beatrice Jones, Beverly noted the changes sweeping through the housing projects and realized that before too long the whole community would look nothing like what they had known growing up. It was time to think about doing something to leave a legacy so that those who came after would know and understand what things once had been like and could and should be again. "Let's think about getting a museum," she said.

She started talking about it to different people and ultimately made contact with Sunny Fischer, executive director of the Richard H. Driehaus Foundation. Fischer was moved by the idea, embraced it wholeheartedly, and became the catalyst for the project. She subsequently took Beverly and four others to New York City to tour the Tenement Museum on the Lower East Side, which they saw as a model for what they had in mind for Chicago.

"We want to show public housing as it was, in photographs, in videos, in testimony," Beverly says. "At one time public housing was good and should continue being as good as it was. We want to showcase that. Without this museum we'll have grandchildren and great-grandchildren who will never know that public housing existed in any meaningful form."

Crystal Palmer, vice chairwoman of the board of the public housing museum and local advisory council president of West Haven (formerly Henry Horner Homes), first moved into that seven-story complex in 1968 when she was about nine years old. "It was a beautiful place," she says. "You could look out my window and see my school, a big field where you could play baseball, and out back was green grass with a low fence. There were gangs, but there was a sense of respect. If something were about to happen they would let the parents know to bring the kids in the house. They would do their thing and nobody got hurt. They didn't harm anybody. It didn't affect us."

She moved into her own apartment when she was about twenty, a time when the building's janitor still lived on site. "When you got ready to go to school your building and grounds were all cleaned. If it had been torn up the night before, we didn't know about it."

By the late 1970s and early 1980s, as jobs began to disappear, things changed for the worse. Gang activity and drug infiltration engulfed public housing. Men with criminal records were barred from living in households with their children, which sped the destruction of the family and the community at large. "They minimized the man," Palmer says. "They took away the ability of the men to protect their families and their community."

The Chicago Housing Authority called the breezeways at the Loomis Courts development, pictured here in 1952, "sidewalks in the air." (Photo by Harry Callahan, courtesy of the Chicago Housing Authority)

In the 1990s the Chicago Housing Authority cut its maintenance budgets and no longer had tradesmen to take care of the buildings. Floors were no longer waxed, walkways were no longer cleaned, people started urinating and doing drugs in the hallways. "It was terrible," Palmer admits. "In a way this was an old plan to move people out and get control of these valuable lands. Older residents knew this was coming thirty years ago. And it all came true."

In 1996 CHA turned over the management of the buildings to private companies and Palmer got a job as a janitor. "The place looked deplorable," she says. "All the CHA staff knew they were leaving and didn't do anything. It was inhuman for people to actually have to live in those conditions."

She expects that the stories told in the National Public Housing Museum will not be only about glorifying public housing or about how terrible it was. "Everyone had a role in this," Palmer says, "the city, CHA, HUD. If you're going to tell the story you have to tell the whole story in its essence, the good, the bad, and the ugly. We want people to understand that the strength of public housing is

A garden at the Trumbull Park Homes. (Photo by Murphy Photography, courtesy of the Chicago Housing Authority)

that it's family oriented. Everybody is part of a big, big family. We are all family. Everybody knows everybody."

Francine Washington moved into Stateway Gardens in 1975 when she was twenty years old. "For some people it was heaven; to others it was hell," she says. "It depends upon which way the mop flopped. If you minded your own business, it was OK. If you didn't, you got caught up."

She stayed on because there were so many people who needed help. They had problems with repairs to their apartments, with their neighbors, with the people at public aid, with reading their mail, filling out forms, and making appointments. She wanted to help these people get the services they needed.

"Stateway Gardens was definitely a community," she says. "Everybody knew your name, they knew your kids, they looked out for you. People helped the elderly go to the store or bring their groceries up to their apartments, find lost children or seniors with Alzheimer's. Back then the majority of people worked. It was a community—not a neighborhood, but a community. If you needed a dollar or a cup of sugar or to borrow a dress or a pair of shoes, you could knock on your neighbor's door."

There were some bad elements, Washington acknowledges, but CHA was not taking care of the buildings and got bonuses based on how much money they could save by deferring maintenance. Public housing was also big business for a lot of contractors who did shoddy work and let the buildings fall down. And as things deteriorated, the housing officials blamed the residents who were the victims.

"If CHA had upheld the lease the way it was written, it wouldn't have gotten run down the way it did. People who were doing bad things knew CHA wouldn't do anything about it, they knew the police wouldn't do anything about it. The renegade police would just come over and get their cut when they needed to pay their mortgage or some other bill."

Even with the drug dealing, all the lights out in the hallways, and the elevators not working, public housing was still safe and home for a lot of people, she says. "Those who have moved out miss the camaraderie we had in public housing. They might live on nice blocks in nice areas, but there's nothing going on—no block parties, no social gatherings, no community organizations. They are just there. People have told me they've lived on a new block for three years before they finally met a neighbor. Some have lived there for twenty-five years and know no one. How could you do that? If you lived in a CHA community you knew over 3,000 people. You knew everyone. If you didn't know them you knew of them."

Washington is extremely proud to be on the board of the National Public Housing Museum and to get the opportunity to tell the world where public housing has been, where it is today, and where it's going. "Public housing did not fail," she says. "The system failed public housing. There are a lot of stories to be told and a lot of people made it in public housing. Public housing helped people send their kids to decent schools and different colleges. Mr. T, Jerry Butler, Mary J. Blige, Curtis Mayfield, the members of Earth, Wind, and Fire, a lot of football and basketball players, people running city departments, judges, people in Fortune 500 companies, Congressman Bobby Rush and a lot of other politicians, policemen, and public officials all came out of public housing. This museum will be unique, it's going to be different, it's going to tell a story, and it's going to leave you mesmerized. It's going to take you a year to come back every day just to get the whole story."

Roberta Feldman, a professor of architecture at the University of Illinois at Chicago, has been working with public housing residents for more than two decades in support of their efforts to save their homes from the wrecking ball. Throughout that time, despite all their public protests when they took to the streets or went through the courts, these people got no support from any quarter.

"I believe this museum is absolutely essential in the United States," says Feldman, who also serves on the Public Housing Museum board of directors. "Public housing has been demonized and the people who live in public housing were stigmatized by outsiders. No one but the residents rose up and complained while the government continued to kill the whole social housing program. In a capitalist country there is absolutely no way the market will provide housing for everyone, so you've got to have government intervention."

The country needed public housing way before it passed its first housing act, she says, and the first projects were touted as employment generators during the Great Depression. But with the economy in collapse, the country faced with overwhelming demands from all sectors, and a flood of negative publicity that portrayed social housing as an infestation of communism, the government provided just a fraction of what it needed and a tiny proportion when compared to that produced in Western Europe.

"The developments themselves were first demonized by urban design professionals who said the Modernist buildings were unfit for living," Feldman says. "But they failed to ask the residents how they felt about these places—that they actually found a tremendous improvement over the absolutely horrendous conditions they were living in in slum neighborhoods.

"Then people like Jane Jacobs ripped the site plans and the notion that a superblock could possibly be a functional space for children to play. That's absolutely absurd because the courtyard schemes of the older low-rise public housing projects work a hell of a lot better than any city street where kids could get killed by cars.

"Then you had the social scientists dumping on the buildings and their effect on people; that somehow the people were made into criminals by these buildings. But the studies did not in any way recognize the fact that the policing was inadequate so that as drug crime went up dealers could easily establish themselves in these buildings and no one in authority gave a damn.

"Then the media treated public housing residents as criminals at best and no one discussed the fact that again, it was the police not policing these neighborhoods that allowed the criminals to move in and cause a terrible living environment for the residents. It wasn't the residents who were the criminals.

"Then the residents became demonized as welfare queens, etc., without any recognition given to the fact that all of the jobs that these people once held have left the country. The only jobs they could get were now in the suburbs where they had to travel two hours in either direction by mass transportation, if they could even get there by mass transportation, which ate away 20 percent of their salaries. And there wasn't any day care provided for low-income families in low-paid jobs and they'd have to give half their pay to daycare providers."

The bottom line, Feldman says, is that the design professionals, the social scientists, and the media, because they did not embed themselves in these communities, did not come to a real understanding of what life there was like, why it was once a wonderful place to live when they were first built, including the high-rises,

Leclaire Courts, an integrated development, 1952. (Courtesy of the Chicago Housing Authority)

why it became a bad place to live, and what could be done about it. Instead, they took their own particular angle on why public housing was a failure.

"The government, which never really wanted to get into the business of public housing in the first place, was let off the hook," she says. "When you get all the media saying public housing is a failure, and the people living there are undeserving, either because they are criminals or won't work, it becomes very easy for government to abandon something it never had a big commitment to. So you wind up with public housing—as a program, as buildings, and as people—as a total failure. It allows the government at this point to completely abandon its commitment to provide safe and decent housing for all Americans."

That is the primary reason, everyone involved agrees, that public housing's story must be told and used to reinvigorate America's commitment to it. And it's particularly important that the museum be located in Chicago, because Chicago epitomizes the lack of commitment by having demolished more than twice the number of units of public housing than any other city in the nation.

"Even more ironic," Feldman says, "is that the building in which this museum will be housed was one of fifty demonstration projects built to prove the viability of

The Altgeld Gardens library in 1945. (Courtesy of the Chicago Housing Authority)

a public housing program. And it wound up on the state registry of historic places because architecturally (three-story walk-ups surrounding courtyards that had places for kids to play safely and residents to build community) it was such an outstanding example of the way to build good housing for families with children."

In January 2007 Susanne Schnell came aboard as director of the museum's planning phase. It was her job to secure its nonprofit 501(c)(3) tax status, identify its mission, and help form a local board and executive committee, a national advisory committee, and a number of other committees and working groups to address site development, fundraising, programming, and architectural and contractor selection.

The National Public Housing Museum will be situated in a forty-two-unit brick apartment building of the Jane Addams Houses that was built in 1937 by FDR's Public Works Administration. Two-thirds of its 35,800 square feet will be devoted to museum uses with open gallery space for revolving exhibits and permanent exhibitions of re-created period apartments modeled in part on the Tenement Museum. The remaining third will include some retail, commercial, and restaurant uses, office space for other nonprofit organizations, and a study center that will focus on housing research and policy.

"I believe there will be national and international interest in this museum," Schnell says. "One core audience is the hundreds of thousands of current and former Chicago public housing residents and the millions who have lived in public housing across the country. We will have an oral-history recording booth within the museum and ways to capture people's stories in other cities as well once we establish chapters in various metropolitan areas across the country. We have talked about ways to organize supporters and friends of the museum in different cities, especially where there are very active public housing communities that would like to have a presence and a voice in this museum. We want to capture various interpretations of the history of public housing coming from current residents, alumni, and others who watched these communities change over time."

Schnell hopes the museum will encourage critical thinking and foster dialog about something that is contentious, that was born out of an idealistic vision, a public policy that had had many successes despite the relentless demonizing and stereotyping of the projects and their residents. "This is about encouraging a serious dialog around how society cares for its most vulnerable citizens in the twenty-first century."

Many of the museum's activities will be generated by the community and involve a range of folks from outside its walls (public housing residents, for example) to advise on and develop exhibitions and programming. "We want there to be an active partnership component in developing content."

The program calls for re-creating period apartments by doing research to understand various families and their stories across the eras and developing a public housing curriculum in partnership with Chicago Public Schools. Working with teachers in history, urban studies, English, and the performing arts, it will relate to children who live in or have families who've lived in public housing while at the same time educating those who do not. The curriculum could be used in suburban schools where there is not much understanding of public housing and related issues.

"We want to help kids understand the differences and similarities among residents growing up in different times and circumstances," Schnell says. "It will also focus on architectural design, urban planning, art, music (rap and hip-hop), things we know have emerged from what we might call a public housing culture. It will expose people to issues of public and affordable housing, public policy, race, class, immigration, and community development. It will provide a broad interdisciplinary curricular experience."

Outside the classroom, the curriculum could also serve in an after-school setting in conjunction with strong community organizations where young people would be trained to interview, go into the field, learn first-hand accounts, and capture oral histories of people in public housing.

"We want to continue to build an archive of oral histories because we want a lot of the exhibition content to be based on the first-voice experiences of people who have been in public housing or part of the public housing configuration," she says. "We hope we can work with other organizations, such as Facing History, the History Makers (which has expertise in oral history interviewing), various centers at big universities that deal with the study of race and culture, and the Center for Cultural Understanding and Change at the Field Museum. We want to challenge young people to think about society's idealistic intentions and to reflect on their own lives, their roles as citizens and neighbors. This is a leadership development exercise as well because they would be looking at the democratic process and how to build community."

Schnell envisions a museum with permanent exhibitions and lecture series and workshops and symposia and photo exhibits. But she also wants to see youth-curated exhibitions on how kids are experiencing the changes in the community. This could be expressed through artwork, the meaning of home, or new designs for affordable housing and mixed-income communities. They will be doing something called Museum in the Streets in conjunction with other organizations that might include live interpretive performances based on experiences in public housing. Musicians, actors, rappers, storytellers, poets, visual artists might perform in little galleries, public libraries, and at neighborhood festivals. To help further tie the museum back into the community, Schnell would like to have neighborhood audio walking tours that tell the stories from residents about how the community has changed, different kinds of small discussions with current residents who would serve as docents interpreting what is in the gallery while continually advising on developing of new content, and a youth camp where high school kids would have an oral-history-based curriculum and some public art activity. Two local theater companies are interested in developing a documentary-style theater piece based on oral histories with public housing residents that would be produced at neighborhood or downtown theaters.

"We are thinking about ways to make the museum interactive and not just exhibition- or gallery-based," she says. "We want to help people look more closely at some of their unexamined beliefs, to think more about the ongoing need for housing, and to consider the roles of government, community, and society at large. We want to look at other models across the globe and what we can learn from them. This is a place that could spawn other civic engagement and public-policy challenges. But it is first a cultural institution and a place for education and dialog regarding public housing and more broadly affordable housing."

Finally the museum board has a concept to house the International Center for the Study of Housing and Society, a global consortium of researchers, practitioners, and public policymakers that will convene workshops, call for papers,

Lowden Tenant Council meeting outdoors, circa 1960. (Courtesy of the Chicago Housing Authority)

and maybe publish a journal. Several distinguished scholars have signed on and declared there is a gap to be filled in study and dialog on innovative policies and best practices in government-sponsored housing.

When up and running, board members would like the National Public Housing Museum to join the International Coalition of Historic Sites Museums of Conscience, which in this country includes the Tenement Museum, the Women's Rights National Historic Park, the Martin Luther King Jr. National Historic Site, the National Civil Rights Museum, and the Japanese-American National Museum.

"Ours will be a living museum of conscience," Schnell says, "that looks at how to link the power of historic place to contemporary social issues and to serve as a catalyst for a lot of dialog: what happened here in the past, how did it affect people's lives, how can this inform the public and their thinking and their future engagement in public policy around this issue."

• • •

This story first appeared in the September/October 2008 edition of *DESIGNER/builder* magazine.

Sarah Singer strikes the classic Rosie the Riveter pose. (Photo by Shirl Buss)

KINGSLEY HAMMETT

ROSIE'S GIRLS SHOW WHAT GIRL POWER IS ABOUT

A GENERATION AGO THE WOMEN'S LIBERATION MOVEMENT RADICALLY altered the traditional view of what it meant to be a woman. Women were finally encouraged to seek their futures in any profession they wanted, including those long considered the bastions of men. Yet today they remain underrepresented in most fields. This is particularly striking in architecture, planning, construction, and real estate development, as well as in blue-collar trades that often come with good wages and generous union or government health, vacation, and retirement benefits.

Research shows that once girls leave the fifth grade, they are in for a couple of rough years. Their bodies begin to change, their confidence plummets, and their self-image is bombarded by dazzling depictions of unattainable perfection served up by television, movies, and magazines. Girls at that age start losing their sense that they can do things; those who were really good in math suddenly say, "Oh, I can't do that." Peer pressure, the desire to attract boys, and the structure of the education system all contribute to moving them from being more communal to being more competitive. They often have a hard time finding their identity and start believing that boys can do things better than they can.

In the months and years after Pearl Harbor, once-sheltered women poured out of the home to fill vital jobs left empty as men marched off to war. They were needed to assemble bombs, weld tanks, rivet ships, and ferry airplanes. Their labor matched that of any man. And their contribution to victory in World War II was symbolized by the mythical Rosie the Riveter, the bicep-flexing poster girl of the female "can-do" spirit of competence and accomplishment.

Young girls today are still in need of a shot of Rosie the Riveter's female empowerment to draw out and reinforce their inherent competence and value and to help them realize they are as worthy as their male counterparts. And that's exactly what's being taught in Santa Monica, California, through a program called Rosie's Girls. Working alongside city maintenance crews during two three-week summer intensives, sixth-, seventh-, and eighth-grade girls are introduced to the basics of carpentry, plumbing, electricity, welding, firefighting, tree trimming, and street repair. They also work through a broad curriculum of female consciousness-raising to counteract the negative images these young girls routinely encounter.

Six years ago native Southern Californian Shirl Buss was asked to help tailor the original model, founded in Burlington, Vermont, to the resources and local character of Santa Monica. Once she saw the potential to help young girls find their way, she jumped at the opportunity to combine her master's in architecture and PhD in urban design with a background in early childhood education, youth services, home repair, and contracting to develop and lead this cutting-edge program for middle-school girls.

Buss had gotten hooked on carpentry and home repair back in the 1970s when she was working at a residential treatment center for children who had nowhere else to live. After someone donated a bunch of hand tools to the youth shelter, she took a class at Santa Monica College to learn how to use them and then passed her new-found passion and knowledge onto the kids.

At that time Santa Monica got some federal Comprehensive Employment and Training Act (CETA) funds to train women in construction, and Buss joined with

Each day the girls take a lunch break and participate in team-building
activities in a nearby park. (Photo by Shirl Buss)

five other women to start what was called the Santa Monica Handywomen's Program. Basically they trained themselves to do home repairs for senior citizens and low-income residents. After a few years they formed a nonprofit contracting collective called Building Women.

The group functioned for six years, primarily doing work for nonprofit organizations, homeless shelters, and an affordable housing corporation in Santa Monica. They survived on grants and payments earned working as conventional contractors and plowed any profits back into the organization. They also held training events on weekends where they taught mothers and children and widows how to repair their homes (how to replace a broken window, how to fix a lock, where the service panel was located, how to turn the gas off), some of the basic things that a lot of women don't know.

Over time the demands on Building Women expanded from fixing broken door locks to doing bigger and bigger things. While working on a women's shelter, they were asked, "Can you build a deck? Can you build a room addition?" Buss felt they could do that and more, but she wasn't a trained designer. So she decided to enroll in architecture school at UCLA to pick up a few skills.

By then it was 1986 and the feminist movement had taken firm hold in the country. Except, as she soon discovered, at UCLA. Despite a number of female students, sexism was rampant among the faculty who routinely referred to architects as men. Coming from a feminist background, Buss was speechless and found that trying to use even something as basic as more inclusive language was tantamount to insurrection. She found salvation in the classes of professor Jacqueline Leavitt and began focusing on planning, the more progressive side of the school, and away from architecture, the stereotypical conservative white side. After getting her master's in architecture, she went on to earn a PhD in urban planning. She then took a teaching position in the design department at San Francisco State University and became a partner in a firm that does exhibit and educational design.

The call to get involved with Rosie's Girls came in 2001 from Renee Cowhig, one of her old Building Women colleagues who got her start in the humble Santa Monica Handywomen's Program and is now in charge of all of the infrastructure maintenance for the city of Santa Monica. Cowhig had been contacted by Elizabeth Shayne, who was then developing the original concept for Rosie's Girls in Burlington, Vermont. Cowhig called Buss to see if she would be interested in meeting with the Vermont people. She was, she did, and she has been with the program ever since.

Carpentry lies at the core of the program, and the first day the girls walk into the carpentry shop their eyes are huge with wonder at how they will ever master the large and seemingly dangerous tools. Three weeks later, decked out in blue jumpsuits and yellow hard hats, they are riding tractors, trimming trees from cherry pickers, learning to fill pot holes, and marveling at what they have built.

"We do probably twenty or thirty things every session," Buss says. "The girls also do a ropes course, a kayaking and a sailing course (both of which are focused on collaboration and teamwork), and because we're in California, we do surfing too. Gotta do that. But whenever the girls evaluate the program, carpentry always rates number one. It's always at the center of it. I think that's because it has rich, creative possibilities and we keep designing more and better projects for the girls to do that are more and more expressive. They really get engaged and love it."

Every session the girls do theme projects that combine their carpentry and welding skills. And at the end of the session they display their creations for three weeks in an arts complex in a converted railroad station. Two summers ago each of them made a clock with the theme "It's Time To …" So they came up with things like "It's Time for Women to Get Busy," or "It's Time for Women to Rule the World." Last summer they did a takeoff on the classic hope chest, with the theme "Your Hopes for Yourself in the Future," "Your Hopes for Your Community," or "Your Hopes for the World." They also each made a lamp of wood and copper called "_____ Lights Up My Life," such as "Friendship Lights Up My Life" or "Music Lights Up My Life."

"Another favorite project was making a little table with the theme 'What I Bring to the Table,'" Buss says. "Everybody had to come up with a theme like, 'I Bring Compassion,' or 'I Bring Peace,' or 'I Bring Diversity,' or 'I Bring Girl Power,' or 'I Bring Love,' or 'I Bring Creativity.' They had to represent their theme in welding and set the welding down into the top of the table they then covered with Plexiglas, so it's sort of like a shadow box within the table."

The girls also have made what they call identity chairs, where they express who they are through their design. One girl loved books, so her chair was all about books, and another girl's was music, so her chair was like a piano.

"One year we built chairs for a daycare center," Buss says. "The girls also make toolboxes and get tools to take home."

Every year Rosie's Girls makes sure there is a project or two for the girls and another for the community. Last summer, for example, girls in the first session designed and built a playhouse for a daycare center. For the second session they made planters for a women's shelter.

"One of the best community service projects we did was to make a chess table and chess pieces for a senior citizens' center," Buss says. "That was great. They got so into those chess pieces you wouldn't believe it. They made them out of wood with these dinky saws used to do detailed work and the knights' horses even had their own little manes. They also made a wood-and-tile coat rack for the senior citizens with tiles they painted and glazed. The theme was 'Rosie Then and Rosie

Riva Santos gets set to use the pneumatic nail gun
to build her hope chest. (Photo by Shirl Buss)

Now,' and they did images of Rosie the Riveter in the 1940s juxtaposed with images of Rosie's Girls and contemporary women."

Outside the shop the girls get involved with a variety of activities that teach media literacy and critical viewing skills. They look at how women are treated in the media and the gender bias that creeps into everyday language—such as mailman, fireman, and policeman—to get the girls to think more critically and to challenge each other not to use those words.

"The first year we had a lot of creative expression around criticizing women's images in the media," Buss says. "We involved the local women's shelter, which gave a little workshop on violence against women and how it starts off as teasing and can escalate to sexual harassment, date rape, and domestic violence. That was a real eye-opener for the girls."

Every year the girls make posters that challenge stereotypes of women. In one consciousness-raising exercise called "Finding the 'Me' in Media," they cut out sexist images and made collages of women in sexist poses, such as selling refrigerators in bathing suits. In a silent exercise, girls write their reactions to these images on Post-Its and devote a day to talking about and debating the images. At the end they create a personal poster to counteract the stereotypical images and put them on what they call the "Wall of Shame and the Wall of Fame."

K. C. Giron learns about heavy equipment from the street-paving crew. (Photo by Shirl Buss)

The girls also have written letters to magazines about the treatment of women. A very strong letter sent to *Seventeen* magazine remarked on the perpetuation of unrealistic images of women's bodies that they felt promoted anorexia and bulimia.

The program also offers the girls workshops with the crew from the city's television department that tapes and broadcasts the city council meetings. And somebody in the city manager's office teaches the girls about budgeting and finance and how the city is run. The girls then hold a mock city council meeting and film it with the city TV crew. "It's a combination of financial literacy, leadership development, and TV production," Buss says. "That's really fun."

Rosie's Girls is very ethnically and economically mixed, Buss says. "There are girls who live in public housing and girls who drive up in Mercedes. At first we weren't able to penetrate the Latino community where families were more interested in exposing their children to Folklórico than carpentry. But eventually the word got out and one summer a girl showed up in her big fluffy dress and changed into her coveralls. It was very cute. In the last five years we have had a really good cadre of Latinas in the program."

Even though Rosie's Girls is designed to raise the consciousness of young girls and to improve their self-esteem, over time it also has been effective in raising the consciousness of all the men who work in the city yards about sexism in general, about language, and about how to really respect young girls in a way that they never did before.

"They start to see how creative these girls are, how talented they are, and how awesome they are," Buss says, "and so their image of girls that age has really improved. But they've also become educators and have had the opportunity to express and convey the pride that they have in their craft and in themselves as the people who take care of the city."

Whether the graduates of Rosie's Girls grow up to join a street maintenance crew or wind up as director of the city's street maintenance department or whatever they choose to do, the skills they learn through the program will give them the self-confidence necessary to meet all kinds of unknown and varied challenges as they move through life. Just ask any great-grandmother who had the opportunity to flex her muscles during World War II and show what she could do.

• • •

This story first appeared in the July/August 2007 edition of *DESIGNER/builder* magazine.

During the show visitors were greeted by life-size photos of nine smiling
guards as they entered the gallery. (Photo by Angus Muller)

KINGSLEY HAMMETT

BEHIND THE BLUE SUIT

MUSEUM GUARDS ARE GENERALLY SILENT AND ANONYMOUS ADJUNCTS to an institution whose main intent is to provide a setting for people to experience art or artifacts. Who are those people who keep an eagle eye on the patrons and protect the objects and art? What are they interested in? Do visitors even notice they are there? Do they ever wonder what the security guards are thinking and what they think about the art that surrounds them all day? Do they ever wonder what the security guards think about *them*?

Robin Pacific did, and when she made the guards the stars of an exhibit at Canada's preeminent art museum, the Art Gallery of Ontario in Toronto, which ran from September 2003 to January 2004, she may have changed the culture of the art museum forever. All of a sudden these quiet, nameless characters became complex human beings with talents, interests, skills, and life histories beyond the gallery walls. This was a show that made everyone, the viewing public as well as the museum staff, sit up and take notice of people long taken for granted. The show challenged established barriers within a very class-bound institution.

"We talk openly and freely about ethnicity and diversity," Pacific says, "but we don't talk much in the arts about social class. This was a way to address that issue in a very embracing, positive, even happy way so people weren't put off by it."

Pacific is an artist who for the last twelve years has done collaborative community-based art projects. She is a co-founder of Art Starts, a storefront community art center that employs 100 artists a year to work in the most multicultural neighborhood in Toronto.

"By making art together we break down the elitism around art," she says, "and help make people visible to each other without trying to soften the struggles between people. We help create an environment where people become active producers of culture rather than passive consumers."

Pacific had often wondered about the guards in museums, and when a friend became director of education at the Art Gallery of Ontario she gave Pacific the name of Patrick Grieve, the shop steward of the Union of Protection Services Officers. Grieve thought the idea for a show on the guards was fabulous, and Pacific got a grant from the Canada Council for the Arts (the counterpart to the National Endowment for the Arts) to put it together.

Of the more than thirty full-time guards employed by the Art Gallery of Ontario, Pacific wound up working with nineteen for the show, including four women. In her initial interviews she asked each guard to name his or her favorite work of art in the collection and to talk about it. She also asked the guards what they wanted to see come out of the project. Everyone said exactly the same thing: They wanted the diverse interests, backgrounds, and other occupations of their fellow guards to be made visible to the public.

Pacific found a wealth of talent among the group and put it to use. One guard interviewed a fellow guard, who was the subject of a video made by a third guard, behind which ran music composed by a fourth guard and performed by himself and a fifth guard. The duo also played for the opening-night reception. And a sixth guard took all the photographs for the show. "It was all about collaboration," Pacific says.

At an initial meeting the guards decided they wanted to be photographed in their uniforms. But Bill McIntyre, a guard in his late fifties who had worked at the gallery for twenty years, had a special request.

"When I asked him to name his favorite work of art," Pacific recalls, "he said his favorite work of art was himself. And he said, 'I want you to photograph me three times: in my uniform; in my house surrounded by my incredible collection of opera recordings, art books, and records; and I want you to photograph me at a bar called the Toolbox.'"

It turns out that McIntyre dresses up every Saturday night in one of twenty-five different official police uniforms and goes to the Toolbox, a gay uniform bar in a fairly rough section of Toronto. "He was coming out of the closet about all this," Pacific says. "Not all his fellow guards knew about it."

McIntyre was hoping to come across as the very complex individual that he is, and he wanted his fellow guards to be seen as more than just faces in the crowd. "We are people who have complex lives," he says.

That gave Pacific two ideas for the project: to photograph other guards out of uniform wherever relevant, and to call the show *Uniform*, using all the plays on that word. They're wearing a uniform, they're not wearing a uniform, there's nothing uniform about these people, etc.

"The way I work," she says, "is to be open to people, to be spontaneous, and to let the project change."

When not standing guard within the Art Gallery of Ontario, Sharon Kiyoshk-Burritt is raising two children and making and selling Aboriginal jewelry. (Photo by Angus Muller)

The show managed to highlight the off-duty interests and supplemental careers of these people who for eight hours a day stand silently against the wall watching other people look at art. One plays in a rock band. Another works as a prison guard. Angus Muller, an expert on ancient Egypt, used to work at the Royal Ontario Museum in the Egyptology and Paleontology departments. He's also a photographer and is the one who took all the shots for the show.

Sharon Kiyoshk-Burritt, married with two children, has a business making and selling contemporary Aboriginal jewelry made from antler, deer bone, deerskin, porcupine quills, and sweetgrass.

Drew Carter had had a successful broadcasting career on the West Coast before coming back to Toronto to take care of his 102-year-old grandmother with the aim of keeping her out of a nursing home.

"We photographed him at home with his grandmother, and they installed it in the gallery's elevator," Pacific says. "On opening night the grandmother just wanted to ride the elevator up and down. People would get in, look at her in the photograph, and then see her in the elevator."

During the show, life-size photos of nine smiling guards greeted visitors as they entered the gallery. Twenty other portraits hung throughout the gallery in places one might ordinarily expect to find a guard. The show also featured a continuously running twelve-minute video of an interview with seventy-five-year-old guard Mike Litnovetsky, the most senior of the group with twenty-five years of service. A Russian Jew, he had been in the Soviet army and had a wealth of stories to tell. The video also included footage of his son Igor, who has been coming to the museum with his father since he was six years old and who now also works there as a guard. Igor has an honors degree in economics and political science, and in his spare time he's a wedding photographer.

Besides the portraits and video, there was a kiosk where visitors could click on the picture of a guard, opening an image of his or her favorite work of art and comments about it.

Before the show many of the guards felt they were second-class citizens, not treated with respect, and one of them said curators didn't give them the time of day because guards can't advance their careers. "But once the show opened the guards had more people from the public and gallery staff talking to them than ever before," Pacific says. "One guard who had worked there for twelve years found senior gallery officials making a point of speaking to her when they never had before. It really had an incredible effect in terms of the culture of the institution."

In fact, the guards took on a kind of celebrity. "After the show was up I can't tell you how many times a staff member would come up and say, 'Oh, I was talking to so-and-so the other day,' like the guards were stars," Pacific says. "People were dropping their names. Suddenly it became the cool thing to be somebody who knew these security guards. In the end several of the museum's guards who originally felt that guards should not be the subject of a show and chose not to participate expressed regret that they hadn't been a part of it."

Uniform was a real departure from Pacific's customary work because it took the art of the people and moved it into a mainstream institution. And it did a lot to highlight the class divisions such institutions represent.

"Here's this institution whose stated goal is to preserve this collection and expose the public to higher ideals of art," she says. "This is one of Canada's most prestigious art galleries. And yet it is a complete hierarchy, a class-bound microcosm of society. This project did something to break down those barriers within the institution."

• • •

This story first appeared in the January/February 2005 edition of *DESIGNER/builder* magazine.

Casa Latina, 151 East 116th St., East Harlem, has been responding to and shaping customer tastes in Latin music in El Barrio for more than fifty years. (Photo by Martha Cooper)

MARKING THE PLACES THAT MATTER

WHEN PEOPLE TALK OF LANDMARK PRESERVATION IN NEW YORK City, the subject is almost always distinctive architecture. But what of Casa Amadeo in the South Bronx, the city's oldest, longest-running Latin music store? Or the Cuyler Church in Brooklyn, which welcomed the nation's first generation of urban Native Americans? Or the Teatro Puerto Rico, a hot spot of Spanish-language vaudeville in the South Bronx? These places are more significant to many people than Federal Hall in the financial district, where George Washington took his first oath of office.

Recognizing and documenting these unsung sites is the focus of an organization called Place Matters. It grew out of a task force within the Municipal Art Society working in conjunction with City Lore: The Center for Urban Folk Culture. Place Matters is the first program to solicit and take seriously the opinions of ordinary New Yorkers about places in the physical landscape that they consider to have historic and cultural value. It is broad-based in its approach, its work encompasses places of interest to all classes and ethnic groups, and it does not prejudge what should be considered significant. If a certain site gets nominated, it is automatically included in the group's Census of Places that Matter. Some sites are selected for further study, and Place Matters uses its findings as tools for public education, to help direct preservation and planning policy, and ultimately to save threatened sites from destruction.

It all began after the Municipal Art Society and City Lore hosted a conference in 1997 at the Museum of the City of New York called "History Happened Here." The conference attracted speakers from all around the country to talk about why places of historical and cultural value were important to strengthening communities and to broadening the historic record.

"It was such a success and so many people expressed real interest in exploring these ideas further that we decided to try to begin a project that would be more proactive," says Marci Reaven, director of Place Matters. City Lore had already done a lot of cultural advocacy, under its program called Endangered Spaces, to gather letters of testimony to help galvanize support for interesting places around the city that were threatened by development or in need of technical assistance. "But we were always coming in very late, when there was already a crisis brewing, as with the Municipal Art Society's losing battle to save the Audubon Ballroom."

To get ahead of the wrecking ball they formed Place Matters to learn more about the city, to learn more about the places people consider valuable, to help sustain those places, and to be in a better position to help protect them if they become threatened. "So from the beginning it was both a history project and an advocacy project," Reaven says.

There are no criteria to nominate a specific site to the Census of Places that Matter. Place Matters requires only that the nominator sign his name so there are no anonymous nominations. Over the years, hundreds of nominations came in over the Internet, by mail, in response to solicitations to particular constituent groups, and from focused neighborhood workshops and community studies.

"In one case, for example, we held a number of public meetings with labor history advocates and labor history organizations to get nominations for labor history sites," she says. "We've also done larger geographic community studies to

William F. Moore Park (aka Spaghetti Park), 108th St., Corona, Queens.
Perhaps the best of a diminishing number of places left to play the
traditional Italian game of bocce. (Photo by Martha Cooper)

Martínez Hand Made Cigars, 171 West 29th St., Manhattan, one of four
Dominican-run hand-rolled cigar makers that continue a traditional master-
apprentice system. Several are owned and operated by men from the
same town in the Dominican Republic. (Photo by Martha Cooper)

survey particular areas of the city, as we are doing now in central Brooklyn. We
take all comers. That was an early decision."

The census is then published both in print and online. Those nominations
deemed particularly significant become the subject of further research with
help from historians, folklorists, anthropologists, historic preservationists, and
urban planners who produce oral histories, secondary historical research, and
building surveys.

"We do that research with the goal of writing a profile about the place,"
Reaven says. "That profile then becomes a story about the significance of the
place and about what goes on there. Then it goes onto the website where we solicit
further comment. That allows local residents to learn more about their area,

and provides information to architects, planners, and students who are doing projects and need to know more about the everyday valuables of the area. The whole point is to make these places visible, both for public education and as a way to protect them."

Once Place Matters has created a knowledge bank about valuable places in the city, the question becomes how to use that information to influence land-use policy, to generate more opportunities for protecting these kinds of places, and to market them. Its answer has been to mount a number of demonstration projects. On one level it works with the state and National Register of Historic Places, which typically recognizes buildings of primarily architectural significance. But Place Matters was able to engage the National Register's New York City field officer to get three nontraditional sites listed.

The first was the former Cuyler Church in Brooklyn's Boerum Hill neighborhood.

Ganesha Temple, Hindu Temple Society of North America, 45-57 Bowne St., Flushing, Queens. Created in India, transported to Queens, and consecrated in 1977, the temple hosts religious and cultural life for the Hindu community. (Photo by Martha Cooper)

Cedar Lane Stables, Linden Boulevard, Howard Beach, Queens. On these 100 acres, the Federation of Black Cowboys introduces local youngsters to the fundamentals of horsemanship and the history of Black Cowboys in the American West. (Photo by Martha Cooper)

Today it's a private residence. But between the 1930s and the 1960s it was a vibrant church serving a community of urban Indians, who had a lot of issues about how to adapt to the city while retaining their traditional culture.

"The pastor at Cuyler Church was David Cory," Reaven says. "He had been incredibly welcoming to the community, and he actually translated some of the hymnals into the Mohawk language. He also encouraged them to recapture, in ways that they found appropriate, their culture. And there's still an important performing group called the Thunderbird American Indian Dancers who used to meet at Cuyler Church."

The second site was Casa Amadeo in the South Bronx, the oldest Latin music store in New York City and a treasure trove of Latin music knowledge. And the third was Bohemian Hall, started by a Czech fraternal organization in Astoria, Queens, and was the city's last beer garden picnic park.

"These three were picked for both their local and national significance," Reaven says. "They were also recognized for what they meant to people whose sites of importance had been left out of any official recognition process."

Place Matters also managed to get the city's Landmarks Preservation Commission to designate the Asch Building, site of the horrific Triangle

Shirtwaist factory fire of 1911, as a landmark, which will protect the structure from future demolition.

"That was a really interesting hearing because all kinds of people who are never involved in these kinds of land-use decisions—labor historians, labor librarians, and union members—came out to talk to the commission about the building," Reaven says. "It was the first labor landmark in the entire city, so we've managed to break the ice and set a precedent."

But there are a lot of sites that for one reason or another are not going to be landmarked, Reaven admits. In such cases the goal is to retain the original use, particularly if it has cultural significance or serves as a community gathering space, an old-time social club, or an important immigrant club.

"We want to keep them going," she says.

Even with its small staff, Place Matters can serve as a broker to connect special places with talented people who are willing to donate their time. In the case of the Bohemian Hall's beer garden, for instance, the group called in a tree expert to see why the giant linden trees shading the garden were dying. If the trees were lost there would be little left but a concrete slab. And Place Matters helped Mike Amadeo, owner of Casa Amadeo, to weather the economic storm that has swept through the South Bronx. After suffering stretches without water or electricity, he's now facing sharply rising rent as the neighborhood makes a comeback.

"It was just a nightmare," she says of Amadeo's experience. "Now that the area has been starting slowly to revive, the management of the building has been trying to take advantage of him as their only stable tenant. We intervened on his behalf, got him press attention, and got a number of articles in the paper about him. We also got some political help to convince the landlord that Mike was a valuable tenant and to get off his back and lower his rent. And they did. It's so ironic; the one guy that's left they try to get rid of."

Part of the Place Matters public awareness campaign has been to develop place markers that use engaging visual forms and graphics beyond the typical bronze plaque. A design competition for markers attracted almost 100 entries, from which a jury chose eight finalists. The Bloomberg administration has taken a very hard stance against public markers, so Place Matters is trying to start with markers that won't get bogged down in years of petitioning and fighting the city for permission.

One choice, called Historic Overlay, is by artist David Provan. It is a simple sculptural piece that stands up from the ground to frame the view of a place from the same vantage point of a historic photograph. "The photograph is imprinted on the piece," Reaven says. "So you look at the photograph and at the place at the same time."

Another marker was designed by Tom Klem and Neill Bogan, both veterans of RepoHistory, the artists' co-op that had marked a number of New York City's

African Burial Ground, 290 Broadway, Lower Manhattan. Unexpectedly unearthed during construction of a federal office building in the early 1990s, this colonial-era cemetery for African American New Yorkers received protection as a burial ground after a long political and legal battle. (Photo by Martha Cooper)

unsung sites and events in the 1980s and '90s. Their idea was to select an iconic image symbolizing the particular site, sculpt an artifact from that image, and embed it in a clear panel to catch the eye of the passerby. They hope the marker's three-dimensional quality will get viewers wondering about the site. As an example, they created a marker for CBGB, a punk rock music joint on the Bowery, that showed a safety pin (the decoration of choice among punk kids) frozen in a Lucite panel with text on another panel, along with a map on a third panel showing interesting related sites nearby.

"This sign is both way-finding and information-providing, and thus thought-provoking," Reaven says.

A third idea, one Place Matters may find far easier to get permitted, would be a combination of window markers and audio stories accessible by phone. When you walk by a place, you see a visually engaging sign in a window that gives you some information and an 800 number. If you dial the number you get a short, beautifully produced audio story about that place.

"There might be an interview, music, or a short narration," she says. "It's quite cool."

Formerly the Asch, now the Brown Building, 23-29 Washington Place, Greenwich Village, Manhattan. To commemorate 146 lives lost in the 1911 Triangle Shirtwaist Fire, union members and supporters gather at the site each year. Firemen extend the ladder to the point where it stopped short in 1911. (Photo by Martha Cooper)

Masjid At-Taqwa, 1184 Fulton St., Bedford-Stuyvesant, Brooklyn. Since 1981, this mosque has served a large, diverse Muslim congregation and played an important role in improving neighborhood safety and fostering local commercial activity. (Photo by Martha Cooper)

Another proposal is to place an elegant postcard-dispensing machine in front of a site. A card might be free or cost as little as a nickel. And once you press a big, beautiful button, out comes a postcard with an image of the site and a bit of its history. You can then stick the card back into the machine for a time and date stamp, so it acts as a souvenir of your visit to the place.

"We're moving forward on some of the eight finalists," Reaven says, "and we'll try to work with as many of them as we can. For the most part they weren't too far out. What we really needed was something that was almost generic, that would be engaging but could be used all over the city. So it couldn't be place-specific."

Place Matters is trying to raise money to do a demonstration project in one part of the city, and the choice of identifying marker may depend on the neighborhood selected. Right now the group is putting a lot of resources into central Brooklyn, an African American area of the city that hasn't been well documented. This area is feeling the intense pressure of gentrification, and a lot of community activity has arisen in response. So it seems like a good time to research significant places, including social clubs, local parks, political centers, and recreational spots that more traditional city planners and community-based plans might overlook.

"We're also working with local historic preservation groups and helping them learn how to do oral histories so that they can better document their area," she says. "The Brooklyn Children's Museum has a huge program for adolescents and they like to do neighborhood research." Another partner has been the Tenement Museum and its affiliate program called the Lower East Side Community Preservation

Project. Place Matters is working with one of its signage finalists to help them mark sites specific to the immigrant experience.

Place Matters co-sponsored a conference on cultural and historical land-marking with the Historic Districts Council, a private organization that has long advocated for New York's historic districts. One of the more interesting areas to win historic status is in Longwood, a section of the South Bronx lined with beautiful townhouses, many of which were occupied in the 1930s and '40s by Cotton Club dancers. It was nearly destroyed in the 1970s when so much of the South Bronx went up in smoke. But because it was largely owner-occupied, the residents secured historic status and managed to protect themselves from the devastation just a block away.

"It's a pretty remarkable story," Reaven says. "Then we worked with the Point Community Development Corporation on a three-year research effort to uncover the previously invisible story of Latin music in the South Bronx. We are making a film with money from Latino Public Broadcasting. We also created an annotated map, titled *From Mambo to Hip-Hop*, which documents the Latin music and hip hop trail through Harlem and the South Bronx. And we have held public programs and concerts."

One of the concerts featured the P.S. 52 All-Stars, a band named after Public School 52, from which Colin Powell graduated along with a number of noted musicians, like Ray Barretto and the Palmieri Brothers.

Our Lady of Mount Carmel Grotto, 36 Amity Street, Rosebank, Staten Island. The city's most elaborate yard shrine dates from 1936 when members of the Society of Mount Carmel volunteered their labor to construct the stone-studded grotto. (Photo by Martha Cooper)

"One summer night we held a reunion concert with all these wonderful guys," she says of the Latin musicians, many now well up in years. "They walked through the elementary school and introduced themselves to the kids and the new principal and the teachers, and the principal ran out and got their files that are still there from the 1930s. It was so sweet. Most of these guys are in their sixties, seventies, and eighties, and they've never been acknowledged before, so it was wonderful."

Place Matters also worked with a local group called Park 52, which cleaned up a junkie park across the street from the school and has been running weekly music concerts and other activities there now for some years.

At one time that section of the Bronx supported a number of Spanish-language vaudeville theaters. The Teatro Puerto Rico is remembered by generations of residents, and Place Matters worked with the The Point to re-create a night of Spanish language vaudeville performances.

Interest in the work of Place Matters is beginning to spread across the country. The organization conducted a workshop at the National Trust for Historic Preservation conference in Denver that was attended by some sixty folklorists, historians, and preservationists from around the country who are interested in paying more attention to places of history and culture that contribute to the vibrancy of their communities.

"I think if you look at all of these different projects that we undertake separately, they can sound a little bit eclectic and all-over-the-place," Reaven says. "But basically what we're engaged in is a broad-based information-gathering effort, which is unusual in itself because in talking about the physical landscape and land use, places are usually valued primarily as property. It's very rare that people get asked why they care about places and in what way the places are adding to the health of their communities or to their personal or community well being."

Place Matters is trying to come up with innovative strategies to then get that information out, which accounts for the concerts, the theater, and the different kinds of place markers. And finally they are trying to stay attentive to when places are endangered, and, when possible, to try to protect them.

"So in my own mind that's what I think ties all this together," she says.

• • •

This story first appeared in the July/August 2004 edition of *DESIGNER/builder* magazine.

JERILOU HAMMETT AND KINGSLEY HAMMETT

NATURALLY OCCURRING RETIREMENT COMMUNITIES
AN INTERVIEW WITH FREDDA VLADECK

Most senior citizens would prefer to grow old in their own homes. But as they age, many need increasing levels of help with their daily routines and monitoring of their health care needs. These roles can be filled by family, friends, or professional home health care workers. But in the absence of such assistance, small problems can quickly lead to major crises and trips to the emergency room or assignment to a nursing home.

As a geriatric social worker at St. Vincent's Hospital in New York City in the mid-1980s, Fredda Vladeck began to notice a lot of older adults coming to the emergency room with preventable conditions. Many lived at Penn South Mutual Redevelopment Houses in nearby Chelsea, a cooperative housing development built in 1962 by the International Ladies Garment Workers Union. A quick survey revealed that Penn South was a community of 2,800 units housing 6,200 residents, almost 5,000 of them seniors. Many had never married and half of those who had married did not have children. Many of them were the old labor organizers who had devoted their lives to the unions, and the result was a population without traditional familial supports.

Working with the board of directors of Penn South, Vladeck designed a unique program that allows these seniors to age in place in what has come to be known as a Naturally Occurring Retirement Community (NORC). In the last twenty years her original concept has spread to include more than fifty similar programs in New York and dozens more around the country.

DESIGNER/BUILDER: How did you first get involved with NORCs?
FREDDA VLADECK: I was trained as a geriatric social worker, and I started my career working in health care settings. While at St. Vincent's Hospital I noticed a lot of

older adults coming into the emergency room with conditions I thought could have been prevented—a lot of falls, a lot of what appeared to be cognitive impairments, some diabetes, and a lot of dehydration resulting from people forgetting to drink. When we scratched the surface, it turned out that in some cases their thyroid levels were not being managed well, which then can mimic dementia. Then you wind up with a whole constellation of problems.

I noticed that the preponderance of these older adults was coming from one particular housing development, Penn South. It was a limited-equity cooperative apartment complex in which people bought shares, similar to the Amalgamated Houses in the Bronx. It was built by the International Ladies Garment Workers Union in 1962 and underwritten by the United Housing Federation. The original residents were union members, plus a few from the neighborhood who had been displaced by its construction. So as with Amalgamated, you had like-minded people who thought they were building a community together.

The community operated for many years with this sense of shared responsibility, mutual aid, and mutual support. It was a community where the residents took responsibility for one another, even across the generations. They had lots of clubs and groups. I'll never forget, some folks wanted to garden on the grounds, and the board actually had a little bit of a battle over how to allocate public space for personal private gardens; how do you make some social good come out of this that benefits the whole community? So the board required that if an older tenant wanted to work a plot of land that had been set aside for community gardening, he had to pair with a child living in the co-op. And you know what? They didn't put a fancy name to it; they didn't call it intergenerational blah, blah, blah. They were already sensing that there was a divide between the generations and they were trying to bridge it, and that was their idea.

By 1984 a lot of the original cooperators were nearing retirement and beginning to show the signs of frailty and deterioration. Initially this community tried to organize a group of volunteers to look out for the older people, but they couldn't sustain it because they weren't trained or able to deal with the range of problems they encountered. They turned to the local senior center, but about all it could do was deliver a meal. People were sensing that they needed something more.

At that time I was in the emergency room at St. Vincent's Hospital, and I noticed this pattern I mentioned before. I called David Smith, the chairman of the board of Penn South, who had a relationship with the folks at the hospital. When a Vladeck (my married name) calls into Penn South, that means something to that community. This wasn't just a hospital mucky-muck calling or a do-gooder social worker; this was a Vladeck calling. Baruch Vladeck was a labor leader, orator, socialist, leader in New York, and within the labor movement they knew the name. He was managing editor of the *Forward*, he was Fiorello La Guardia's minority whip, he was a Bundist, and he had been a revolutionary in Russia. He actually convinced La Guardia that they needed to go to FDR to get the feds involved in funding public housing in New York, and the two of them went to see the president and actually got the feds to start financing public housing. He was also on the first board of supervisors of the Public Housing Authority.

DESIGNER/BUILDER: What was David Smith's reaction to your call?

FREDDA VLADECK: He confirmed for me that the board was very concerned about all of these older, frail residents who had been the pioneers in their union, and the strain it was putting on the community, which was pained by its inability to help or address these needs. They wanted the hospital to send a social worker and maybe a nurse to go in and help people who they thought were in trouble. I told them that there was a reason why these folks were not coming to the attention sooner of people who could help them: they wanted to remain hidden, they were frightened, and they didn't want to leave their homes. So we needed to figure out how to get to people before they were in crisis.

If you just set it up for a social worker to go in when you notice a problem, they won't get in. The way our service system is organized, it's stigmatizing. We needed to come up with a way to change the dynamics so that people felt comfortable connecting to professionals who could help before there was a crisis. We needed to think about how to design a program that could get the older adults involved in shaping and re-shaping the kind of community they wanted to live in as they grew older.

There was a lot of deliberation among the board of directors about what to do. There was actually a battle. We're a housing company, they said; we're not a social service agency. But David Smith prevailed. I think what he said was something like: Just as we have to take care of the bricks and the mortar, we also have to take care of the people who live within the bricks and mortar, and we have a responsibility to shape the kind of place we are as a community.

DESIGNER/BUILDER: How did you propose to meet that challenge?

FREDDA VLADECK: I worked with David and a few people who lived at Penn South to think through what a program would look like, what it was we were trying to accomplish. They accepted my conviction that we couldn't just target people who appeared to be in trouble, because by that point it's too late. That doesn't get you ahead of the game. You're always catching up. A task force of the board was formed, and we worked through the design of a program that was structured to get older adults engaged, to get them to become contributing members of the community as well as receivers of services when they needed them, and to provide a safety net for the most frail and fragile.

The program officially opened on November 14, 1986, the first time anything like this had ever been done. We didn't know at that point that this was what would become known as a NORC program. NORCs were first identified in 1984 by Professor Michael Hunt in the School of Architecture and Urban Planning at the University of Wisconsin. He had noticed that one building in downtown Madison, which had maybe 100 units, seemed to have a lot of older people in it. He went and looked and talked to the folks, and realized that while the building was not built for older adults, people retiring were migrating to it because it was close to downtown and they could take advantage of things going on at the university. So he coined the phrase "Naturally Occurring Retirement Community," which he defined as a community that had not been built for seniors where 50 percent of the residents are sixty and older. His building became a NORC because of in-migration. The Penn South co-op became a NORC because of evolution, because of an aging-in process. And there's a third type, which you see a lot in rural areas, of out-migration of the younger working folks, leaving the older folks behind.

The board of directors of Penn South, the committee, and I developed a program for all older adults living in the complex, no matter what their abilities, their talents, their interests, or their needs, that brought group services, individual social services, and health care services together under one roof. Our goal was to change the experience of aging in that community. We called the program the Penn South Program for Seniors. To make it work we needed social workers, a geriatric nurse, and the residents themselves. Penn South took one of its community rooms and converted it into an office and a center for the program, and it was funded for the first three years by a family foundation of the United Jewish Appeal-Federation of New York.

DESIGNER/BUILDER: Specifically, how did the program work?
FREDDA VLADECK: On the health care side, we started to systematically address the issues of helping people manage their chronic conditions. Because I came out of St. Vincent's, which was the emergency receiving hospital for that area, we purposely connected back to St. Vincent's, both to its social work department and its ER department.

The public face of the program was what we called the group services side: the activities, the lectures, the art classes, the social gatherings, the bridge club. Basically we used building captains (the old volunteer corps that had tried to deal with individual issues as they came up) to get people to come and be a part of the activities and especially to convey that the residents had a role in building the kind of program they wanted. We needed their talent. Some of them became the teachers in these group programs. Some of them organized theater trips. They were the heart of the group services program. These were often the younger, healthier, more mobile members of the older population.

They also helped to identify who they were worried about on their floor, and we would then be able to send a nurse. We couldn't always send social workers up to visit somebody, because to them the idea of a social worker meant that they might have to go to a nursing home. We found ways to get the nurse into the apartments first and with her taking the lead we were then able to get social workers in to try to address some of the support issues.

DESIGNER/BUILDER: Why did this program work?

FREDDA VLADECK: What was critical here was the role of the visionary, and that wasn't me. I was the director and facilitator who gave voice and action to the vision. The true visionary was David Smith, and he led his board and the community through this. He recognized that housing management and the board had a major role in getting all the residents to participate and to help make this program meaningful and valuable. He truly believed that this would change the face of the community, that you would no longer see disheveled people schlepping along the walkways; that you would no longer see dirty, demented people talking to themselves, sitting on the benches all by themselves, clearly out of it. The goal was to begin to start trying to connect to these people before they fell and wound up in the emergency room and then in a psych ward or in a nursing home. It took a number of years to get those most frail and fragile to trust the nurse/social worker teams, which put in place services and supports to work with their doctors to make sense out of their medications and to work with the family or neighbors to look in on them. It took a couple of years for the community to trust that we weren't there to just get them out of their apartments and into a nursing home. But we did it. We succeeded.

There were some remarkable folks who lived at Penn South. The guy who wrote *Bread and Roses*, he and his wife lived in this community. A. Philip Randolph lived in this community. It was an amazing place, where singing and culture were happening all the time. And much of that vibrancy had been diminished as the community got older. The program started to resurrect that original spirit. All of a sudden we now had a chorus going again. They practiced every Friday next to my office, and some of these songs were songs that I was raised on, all the union songs and the Yiddish songs. They always had community rooms, but because the original cooperators were getting old and losing some of their ability to organize and keep these things going, they needed help. We provided that help and did the mechanics for the community. There was a monthly flyer that went under each door. We did art classes. There were some incredible artists there. We started a writing club. There was definitely a social action committee, and that was one of the most lively groups. Eli Stern led the weekly discussion about the news. And let me tell you, it really brought this community to life—socialists, a few communists, some regular Democrats, a couple of anarchists, and maybe one or two

Republicans, all in the same room. Politics was the lifeblood in the community because these were the old organizers. A gathering wasn't a good gathering unless we could have a political discussion and argue. And so there were real battles in this community, but somehow it all worked.

What this program did was provide a way and a place for people to come together, which had been lost. And that's a very important thing in all communities that have large concentrations of older adults. They are not going to go to the playground or the sandbox. They're not going to see each other at the school. Where do they go to find one another? It's a question that I ask whenever I'm visiting a community that might be demographically a NORC. How do people in this community come together and make community? Because that's indeed what is needed in all of these communities. Our aging services, our formal service system, don't ask that question. They merely ask: what do we need to give that person? Do they need a meal, do they need housekeeping? What can we do just to shore up their needs so that they can stay in their house? They'll be trapped behind their front door, because they have to be homebound to get any of those services. This is our traditional system. This was what I was reacting to in the mid-1980s, and some of what I was asking this community to rethink. This was the first time older adults had been invited to re-fashion their community in their image, in the way they wanted to live.

DESIGNER/BUILDER: How was the program financed?
FREDDA VLADECK: In 1989, having had three years of philanthropic support provided by the UJA Federation, we realized that this program was valued and important and that we needed to find more stable funding. At that point David Smith, the visionary, said we have a shared responsibility here and as the housing corporation we need to support it out of our operating budget rather than have people pay for it as they use it. I knew that if it were "fee for service," people would not come because it would be too costly. I am a believer in social insurance, which spreads the risk and shares the responsibility. And David figured out that by adding one dollar to the monthly carrying charges on all 2,800 units, they could actually support a good chunk of this. And the residents themselves were raising somewhere between $30,000 and $40,000 to fund activities and to help subsidize those who were less fortunate.

DESIGNER/BUILDER: How did the NORC programs spread around New York?
FREDDA VLADECK: I left Penn South in 1992, thinking the program was on sound footing and wanting to go on to something else. By that point, the UJA Federation was already working to replicate the NORC concept in other similar communities. We needed to answer the question, was Penn South so unique that you could

never do this anyplace else? We knew that there were approximately 400,000 units of this kind of affordable housing in the city that were demographically becoming NORCs. We knew that this was potentially a large issue in New York. And with the replication in 1992 of projects at Warbasse Houses on Coney Island and at Co-op Village on the Lower East Side, we confirmed that this was doable.

By 1994 we had four programs operating: three in moderate-income and one in public housing. We knew by then we could change the dynamic in a community, move it from a place where people were waiting to die, where the community itself was overrun and beset by problems, to one in which it was building something for the residents that would enable them to take care of their own and become a place of living again.

The Coordinating Council of Cooperatives (CCC), which represented cooperative housing complexes in the city, saw that this was working and believed it was time to see about creating some public policy to broaden the approach of shared financial responsibility, of public and private funding, and see if you couldn't make this available to more housing developments in New York. In 1994 the CCC, health care and social service providers, and residents organized and got legislation passed that established the NORC Supportive Service Programs (SSP) model as something that the state would fund. Starting in 1995 the state approved public financing to match private financing and twelve programs began in New York State, ten of them down here in New York City. In 1999 the New York City Council, not to be outdone by the state legislature, decided that it wanted to get in on the act. It allocated $4 million to be matched by the housing companies and other private support for more NORC supportive service programs in moderate- and low-income housing. Then in 2005 and 2006 the amount of money actually increased at both the state and the city levels. So today in New York there is something on the order of $11 million in public funds from the state and the city being matched by roughly the same amount from the private sector.

DESIGNER/BUILDER: Can you do a NORC program in a setting other than an apartment complex?

FREDDA VLADECK: About four years ago we realized that we were going to have to figure out how to organize a community where you've got a neighborhood of people living in unaffiliated housing without a housing management entity. With funding from a local foundation a prototype was done in a community in northeast Queens that had been built right after World War II for returning vets. It was called the NORC-WOW Program (NORC Without Walls). This was an area of very modest homes built in the middle of what had been farmland with nothing else around. So these people had to make their own community. They were the pioneers who made sure that the sidewalks got built, that schools got built. By

2003 this had become largely a community of very old, white, retired teachers, shopkeepers, librarians, and blue-collar workers. Some serious community organizing needed to be done.

Today it's going like gangbusters, so much so that in 2005 the state legislature introduced a bill to fund Neighborhood NORC programs using NORC-WOW as a model. The key question was what was going to take the place of the co-op board as we tried to find a community space and structure the program. You can't do that without a year or two of good old-fashioned community organizing and getting the politicians, the shopkeepers, the informal leaders, the key leaders involved. There are a whole variety of ways that you can start making connections, beginning with getting people to start talking about what will make this a good community to grow old in. Nine-tenths of this is about giving people the permission to dream, and telling them that they can affect their environment.

What we've accomplished is about changing the discussion from long-term care to long-term living. It's moving the mindset and recognizing that older adults, as old and as frail and as fragile as they are, have roles to fill in their community. It's up to us to find those appropriate roles and recognize that it's not just about putting in a service; it's about addressing the quality of life of older adults.

There's a major push right now among public policy folks in the aging and long-term care world to do what's called community-based care. I'm not exactly sure what that means. I think the larger question here is we need to be thinking about the role of older adults in communities and how they can continue to be valued contributors. At Penn South we told people in wheelchairs, who ordinarily would have been stuck in their apartments, that there was stuff they could do here to help this community and this program. We told them, bring your home care worker, too. That's fine. You have a role in this community and in this society, and our job is to help you realize your potential.

DESIGNER/BUILDER: What are you doing these days?

FREDDA VLADECK: Now I am working at the United Hospital Fund, where I direct the aging-in-place initiative that is a resource to those interested in developing NORC programs. We are also working to show the impact these programs have had on the health of the NORC communities and the older adults who live in them.

• • •

This story first appeared in the January/February 2007 edition of *DESIGNER/builder* magazine.

Older children in Moo Ban Nua help their younger sibling explore the more challenging play structures. (Photo by Katherine Melcher)

KATHERINE MELCHER

HEALING COMMUNITY THROUGH PLAY

...the preservation (or restoration) of communal forms of life must become a
lasting concern, not only for those charged with healing the wounds of acute
disaster but for those charged with planning a truly human future.
—Kai T. Erikson, *Everything in Its Path:*
Destruction of Community in the Buffalo Creek Flood

WRITTEN IN 1976 AFTER ERIKSON HAD WORKED WITH AN
Appalachian community destroyed by flood and landslide, these words still have
relevance today. In the aftermath of recent hurricanes, tsunamis, earthquakes,
and war, ways to heal the wounds of acute disaster are needed now more than ever.
And in light of growing evidence that health and happiness depend on our connections with others, preserving and restoring communities must become priorities for planners, designers, and citizens undertaking the task of rebuilding.

In August 2005, I got the opportunity to explore how landscape architecture
can contribute to a community recovering from a disaster. I volunteered with the
Crisis Corps, a division of the Peace Corps, to help a tsunami-impacted village in
Thailand design and construct a playground.

I arrived in Suksamran, Ranong Province, six months after the tsunami. In
some places along the Andaman Sea, like the resort of Khao Lak, debris such as
hotel shampoo bottles, backpacks, flip-flops, and stuffed animals was still washing
ashore. But Suksamran had been largely rebuilt. The Thai government had built
housing for people who had lost homes and had created a new dock for fishing
boats. Approximately forty homes were built in Moo Ban Tap Nua, a stretch of
beach in Suksamran between the sea and a mangrove swamp. Moo Ban Tap Nua is
an ideal place to live for those who rely on the sea for their livelihood, as these
fishermen do. But the danger of another tsunami remains real.

Because of the fear of future tsunamis, the fear of ghosts, and the lack of a reliable water source, when I arrived many families had not relocated to their new housing at Moo Ban Tap Nua. They preferred to stay inland with relatives in the sister village of Moo Ban Nua. Even those who did move back were hesitant to have their children stay on the beach. Moo Ban Nua, as a consequence, was inundated with children.

Moo Ban Nua is a tight-knit Muslim village whose residents rely largely on fishing and small-scale agriculture for income. In addition to the children who live in Moo Ban Nua, over a hundred children come to the village on weekends for religious schooling. The leaders of the village mosque requested help in creating a new playground due to the influx of children, the unsafe conditions on other playgrounds, and the numerous children playing on the busy street.

Throughout my stay in Moo Ban Nua, I never met the leaders of the village mosque. I assumed it was not proper for me as a non-Muslim female to meet with them, even if it was for business. At first I was not sure how the village would accept a single American female with almost no Thai language skills. Still, I set out to do a community design process much like I would at home. The first workshop introduced the adults to the project and the proposed playground location. We broke into small groups, each with a site map and cutouts of the different equipment and amenities that could be placed on the site.

The use of small groups brought in more participation and new ideas than I had expected. In a culture that is used to rote learning, lectures, and separation of the sexes, it was great to see women earnestly discussing the design and the men in another group coming up with different ideas. Most groups tried to fit in all the elements I gave them by piling them on top of each other and overflowing the edges of the maps. As one man explained to me, "We want everything."

One group of women added a private room for aerobics to their design and then convinced other groups to add one as well. Aerobics is popular in Thailand, and it is common in city parks to see aerobics instructors leading large crowds in exercise. But this type of public display would be highly inappropriate for Muslim women.

Although the playground site was too small for an aerobics building and the primary goal of the playground was to create a safe place for the children to play, I wanted to include space in the playground where women could gather and socialize. I realized that these women really have no public, social space of their own. The men spend time at the mosque and cafés, while women mostly spend their time at each other's houses.

To involve the children in the design process, we asked them to draw two things: their favorite outdoor places and what they would like in a playground. Most children drew the beach and sea as their favorite places, while others included houses, flowers, mountains, and trees. Much of what they wanted in the

In a community workshop, women and their children help design the playground. (Photo by Katherine Melcher)

playground was the standard equipment they already had at their school playground. But the children also came up with haunted houses, trains, badminton courts, and swings with flower vines as chains.

My relationship with the village at this time was still distant and uncertain. My neighbors would watch me with amused curiosity but never really approach me. A few days after the children did their drawings, three girls came to my porch asking for something. I could not tell what. They pulled out a Thai-English computerized translator. What they typed in came out as "to create a frame." Eventually, after a lot of pointing and gesturing, I realized they wanted to draw a picture. I gave them paper and markers and taped the three drawings up on my porch wall when they were done.

Soon I was surrounded by children asking for *wah-doop* (markers) and insisting that I put up their drawings too. By mid-afternoon, the drawings wrapped all the way around my porch. I left for the market and when I came back, even more drawings had appeared on my walls.

I had made friends. The girls took me by the hands and led me to the river to *ab-nam khlong* (swim in the river). They became my best friends; they would come to my porch to draw, swing in my hammock, sing "Jingle Bells," and try to teach me Thai. The children broke down the barriers, and the women, despite our lack of a common language, soon followed and became my friends too.

From the input of the first meeting, I came up with a plan that tried to squeeze in as much as possible without sacrificing safety. Playgrounds in Thai city parks might have fall zones and soft surfaces underneath play equipment, but in small

Local carpenters devise a way to construct a wooden slide. (Photo by Katherine Melcher)

villages this was not common. The typical playground I saw in Thailand consisted of thin metal structures fastened to a concrete slab. The year before I arrived, a boy in the village died when he slam-dunked a basketball in a poorly anchored hoop; the post came loose and fell on top of him. For the village, safety zones and strong, durable equipment with a soft surface underneath were a priority.

Even though safety was of the utmost importance, I did not want to use a prefabricated powder-coated pipe structure like those found often in playgrounds in the United States. I wanted to use local materials so people in the village could repair the equipment as necessary and also so they could build more playgrounds if the opportunity arose. Plus, I welcomed the challenge of designing a playground from the ground up, using local construction techniques and materials, resulting (I hoped) in a unique playground expressive of the local culture.

The plan, much like playgrounds designed in the United States, consisted of a play structure geared toward two- to five-year-olds and a larger one for five- to twelve-year-olds. The smaller structure contained a small boat and dock representing the sea and the village; the taller structure near the existing trees represented the forest and the mountains. I included a covered stage for performances and gatherings and a space with removable curtains for semiprivate aerobics. In a tropical climate where it is either pouring rain or burning hot, the stage also provides protection from each extreme. The play structures and stage are oriented around a small open field that can be used for Chinese jump rope, badminton, and small games of *takraw* (a popular Thai sport) or volleyball.

In the United States we would take the playground plan, develop construction documents, and find a contractor. But in rural Thailand, I was not sure how to get the project built. During the design process, I stopped to watch construction techniques whenever I came upon a house under construction. I also spent hours wandering in hardware stores and art supply stores, seeing what materials were locally available. Still, I had a list of very basic questions that I did not have the answers to:

- What construction materials are low cost and locally available? How strong and durable are those materials?
- Who would build the play structures? Does the village have skilled laborers who could build them?
- Who will take care of the playground, once built, and supervise its use?

We held a second community meeting to get feedback on the plan and to try to answer some of these questions. Four different stations gave people the opportunity to comment on four different topics. The first station displayed the playground plan and sketches and asked if it fit with what the community wanted. The second presented potential materials, including bamboo, river rocks, and old tires, and asked what would be easy to find and what the village would be willing to donate to the project. The third asked about labor—who would be willing to volunteer their time and what skills they had. And the fourth discussed maintenance responsibilities—who would look after the playground, who would regularly inspect and repair the structures, and where would the funds for repairs come from.

From this information, I put together a budget and grant proposal for submittal to the Peace Corps Partnership Tsunami Fund. With the donation of land, labor, and some materials (bamboo, rocks, etc.), the village's contribution was approximately $6,000, 25 percent of the total project budget.

A landscape architect once told me that there are two keys to a successful project: a good client and a good contractor. In Thailand I was lucky to have both:

my client, Khun Abdullah, a local village leader, and my contractor, Khun Faori, a local carpenter.

Khun Abdullah, my client and work supervisor, is a local government representative for Moo Ban Nua. He is also a father of four who is well respected in the village for his dedication to the community. Although we often had no idea what the other was trying to say, he was more than tolerant of my ideas and questions. He met my odd requests for things such as used tires and pipes with holes punched in them with a smile, and often the materials would quietly show up in the next couple of days.

Our first construction challenge was the drainage. Ranong Province has one of the highest rainfall rates in Thailand. Yet drainage systems we use in the United States, such as surface swales, trench drains, permeable paving, and even drainage pipes, are not commonplace in Thai villages. The Thais simply build their houses on piers and let the floods come and go. I appreciate the simplicity and light touch of this solution, yet I wanted the playground to be functional year-round. Also, increased development in the village and more concrete roads and house foundations are exacerbating local drainage problems. The playground provided an opportunity to demonstrate some simple solutions that anyone could implement, such as drain trenches and permeable pathways set on a gravel bed.

When the backhoe arrived to dig out the play areas and trenches, it drew a crowd. When the work was done, we were left with something that looked like the trenches of World War I, but the children loved it. They were already treating it like a playground, hiding in the trenches and running up and down the piles of dirt. A neighbor asked me if we were building a swimming pool. In a culture where one usually builds up to avoid floods rather than down, the technique was counterintuitive to them.

The second key to the playground's success was our carpenter, Khun Faori, and his assistants. Faori, whose nickname is Dtong, or "golden," was truly worth his weight in gold. Normally a house carpenter, he took our plans and sketches, tried new things, and added his own style and ideas to the project. And he did it all with a sense of humor and fun appropriate to the task at hand.

Traditional wood houses in the village are built on concrete posts to avoid the problems of termites and rot. We created similar structures for the play equipment. Faori, Dean (a carpenter from England who volunteered his time on the project), and I had many discussions about how to make sure that the structures, especially the taller ones, were stable and could withstand the rowdiest children and the heaviest adults. The result was a combination of techniques from each of us, such as designing the decks to be interconnected to support each other, sinking the posts deep in the earth, and reinforcing the taller structure with rebar and concrete below and diagonal wood trusses above.

To incorporate art into the site, children paint rocks for lining the edges of the playground. (Photo by Katherine Melcher)

Once the play structure decks were up, Khun Faori added his own creative touches to the project. On the railing, he twisted every other baluster 45 degrees because he considered it more attractive. He built all staircases to have an odd number of steps because it is bad luck in their culture to have an even number of steps.

When it came time to construct the slides, we started negotiating with a metal manufacturer to have them custom built. But Faori decided he could do it cheaper out of wood. I trusted him, gave him the dimensions, and he created beautiful slides, even though he had probably never seen a wooden slide before in his life.

The most exciting part of the project was watching the children's reactions to the playground as it came together. From playing in the trenches to trying out the sliding pole and monkey bars, the neighborhood children enthusiastically embraced the playground. Separating the play structures by age was almost not necessary since older children would carry their younger siblings on their backs up the larger one. Girls from the weekend religious school would drape their *hijabs* on the play structure, respectfully remove their shoes, and climb up onto them. Boys from the religious school would watch the carpenters at work and then build their own play fort in the trees nearby.

One day stands out in my mind as the day when I first saw how the playground was truly becoming a center of the community. Most of the equipment was up and surfacing installed. Children brought hula hoops and were running around the equipment. Others sat underneath the structures and on tires, talking and hanging out. A man selling ice cream from the back of his motorcycle stopped by. Parents watched from the porches next door. The children's bicycles lined the front of the playground and spilled out onto the street. At the end of the day some of the children drew a sign that said "Bicycle Parking" and posted it in front of the playground.

Once the structures were built, we had fun with the finishing touches. The children painted rocks that we used to line the play area edges. We hired a local batik artist to paint plants and animals representing the forest and sea on the play structures. We attached pulleys with buckets, connected plastic tubes and funnels for a telephone, and fastened recycled steering wheels to the play structures. In the sea area, we hung colorful, recycled buoys from the deck. In the village area, we installed a hammock.

Children play in the almost-finished playground. (Photo by Katherine Melcher)

One day, while walking to the market, I saw an old plastic lifeboat sitting in front of someone's house. It had several holes and was obviously waiting to be thrown away. We negotiated with the owner and bought the boat, and the children helped me wash it out. Khun Faori figured out a way to attach it to the ground so it could rock back and forth as if it was on the water. I bought an old plastic fan blade to serve as a rudder. Khun Bow, one of the carpenter's assistants, attached it to a piece of bamboo and string and placed a steering wheel at the front that would turn the rudder.

Every project is a learning experience that contains some regrets. My biggest regret at the Moo Ban Nua playground is that we ran out of time. Many of the smaller projects I wish we could have done, such as having the children paint concrete tunnels and create tile stepping-stones, we did not have time to do. I also wonder how long the playground will last. Although the play structures are sturdy and will last a long time, the smaller elements, such as rope rails and buckets and pulleys, can wear down quickly with lots of use. My biggest fear is that I'll return and find the playground falling apart and abandoned.

The best reassurance I have that it will last are the ways people demonstrated how the playground has become a part of the community. My neighbor took the initiative to sweep up the trash that was collecting there. Another woman coming back from Bangkok gathered the women on the stage to show them the clothes she brought back. Another neighbor set up a stand on her porch to sell snacks and drinks to the children. The ice cream vendor started coming by as a part of his regular route. People use the swings as a place to sit and talk with friends. To me this indicates that the playground has become a true communal space and that the community will continue to take care of it. For me, seeing how people in the village adapted the playground into their lives is the best indication of a successful design.

Now back in the United States living in a community where I don't greet my neighbors every day and children don't just stop by to hang out with me, where I search for community in coffee shops and farmer's markets, I realize that Moo Ban Nua was in little danger of losing what Erikson called "communal forms of life." Moo Ban Nua's sense of community remained strong despite the tsunami, and I am grateful they welcomed me as a temporary part of it.

My challenge to myself and to the design professions is to no longer wait for acute disasters for the opportunity to design for stronger communities, but to find ways to advocate for it in our day-to-day practice. Because, as Erikson implied, community is vital to what makes us truly human.

• • •

This story first appeared in the May/June 2007 edition of *DESIGNER/builder* magazine.

The Moreno family at the groundbreaking for their house. (Photo by Bryan Bell)

KINGSLEY HAMMETT

SELF-HELP HOUSING

BY ANY STANDARD MEASURE, BRYAN BELL HAD IT MADE. AFTER earning a bachelor's degree in architectural history from Princeton and a master's in architecture from Yale, he found himself in New York City in 1988 working for a prominent architectural firm.

"I guess you could say I was lucky," he says. "I picked the firm I wanted to work for, got the job and, I suppose, from a traditional architectural point of view, it was a great year. We won an international competition, two Progressive Architecture Awards, and some other big, fancy stuff."

But after six months he was miserable and became increasingly disappointed in what the firm and everyone in it was doing.

"Somebody once told me that in New York City you have PhDs competing to design doorknobs," he says, "whereas in huge segments of the United States there is no one who cares about design. I felt redundant. And I also saw very little real design work going on."

At the time his younger sister was working for Legal Services in central Pennsylvania, filing suit against fruit growers for housing violations.

"It hit me that that was probably a place where they could use an architect," Bell says. "I started making phone calls, talking to housing authorities and non-profits, and I finally found an organization called Rural Opportunities. They had been involved in migrant job training, helping migrants get out of farm work, operated a migrant Head Start, and were just beginning a housing program."

So he made them an offer they couldn't refuse: he would get a grant to pay him to survey and interview farmworkers and, based on that research, come up with some designs that would be useful for their new housing program. He got his first grant from the American Institute of Architects, another from the National

Endowment for the Arts, and spent the next five years working with Rural Opportunities designing housing for migrant laborers.

Bell came to understand that the notion that every migrant worker wants to live and work in the United States is a myth. Many of the single migrants he met didn't want to stay in Pennsylvania. They wanted to come, do the work, make some money, and then go back home to their families.

But for the families traveling in the stream it was often different, particularly after passage of the Immigration Reform and Control Act of 1986. Many were desperate to leave the migrant life, specifically for the sake of their children's education. Many of them were settling down as part of an extended network of family and friends, bringing much of their community with them. To help them find the permanence they sought, Rural Opportunities found a federal program called Rural Housing Services, funded under the U.S. Department of Agriculture, that would help them build their own homes.

Rural Housing Services, essentially the rural equivalent of the Department of Housing and Urban Development, serves towns and rural areas with populations below 10,000. The program started during the Great Depression when the droughts of the 1930s forced small farming families to flee their homes in search of work elsewhere. In one five-month span alone, a total of 37,331 migratory job seekers and their families arrived in California from the Midwest.

To respond to their need for housing, a group of visionaries founded the Resettlement Administration. To promote the need for the new program, they hired Dorothea Lange, one of America's foremost photographers, to document the plight of migrant families. And since there was no job description for a "Photographer," some of the most memorable images of the Dust Bowl years were taken by a "Typist."

Over subsequent generations, the program became known as the Farm Security Administration and the Farmers Home Administration. Eventually it got bogged down in rules, regulations, and the standardization of house design and fell out of touch with the vision that gave it birth. In 1996 design restraints were removed, freeing it from its generic three-bedroom, bath-and-a-half ranch, opening the program to new creative approaches in meeting the permanent needs of thousands of families.

Since 1952 this program has provided several million rural families with their own homes. In 1997, 55,000 single-family detached homes were financed by Rural Housing Services. All the families earned below 60 percent of median income, opening homeownership to people earning $12,000 a year.

One of the unique features of Rural Housing Services is its Self Help Program, which has operated in more than thirty states and is locally administered by non-profit organizations. Out of those 55,000 homes, 15,000 were constructed by families who earned a "down payment" of $12,000 to $15,000 by providing 60 percent of the value of the house through their own labor. Mortgages with interest as low as 1 percent allow for payments as low as $230 a month. Experience in construction is not necessary, but each family can expect to work thirty hours each week for six months. The families work in groups. Everyone works on everyone else's house, and no one moves in until all the houses are completed. The work that cannot be done by sweat equity is contracted out to professionals. It varies with each group, but these tasks typically include excavation, electrical, plumbing, heating, and roofing.

"Fortunately, the credit as defined by this program matched the credit of our farmworker families very well," Bell says. "To establish good credit all they had to do was pay all their bills on time for the last year. A conventional bank never would have considered these families because it wants to see performance in paying off past debt. But the families we work with don't go into debt. They pay cash, and so as far as this program was concerned, they had perfect credit."

One of the first projects Bell designed was for a farmworker family with three boys, one of whom was having difficulty in school and had been diagnosed with attention deficit disorder. The only place for him to study was in the family's one room, used for cooking, eating, conversation, and television, in their previous 600-square-foot apartment owned by the farmer/employer.

Krisztina Tokes working with the Solis family, originally from Puerto Rico, on the design for their house. (Photo by Bryan Bell)

"It was clear after talking to them that no one could do schoolwork in that tight a quarters," Bell says. "He was having great distractions, not because of ADD, but because of the architecture."

Together they designed a three-bedroom house with the boys' bedroom and a quiet area on the second floor for studying, away from the group activities below. They built their home with two other families. And since moving in, the boy is doing very well in school.

In another case a single mother with two children had a partner who worked the night shift. The architectural solution was a split-level design with the children on the lower floor and the mother and her partner above.

In a third case, the mother told Bell she didn't want fourteen stairs.

"I was a little confused by that," he says, "but after talking I realized that she, being pregnant, found it very tiring to go up and down. At the same time they made it very clear they wanted a two-story house. So we worked on it together and came up with a split stair with a landing and window seat halfway up as a place for either physical or visual rest."

Bell is the first one to admit that he is no expert in sociology or anthropology. What he knows is, "All you have to do is ask and communicate. The clients are the experts. They will tell you."

After working five years with Rural Opportunities, Bell decided he could do much more design work if he had some help. So he formed a nonprofit organization called Design Corps and reached out to students and young professionals eager to do something other than design homes for yuppies.

"Yuppies need design too," Bell concedes, "but they have the monopoly on architects."

In most years just 2 percent of all new home buyers work directly with an architect. At the same time, 22 percent of 32,000 architecture students surveyed by the Carnegie Foundation's Boyer Report had stated that they chose architecture as a profession to improve the quality of life in communities. The disconnect between these two facts demonstrates that architecture is the province of the rich, while many architects want to work with the poor.

"What opportunities do these students have to do that?" Bell asks. "As far as I know, it's not zero. But it's very difficult."

Bell counts himself among that 22 percent who go into architecture hoping to serve humanity and seek social solutions. To find some like-minded interns he mailed a notice to the 100 schools of architecture around the country, inviting students to come work with him during the summer. He found them housing, paid them a stipend, and very quickly saw how much they could contribute and how much the families appreciated their help.

"Generally they want to learn about the spectrum of affordable housing and work directly with a family, which is something they never get the opportunity to do while at school," Bell says. "Schools are horrible in teaching designers how to treat people as other than fiction."

Communications skills are not taught in school, Bell says, and after graduation young architects feel that the real client is just getting in the way of their fictional one. Even in a program like the Yale Building Project they don't select the family before they build the house. They design a house and then select a family, so there is no relationship between the two.

"When I started I realized I didn't know anything about migrants," Bell admits, "and that if I was going to help them I had to start my education. I was guided by a quote from Henry Glassie: 'All architectural practice must be preceded by intense field study among the people for whom the architect plans to build, from whom he has stolen the right to design.'"

Bell found the experience of helping low-income people design their own homes a humbling one. In an early encounter, when asking families what their ideal home would be he expected them to say the biggest, fanciest one they could get. Instead, the answer generally was just one that they could afford.

"That was nice because I don't have to constantly remind them of their limited budget," he says. "We're talking about people who make an average of $14,000 a year."

Design Corps continues to have a year-long program for interns. The ideal candidate is one who has gone to graduate school, become disillusioned with the state of the architecture profession, has reached a confusion crisis, and wants to take a year off.

Some students who come to Design Corps initially want to build the last project they did in studio. But when they sit down with a family they soon see that what they design is either going to be a burden or a help to this family.

"Then they are able to put a lot of their baggage away," Bell says. "They aren't talking about 'Mexicans' as a research project. This is a family with individual needs and tastes. Good design is about consideration, not about cost. In other words, regardless of the cost of a project, there is the opportunity for great design to accommodate daily living."

The mission of Design Corps is to ensure that the benefits of good design are available to those who do not have access to designers.

"In our 'Direct-To-You' design program," Bell says, we introduce a process for each family to create a house that meets their own needs, culture, taste, and dreams. We don't expect everyone to be an architect or even to be able to read a blueprint. But we do believe that the families know more about what they need than we do. We talk about how they use space. They are comfortable with this. And they are the experts on this."

Drawing on the work of Ellen Pader, Bell came to understand the relationship between public and private spaces within the traditional Mexican home versus a 1950s-style United States bungalow. In the latter case a great deal of space was wasted on hallways, and if a family did not require that strict hierarchical separation of public to private, then that space could be put to better use.

"This is the biggest investment most of these families will ever make," says Kristine Wade, one of the Design Corps volunteer designers. "This is where they will live for possibly several generations. We feel that they ought to have as much input into their environment as possible. We don't increase the budgets; we just let the families have more control over how their money is spent."

The self-design process occurs over five meetings. The first step is to determine the family's own budget in order to determine how much house they can afford. This suggests a number of square feet that they can allot among rooms. The families are then given a questionnaire on how they live and use space day to day, such as how many people cook at one time and how many people eat together at one table. Reviewing their answers together, a staff architect and the family decide what spaces are most important. Extras, such as garages, fireplaces, and porches are also given costs, and the family is free to trade square feet inside for such additions if they feel they are important.

"We also create a wish list for items that probably won't be within the budget," Bell says. "This is prioritized in case the bids from the subcontractors come in below expectation and some wishes can be included."

The final meeting consists of viewing perspective sketches of inside spaces, often with actual furniture placement of pieces the family may own or have in mind.

"We measure our success solely by the opinion of the families we serve," Bell says. "In a survey we ask questions such as: were you treated respectfully and appreciated as an individual (or a family) during the design process; was the design staff capable of listening to you and understanding your wishes; how comfortable were you in giving your input during the design process; considering your family's budget, were you satisfied with the choices that were made for your house?"

Bell discourages his volunteers from just sitting at the drafting table and drawing anything that looks like the one-story ranch that graces the cover of the Rural Housing Services regulations manual.

"We want our interns to understand how projects are funded, how projects are defined, how communities come together, and to reconsider the role of the architect," he says. "Our hope is that when they go back to their communities they have the tools to initiate community-based design. In fact, the model for Design Corps is Legal Services."

Design Corps received $1500 for each house it designed through funds that were earmarked for affordable housing in the wake of the savings and loan debacle.

When the federal government bailed out the S&Ls it stipulated that once they made a profit again they had to contribute 10 percent to affordable housing. That money is now administered by the Federal Home Loan Bank.

Design Corps interns are paid through Volunteers In Service To America, and Bell heavily recruits bilingual interns.

"It took me five years to figure out how I could make the contribution I wanted to make," Bell says. "Once I figured out how I could contribute to the people who had no access to designers, I wanted to help other young designers do it as well."

. . .

This story first appeared in the July 1998 edition of *DESIGNER/builder* magazine.

Sister Mary Paul Janchill (left) and Sister Geraldine Tobia, co-founders of the Center for Family Life, in the Sunset Park neighborhood of Brooklyn. (Photo courtesy of SCO Family of Services/Center for Family Life)

KINGSLEY HAMMETT

IT TAKES A COMMUNITY TO RAISE A FAMILY

IT MAY HAVE TAKEN FORMER FIRST LADY HILLARY RODHAM CLINTON to make a best-seller out of the axiom "It Takes a Village to Raise a Child." But she got it only partly right. The fact is it takes a community to help a family to raise a child.

The common model in social services is to focus on individuals within the family, but not on the family as a whole. This approach often fails to strengthen the threads that bind the family together, which collectively weave the fabric that creates an intact community. This is what Sister Mary Paul Janchill and Sister Geraldine Tobia understood when the two Sisters of the Good Shepherd opened the Center for Family Life in Sunset Park, Brooklyn, in 1978 in a former residence hall of a community of religious brothers that had been abandoned twenty-five years before. They started with a check for $5,000, which a couple gave them as a small challenge grant, and a deep conviction: that families formed the core of communities, and to strengthen the community it was essential to support and strengthen families.

After an earlier experience doing family work in nearby Park Slope, the two Sisters were strongly urged by the city's then-commissioner of child welfare, the district superintendent of schools, and the local community board to bring a family program into Sunset Park, an extremely disadvantaged and underserved area. Basically an immigrant community, it has the third-largest Chinese population in the city and many South and Central Americans. The most recent influx has come from Mexico and the Middle East. And the problems are severe.

"We went to funerals one after the other," Sister Mary Paul recalls. "It was very brutal. The community needed so much."

By 2005 the Center for Family Life had a budget of $5 million and a staff of sixty full-time workers. It operates a main center; seven-day-a-week programs at three area schools (after-school programs, evening centers, and summer day camps); a program for adult employment (that tries to bring skills up to par, to create job readiness, and provides English as a Second Language, computer skills, and job counseling and placement); and a storefront where the Center provides advocacy services, an emergency food program, and a thrift shop that can distribute clothing and household necessities. Rarely does the Center use minimum-wage job placement, and it follows clients for at least a year to assure job retention.

"If a job falls through," Sister Mary Paul says, "they just try a second or third time. People have learned we're here for the long haul."

The Center employs many young people, most part time, who work in the school programs. They use the camp model where kids who start out in the after-school programs grow up to become Counselors in Training at the age of thirteen or fourteen. Once they reach the age of sixteen they can get paid to help with the younger children. And there are more than thirty students in college who work part-time. In the summer between 700 and 800 teens work as interns in programs and institutions throughout Sunset Park, including every hospital, day care center, school-based program, army base, and police precinct.

"Every system in the country, and certainly in New York, tends to focus on an individual with a problem," says Sister Mary Paul, who with Sister Geraldine (who passed away in 2000) immediately recognized that behind every troubled child was a troubled family and no one to deal with it. "We don't blame the family; it's just that there is some family story there."

The Sisters realized that in order to help families they needed the support of the entire community. They asked the Commissioner of Human Resources to establish a cabinet just for Sunset Park that would have the leaders of various public service agencies join the Sisters and other community groups in addressing the broad human service needs of the community. In the process they found a helpful partner in Lutheran Medical Center, which lobbied with them for more day care and worked closely to avoid duplication of services.

"Nobody had adequate public support," Sister Mary Paul says. "We just created it by working with each other. If somebody did day care, we didn't do it. We just complemented each other. And we knew we had to work with families."

When they encountered trouble with teenagers—and in the beginning they did, with slashed tires, graffiti, and so forth—they went to look for the family, talked to them in their home, and said, "We want to help families. But if you slash the tires and somebody gets sick and we have to take them to the hospital, we won't be able to." Once those kids got to see that the Sisters knew their mothers and fathers, their little sisters and brothers, it was a different story.

"It may have looked like the teens were alienated from their parents," Sister

Luis Castro learned how to manage his rage in circumstances beyond his control from Sister Geraldine Tobia, co-founder of the Center for Family Life. (Photo by Jennifer Huegel, courtesy of Public Policy Productions, Inc., from the documentary *A Brooklyn Family Tale*)

Mary Paul says, "but they did respond." Particularly once they saw the Sisters providing a once-weekly family night where they got together to chat and plan family outings to sports events, famous sites in Manhattan, museums, an aquarium, or other recreational sites, all with reduced-fare subway passes. "It was just to keep families sharing with one another, knowing each other, and supporting each other. And they really did help each other, like baby sitting for each other or having someone stay with the children if they had to go to the doctor."

The Sisters knew that the only hope was early family intervention before a child came to the attention of a public agency and was forced into foster care. Speaking, shortly before her untimely death, on a video titled *A Brooklyn Family Tale* (that was produced and directed by Roger Weisberg and Murray Nossel), Sister Geraldine detailed the mission of the Center for Family Life. "The absolutely major goal of the Center is to help each individual person be everything they can possibly become," she said. "We're not here to label people, but to look for people's strength and not just their pathology."

Sister Geraldine expressed a strong belief that we all come into the world broken and divided within ourselves, and that our journey through life is finding integrity and wholeness. And that is where she saw the vital role of family and community. "Often we are broken families or we are broken communities," she said. "And working on that wholeness is to me a holy act."

Fortunately for the young people of Sunset Park, the Sisters understood the pull of the street, the power of a street culture that gives young people fast money and sometimes quick prestige, and that gangs, or groups of young people, are a normal fact of adolescent life. But they sought to bring that street life indoors and create a different context, where adolescents could be leaders, put their energy to positive use in the after-school program, and have a place in the community where they were valued and not shunned.

"It helps young people understand how they can be giving, powerful, and capable by showing the same strength and the same skills in a different way," Sister Geraldine said. "Let's give them the role they have that's anti-social in a social environment."

Many girls in poor neighborhoods get pregnant early. But Sister Geraldine understood it was not their role to stop them. "People need to see their way them-selves," she said. "And that's not for us to define, to spell out, or to prescribe. That's not my role. My role is to be in the journey with people, to give them a sense of 'You can go somewhere' rather than 'You're the dregs of the earth and we're here to save you.' It's more like 'Why are you not seeing all that you have to offer?'"

Over the years Sister Geraldine saw that families with histories of being beaten down get messages both from within their immediate family and from the world outside that they are not capable. They then become comfortable with the negative identities and are not comfortable with their strengths and their positives.

"I wouldn't want to become Pollyannaish," she said. "People need you to be able to get in there and honestly help them see what they are struggling with. They don't want that to be watered down. They want to be able to trust enough to be able to tell you their negative feelings about themselves. And we need to be able to honestly know those people so we see their strengths as well."

The Center for Family Life has counselors available seven days a week. Neighbors come to discuss marital issues as well as parent/child issues. The goal is to help families in a timely way before a situation deteriorates and a child has to be separated from its family. "We felt it was important to just be available when they wanted to come," Sister Mary Paul says, "to be available for them to ask for help and discuss a problem without judgment, shame, or blame. From the beginning that was very important to us."

There was another important difference that engendered trust and made the Center a safe haven. The Sisters insisted that confidential client records remain within the Center despite regulations at the time that required that any organiza-tion receiving public funding submit records to the funding agency.

"We said this could not be. Nobody would come to us," Sister Mary Paul says. "If they were addicted to drugs they wouldn't easily come and tell us about it if we were going to copy the record and send it to a government office. That became a major challenge."

When the Center was threatened with being cut off from public funding, the Sisters got a pro-bono law firm that sent word they would sue to maintain client privacy. The case was headed for the United States Supreme Court. But before a trial date was set they reached a settlement with the city and state that would allow officials to review client records on site but not take copies away. The only exception is when there has been documented evidence—not just a complaint—of neglect or abuse.

"When and if we receive public funding, we always insist on confidentiality," she says. "Now people know they can come to us and trust they will get help without being stigmatized by having their records all over the place."

Today there are more children known to the city in preventive care programs than there ever were in foster care. "Preventive services have worked," Sister Mary Paul says, "and confidentiality has helped them to work, helped children and families to be safe. That word is so important to me. I want them to be safe and I want them to grow."

The Center for Family Life has been a lever in the community to help bring it together, she says. "The community context is a very important factor because people take their values, their sense of themselves, and their sense of their futures from the cues they get from those around them."

After dropping out of school, having a baby, and attempting suicide, fourteen-year-old Elena Castro (center), along with her mother, Rosa Cruz, gets some helpful counseling from Sister Geraldine Tobia. (Photo by Jennifer Huegel, courtesy of Public Policy Productions, Inc., from the documentary *A Brooklyn Family Tale*)

Much of the gang activity has been reduced, although the problem resurfaces periodically. Four years ago gangs took over a large schoolyard next to one of the schools where the Center for Family Life was active. So John Kixmiller, head of the Outdoor Neighborhood Center at that school, created what he called a neighborhood plaza. He took the yard back and replaced the drug activity with wholesome activities for the entire family.

Kixmiller was hired in 1983 to open a school-age child care program at P.S. 314, a new facility that had been designed as a high school but opened as a huge elementary school that now has nearly 2,000 students. Ten years later the school stayed open day and evening with after-school programs in art, theater, sports, GED, and ESL.

The P.S. 314 program has four different components. The first is an after-school child care program from 3 p.m. to 6 p.m. for 350 children every day and day camp in summer. The second is the Neighborhood Center program for families, open from 4 p.m. to 9 p.m. and on weekends, which offers soccer, basketball, games, creative arts activities, gardening, a lending library, literacy activities, homework help, and snacks. The third is a youth leadership program where approximately 100 teenage Counselors in Training receive a small stipend for an internship in every aspect of the program. And the fourth is the adult education program that offers classes in ESL for both Spanish and Chinese speakers.

"Parent leadership is a part of this whole model," Kixmiller says. "We have a parent council that advises directors, raises money, creates festivals and fund-raising activities, and serves as a motivating force."

At Middle School 136, the Center for Family Life has an extensive community arts program, which includes improvisational drama, music, dance, and visual art. It won the national Coming Up Taller award, which was presented at the White House. The program's staff also works during in-school hours to integrate art into the school curriculum.

Kixmiller looks at community as a web of relationships and activities. And he sees his job as creating access to that matrix so families can enter in a constructive way and access what will work for them. "It works for people," he says, "especially in a neighborhood where there are new immigrants who don't necessarily speak English, who don't know how to negotiate the school system, and who may be undocumented."

The Center for Family Life is very user friendly, Kixmiller adds. "It makes the community better and stronger because people are able to make the connections they need to develop their lives. And the more complex the network of relationships and activities, the more chances there are to get people involved, to draw in more family members, and to be enriched."

"This is a community that has come together," says Sister Mary Paul. "And as a result we have one of the lowest rates of children being sent into foster care in all of the City of New York."

The Sisters knew that there will always be troubled families. The idea is not to exclude them, but to bring them in. "At any time, any one of us here in Sunset Park needs something, and we have something to give," Sister Geraldine said in the video. "And I hope that the Center has been that place where the possibilities for that give and take, take place."

• • •

This story first appeared in the May/June 2005 edition of *DESIGNER/builder* magazine.

KINGSLEY HAMMETT

COMMUNITY WITHOUT WALLS
BUILDS COMMUNITY AMONG SENIORS

AT A TIME WHEN INDIVIDUAL AMERICANS ARE LIVING LONGER, American families are more scattered and communities less connected, leaving many seniors unnoticed, alone, and isolated. Most of them would prefer to remain in their own homes as they age. But in a society short on caring, personal contact, and the social networks that would make that possible, too many are forced to move into retirement centers before moving on to nursing homes.

That eventuality became all too real for Richard Bergman and his wife, Vicky. After his father died following a long illness, Richard's mother announced she couldn't stay in the home she and her husband had shared. She chose instead to live with the Bergmans for a few months before moving into the assisted-living section of a retirement community.

"She lived there for four years," Richard says. "We went to see her three or four times a week, so she had lots of company. But she was never happy and eventually she passed away."

Not looking forward to something similar for themselves, the Bergmans, whose children live far from their New Jersey home, began to think about their own options for aging. As for most seniors, the time would come when they would need a hand with home repairs, a ride to the doctor's office, or just some company. But that takes community, something missing from the lives of too many Americans. Their answer was to start what they call Community Without Walls, a group of people drawn from among their Princeton-area friends and neighbors who came together in an effort to develop and provide sorely needed social support.

The Bergmans' idea was sparked by a flyer announcing a conference in Manhattan on conscious aging sponsored by the Omega Institute. Thinking this might hold some answers to questions they had about retirement, they attended and found a smorgasbord of speakers and information booths that offered everything from yoga to housing to financial planning. There they met fellow Princetonian Harriet Bogdonoff, a geriatric social worker, who was looking for something not only for herself but for her patients. She had begun to see that as people got older and started to decline, their biggest problem, even if they had enough money, seemed to be a lack of social support. She and the Bergmans agreed to explore the issue further and were soon joined by Roz Denard, who had just retired as managing director of the Princeton Packet, the local newspaper. All four wanted to remain in their own homes, all were active in the community, and the focus of their conversations was how to best age in place.

"We wanted to look at the options available that were missing from our parents' and grandparents' generations and to see how our aging could be different from the existing models," Vicky says.

Today there are parents in their nineties with children in their seventies who might have children in their forties. Fifty or 100 years ago, most of them would have been dead before they had to worry about retirement plans. But today's seniors are more educated than ever before, are more curious, and are bringing more thoughtfulness to the process. The Princeton group got together to explore how they could ease their transition into old age.

"But back in 1992," Richard says, "people just didn't talk about getting old. Of course, at one time no one talked about cancer, either. Now you can't open a newspaper without seeing somebody's story."

Unsure exactly what they were setting out to do, where to begin, or what they'd be getting into, they did know a number of smart, well-educated people asking the same questions who wanted to explore what getting older would mean for them. So they invited eighty people to their home and, much to their surprise, all eighty showed up.

"There was an incredible amount of interest and curiosity," Vicky says, "and what we finally figured out after about a year was that the medium was the message: what we were doing was it. We were building community, and by building community we expanded our social networks."

They continued to meet on a monthly basis for almost three years to discuss and refine what it meant to age, what they were interested in, and issues around housing and health. They invited a variety of outside experts who gave talks on everything from housing to memory loss to changes in smell and taste (by the age of eighty most people experience a serious reduction in smell, which affects how they eat and whether they enjoy their food). A few of the initial eighty dropped out, but most kept coming to meetings, including a number of social workers.

"If you want people to be there for you when you need social support as you get older, you have to develop a community so people have some sense of relationship and possibly even affection for each other," Richard says. "That takes a long time."

Over the ensuing years Community Without Walls has created a number of subgroups to address a range of specific needs. First came one called Chores-R-Us, which was prompted by a widow who needed help with certain household chores, such as programming her VCR. Others needed to be driven to the doctor or to get something in their house repaired. And if the request was beyond the capability of any available volunteer, Community Without Walls had a list of preferred service providers.

A second group they called Friendly Support, wherein members give assistance to other members when called upon, such as driving someone to and from the hospital for follow-up visits or putting out food after a funeral.

Other members have come together in separate groups to read plays, to write poetry, to discuss sex after seventy, to explore memoir writing, to investigate available options in conscious dying, to share new passions discovered in retirement, and to go out to eat at different ethnic restaurants. And a group of widows calls itself the JULIETs (Just Us Ladies Into Eating Together).

"That's what we do," Richard says. "That's how we build community. Every year somebody gets a new idea about a new group they want to start. The whole thing is to keep the community thing going, because everything comes out of that."

Once the original group, which came to be called House One, reached its membership capacity of 100, someone volunteered to start a second house. The expansion signaled it was time to get a little more organized, start a steering committee to give the group more structure, secure nonprofit status, draw up bylaws and a four-point mission statement (social support, information, education, and advocacy), and set annual dues at $10. House Two capped its membership at sixty, and eighteen months later, after both houses had accumulated waiting lists, volunteers chartered House Three. Each house has a monthly meeting, generally with an invited speaker, and they all get together under an umbrella organization for an annual meeting in September.

Some houses have established a buddy system. The members make another person in their house privy to certain personal information, such as how to contact their children, their doctors, and their attorneys, and many turn over a set of keys to their homes. If something happens to an individual member, that person's contact will take the lead responsibility for coordinating his or her needs.

Two or three years into Community Without Walls, the Bergmans began to notice some interesting changes taking root among members. Its community-building efforts were giving people permission to be more open about what was happening in their lives and making them freer to both ask for and offer help.

"People once said, 'I don't want to intrude,'" Vicky says. "A few years ago they might have thought they were imposing. But now, because of Community Without Walls, they make that call."

• • •

This story first appeared in the September/October 2007 edition of *DESIGNER/builder* magazine.

Elaine Ostroff, pioneer in universal
design and user-friendly environments.
(Photo by Noelle Teixeira)

KINGSLEY HAMMETT

THE EVOLUTION OF UNIVERSAL DESIGN

WITH AN AGING POPULATION, THE NEED FOR MORE UNIVERSAL design becomes more critical with each passing year. And as more elderly people want to spend their final years in their own homes and neighborhoods and take part in community life, builders will find it good for business to stop building homes that become obsolete. But the central issue isn't just about a growing market for the aging. It's about equity and inclusion. Design has the power to enable people or disable them, to include them or exclude them.

"The challenges of designing for the twenty-first century require a level of collaboration among designers, policy and decision makers, and user/experts who can advise us based on their own experience," says Elaine Ostroff, a pioneer in universal design and user-friendly environments. "We need a much higher level of flexibility and professional collaboration. Architects can no longer assume that the people they design something for will be the only ones to use it. The question is: how do we rethink the way we design our communities—our homes, schools, and public buildings—so that they work well for most people, most of the time?"

The challenge is to build in resilience, transformability, and accessibility in the broadest sense, while making it wonderful and nonstigmatizing, she says. Developers don't want to make housing that looks "handicapped," and people don't want reminders of their changing abilities. Good design will have its potential built in so gracefully that all that's visible is convenience and comfort, not institutional rigging that reminds people that they are no longer as strong as they used to be.

Ostroff's path to becoming an outspoken advocate of universal design is a long and winding one that began in 1961 when she was an earnest mother of a four- and five-year-old. One day she took them to a children's theater performance at a junior high school, organized by the Junior League in Providence, Rhode Island. It was incredibly boring, the actors were wooden, and very soon the young audience was restless and running around. Finally the anxious chairperson of the Junior League stood up and very piously blamed the audience for its terrible behavior, said they didn't appreciate culture, and essentially browbeat them all into sitting down.

"As the play progressed an actor suddenly climbed up on a chair and pantomimed reaching for something," Ostroff recalls. "The audience immediately got engaged because it was live action and it was real. So I had an insight: if you are going to do theater for children, it has to be authentic, have a lot of action, and be engaging. What we had seen was a fraud and I was outraged that the Junior League was blaming the victim."

She took her kids home and got some friends together to start their own children's participatory theater group, which they called the Looking Glass Theater and which is still going strong. Despite having no experience in theater, Ostroff did what she's always done: experience a problem, get some idea about what to do about it, and pull together people who know more than she does about how to develop a solution. They mounted their first production for the academic community at Brown University. It was based on the children's story of Ferdinand the Bull—the bull who didn't like to fight and loved to smell the flowers. The available room didn't have a stage, so the performance was done as theater-in-the-round, a circumstance that supported the interactive nature of the performance. Ostroff helped invent ways for the audience to be part of the action, and that became the hallmark of all future productions.

Teachers in the audience were astounded at what they saw as the magical control over the children, who were engaged throughout the drama by being called upon periodically to jump up and be the rain, the thunder, and the wolves. And when it was time to be quiet they listened intently. Afterwards the teachers asked Ostroff if she could develop workshops to teach how to have that kind of involvement with the children in the classroom.

"I suddenly had my second big idea," she says. "What we had been learning about in our interactive, audience-centered theater had a lot of relevance to education. I felt that if one wanted to change the world one had to change the way teachers were educated so the education they provide to kids was worthy of the kids and not just the teachers or the administration. I saw that systems that are designed to perpetuate themselves needed to be reoriented to enhance and enable the user."

She believed that the way they broke down the wall between the actors and the audience, and how they helped the actors find ways to engage and listen to the audience, could help teachers work better with children. They need to be able to improvise, yet be well prepared with an adaptable structure.

As Ostroff began working with classroom teachers to use improvisational movement and other kinds of theater techniques, she realized how important it was for people working with children, especially ones with limited language skills, to be more physically expressive. The images and messages people need to give are not always ones they can express verbally. Creative movement is very important, and the structure of the environment determines whether participation is possible.

In later years, when the theater was well established, Ostroff won a Radcliffe Institute Fellowship that allowed her to attend the Harvard Graduate School of Education and create an independent program enabling her to build some theory around teacher education and improvisational theater. She then took a job with the Massachusetts Department of Mental Health in a program that used artists to work with children with developmental disabilities.

"I explained that I wanted to work with the teachers, not the children, and the program directors were delighted," she says. "So I was hired to coordinate in-service education for pre-school teachers in a mental retardation program. I had absolutely no background in special education, just my experience in education, adult development, and creativity, and my notion of what I wanted to accomplish."

As she traveled around the state to visit the 104 classrooms in various institutions and church basements, she was suddenly struck by the rotten environments people were working in. Everywhere she found earnest teachers working very hard in places that undermined everything they were trying to do.

For example, one little boy kept going down a slide and interrupting another boy who was reading in the reading corner. Did they think about moving the reading corner? No. Instead, they did behavior modification with the boy on the slide, once again blaming the victim. At that time (the early 1970s), everyone was embracing the concept of open education and open classrooms. But the special education facilities she visited were decades behind, and none of the thinking about openness had penetrated.

That got Ostroff thinking about the teachers' physical environments, and she set to work with the teachers to create powerful settings that would provide expressive play opportunities and also meet the educational goals.

"The teachers didn't know that they could adapt the spaces that they worked in," she says. "So I worked with them to help figure out how we could re-create those spaces, in very temporary ways, since many of them had to become church meeting rooms over the weekend. It was the theater all over again."

Ostroff then got a federal grant to assemble a resource team of artists, developmental psychologists, and environmental designers to work with the teachers and parents to help create solutions to individual and classroom needs through the arts and environmental design. Over time it became more and more obvious that nobody was paying attention to the impact of the physical environment. So she focused her attention on the question, What role could the environmental designer, who understood how space worked in relation to people, play in education?

"I started to see that the skills in space and environmental planning were absolutely essential for anybody who was going to be involved with the education of children with developmental disabilities," Ostroff says. "The more vulnerable a person is in a physical or sensory sense, the more impact the environment has, either negatively or positively. Most traditional special educators believed in the 'some children will never learn' theory and that 'some people will never live in the community.' We set out to help classroom teachers believe that it is possible for children who have spent their lives on their backs, kids who have never spoken, and kids who jitter and shake to learn something."

The environment was key. With an improved environment the children could show their potential. And teachers kept asking for help in environmental design. So in 1976 Ostroff developed the Adaptive Environment Center, a resource center for teachers and parents to learn how the built environment could be factored into the education of children with disabilities.

She also began to see that in order for adults to be able to give something away, they had to experience it in their own lives first. Teachers can't help children to be creative if in fact they don't see creativity in themselves. So the low expectations the teachers had about the children were really an extension of the way they thought about themselves.

By 1980 the Adaptive Environment Center started getting phone calls from individuals who had all sorts of access and adaptive design issues and had no place to turn for help and information. Apparently, there was a tremendous need for adaptation in homes as well as out in the community that no one was addressing.

"It felt like an access emergency room," she says. "People called us with horror stories about their access problems. One woman could not climb down the stairs without falling. Her husband used to help her but he died. We installed a handrail—that would help for a while. A father whose son had lost his legs in a train-crossing accident reached us after twelve unsuccessful calls. He needed advice, he needed funding, and he needed good carpenters to do what needed to be done."

The Center heard about existing buildings that didn't work, and brought in architects who had some feel about the issues but little experience with a participatory approach. They went into homes to give free consultations, which gave birth to the Homes Initiative. As word spread they began to hear about other architects and other educators who were thinking about the problems of inaccessible environments. And they got a grant from the National Endowment for the Arts to convene a meeting of architects and designers to teach them about adaptive environments.

In 1982 they hosted another meeting of designers and design educators. Out of that came the desire to get beyond single-purpose design and adaptations of existing environments, and more into designs that work for more people. How do you design for the real world involving the needs of people with disabilities to make something that's better for everyone? How do you move beyond ramps and think about designs that serve everyone? How do you bring disabled people into the architecture studio to teach architects to design for people unlike themselves?

"That meeting in 1982 was a milestone," she says, "a giant platform out of which sprang all the work happening now in universal design education. We built upon our earlier work and created something called the Universal Design Education Project that incorporated those ideas. We raised money to offer stipends to college faculty in five major design disciplines to come up with ideas on how they could shift their curriculum so that the basic teaching of design would be more inclusive. We wanted to get beyond the double-standard where we had good design on the one hand and handicapped design on the other. The question became: how do we begin to infuse an approach for universal design with the basic academic teaching of design professionals?"

But even with that promising beginning, Ostroff still sees architects who find it very difficult to distinguish between the accessible design standards of the Americans with Disabilities Act and the concept of universal design. Many of these designers think that universal design is just a politically correct, trendy term for talking about design standards. But universal design is much broader. It goes beyond the standards to look at the needs of user groups in any setting, whether it comes with design standards or not.

"While the ADA inspired the creation of the Universal Design Education Project," she says, "it had an unexpected effect on many architects who could only see the well-publicized requirements as limiting their creativity. For many firms, the requirements were seen as an add-on that was not considered until too late in the design process to be integral to the design."

The resulting hostility and the lack of understanding of the range of diversity across society—particularly among children and the elderly, all with different levels of reach, grasp, and intelligence—are interfering with the creative process, she says. There are many conditions people operate under all the time that need designs that are more tolerant. But the architects get stuck on the minimum standards and can't think beyond them. They have a very distorted image of who is average, and the idea that 97 percent of the people can use such-and-such is based on an outdated notion of who the average person is.

"That hasn't come into people's consciousness yet," she says. "We want their imagination, not just limited compliance. The American Institute of Architects Diversity Committee is working to change this narrow perception. But architects still exhibit a limited interest in people unlike themselves. At the university level there may be more interest among students than faculty. 'User needs' is not a new concept in design. But it is not a strong theme in many programs."

• • •

This story first appeared in the June 2000 edition of *DESIGNER/builder* magazine.

Kelee Katillac. (Photo by Roy Inman)

KINGSLEY HAMMETT

THE BEST LITTLE TRAILER HOUSE IN KANSAS

WHETHER YOU'VE RECENTLY REDECORATED YOUR HOME WITH THE help of a professional or a trip to Cost Plus, does the end result truly reflect who you are? Too often it mirrors better the taste of the designer or the look du jour, leaving you wondering, "How long can I live with this?"

To end up with a nest that genuinely fits you and your values, nationally celebrated interior decorator Kelee Katillac counsels you to look deep within yourself and decorate your home with things that represent the inner you. She has developed a philosophy she calls "House of Belief," which holds that the home is a tool to help unlock the creative spirit that resides in us all. When your spiritual qualities become the catalyst for your creative actions, she says, the result is a home that represents your beliefs, goals, values, dreams, memories, and cultural heritage. Then you have moved from living in an adorned cave to becoming a cave painter. You have taken an active role in the age-old ritual of bringing into a tangible form that which you see, feel, hear, experience, and believe to be good and true and beautiful.

"As we use our home to creatively express what we are inside in an outward, visual form, we inspire ourselves," she says. "And we find proof that we have more within us, more than we think, because when we see it we do believe."

Katillac ought to know. In 1982 she was twenty-two years old, poor, suicidally depressed, and living in a trailer house on the wrong side of the tracks in a small town in rural Kansas. She suffered from low self-esteem and a nagging worry that she had been given no special gifts in this life. Her routine consisted of rising at noon and taking a brief walk to the nearby convenience store past life's castoffs, from discarded furniture to worn-out clothing to broken car parts—a ritual that accounted for the bulk of her daily activity. "I had walked past this stuff lots of times," she recalls. "But there was nothing special about it, no poetry in it."

Until the day she encountered an abandoned chair that constituted an accurate reflection of her present condition: it was dirty, with torn fabric and one missing leg, about as beyond repair as a chair could get. Something impelled her to drag the relic back to her trailer, and after a few weeks of contemplation she began its restoration using whatever materials she could find. "I essentially applied what was left within me to that chair," she says.

Katillac's experience with the discarded chair taught her to take one small action and make something you can see that causes you to begin to believe. Your belief will in turn lead you to another act of creativity, and the quality of your actions and the size of your projects will increase ad infinitum. After remaking her derelict chair, Katillac spent the next eighteen months redecorating the entire trailer house. She made new curtains, covered the plastic paneling with fabric, repainted the woodwork, and fashioned furniture and picture frames from found objects. "Within a year and a half I began to get decorating jobs based on what people saw in the trailer," she says.

Within a few more months, despite having no design background, Katillac was working at a big interior-design firm in Kansas City. A year after that she had a project published in *House Beautiful*. From Kansas City she moved on to New York City, and by 1990 she had had projects published in more than thirty national magazines. But she found herself trapped in the current design paradigm, at that time the Americanized view of English Country. At the outset of a particular assignment she might get some clue of what the client liked, but the end result would be from her own inner vision. And because she made her living by earning a commission on what she sold the client, she found herself creating little more than gilded cages for the wealthy.

"Because you have spent all this money on these lavish draperies and this color-coordinated interior, you can't change it," she says. "But we are constantly, daily, moment by moment evolving and changing and growing. So the home in which we have too much respect (because of the money we have spent on a one-time decision) becomes a gilded cage to which the creative spirit of the individual who lives therein has no key."

On a return visit to Kansas City, she met two individuals who said some of her former clients were claiming sole credit for the work she had done for them. She was disturbed by the news, but was forced to recognize that clients really wanted to be creative and just didn't know how. On further self-examination she had to concede that what she had been doing was in large measure a crime. She had been putting her own vision within other people's sacred spaces and locking them out. Perhaps not coincidentally, she had to admit that there was always something wrong with her client relationships. Despite her meticulous and virtuous attention to detail, she always felt a little guilty and was ready for the client to be unhappy. "And they usually were," she admits, "but usually for some crazy reason, maybe about the bill, or some loose stitches, or the color of the paint."

She immediately quit her job in New York, pulled out of design completely, moved back to Kansas City, and enrolled in the graduate art history program at the University of Missouri-Kansas City. There, through the Arts and Crafts writings of Morris and Ruskin and those of the Transcendentalists, like Emerson and others, she quickly found the missing link she had been searching for. Morris, particularly, saw artisans leaving their individual workshops to toil anonymously on the factory floor and predicted that within 100 years the human spirit would become totally alienated as man became cut off from his creativity. Adopting the Arts and Crafts spirit, Katillac spent the next two years delving into her own creativity, working on designs for clothing, furniture, stained-glass windows, and bookmaking while trying to cleanse her mind of the poisonous dictates of the interior-design industry, the totalitarianism of style, and the elevation of the certifiably creative above everyone else.

"I simply was seeking a way to make interior design meaningful once again," she says, "to make it representative of the person who lives in the dwelling, to make their dwelling a personal cathedral of belief and creativity, and to give them a place to enact their own rituals of creativity."

The process she developed begins by having clients focus on what they believe and value. Then she has them tour their houses and ask of every object its story, what it means, where it came from, and what it symbolizes. Maybe you still have a couch you bought from a cheap furniture store when you first got out of college. Do you want to keep around you an object that takes you back to a time you'd rather forget? Or does the cheap couch represent a struggle over adversity?

"This is not rule-bound," she says of her discovery process. "This is completely personal to your own perception. And it doesn't mean you have to launch into making a stained-glass window. It means to think creatively about what you have, to be conscious of meaning."

The next step—to begin thinking like an artist about your home—is to become conscious of what's meaningful. So she has clients create visual symbols for the beliefs and values, goals and dreams they've identified. "It can be difficult in our time for people to really think about what they believe and to find an image to represent that," she says. It could be buttons from an immigrant grandmother who went on to financial success and the ability to buy any clothes she wanted. Buttons might then find their way into pillows and window coverings to remind you of the power of hard work.

Katillac then takes clients back to the childhood rooms that celebrated what they loved, who they admired, and who they wanted to be like. Perhaps you want to shed your corporate suit for the life of a writer. She'd have you create a model of your ideal writing space. That helps the average person who still has reservations about his or her creativity to manifest a new idea in an unintimidating way.

Then he or she can blow the model up into life-size form somewhere in the home and maybe actually begin to live the dream.

In 1990 Katillac decided to go back into design. But now her ideal was to put herself out of a job as soon as possible, to empower her clients to find their own creativity and help them design their own space. For the next seven years she worked with people from all walks of life and cultural backgrounds, and in that time she reaffirmed her belief over and over again that one common truth runs through every project: we're all creative, and when we represent that in our homes we have a more meaningful existence within that space. "It works the same whether you have an unlimited or a limited income," she says.

In 1997, because of where she started as a low-income person in a trailer house, Katillac once again left her professional design work behind, this time to work sixteen hours a day to develop a twelve-workshop series (along with twelve videos) on her design philosophy, and began creating a community House of Belief with Habitat for Humanity. Just as Morris had tried to reinvigorate his community with the creativity of arts and crafts, she believed that by bringing together the Habitat homeowners they would get to know each other and begin to bond. In a workshop called "Reupholster Your Life," for example, she had eight to ten people talk about negative experiences in their lives. Each then found an old abandoned chair, wrote the negative ideas all over the chair, sanded them away, and refinished the chair with new positive symbols and words.

"This gives the low-income homeowners a way to let go of the old, embrace the new, and learn a skill to furnish their Habitat home and maybe even earn a living from," she says.

In the process she taught them all of the skills involved in refinishing a house, and several homeowners have gone on to establish their own businesses. One woman, who had grown up in the Watts district of Los Angeles with no belief in herself and no support, had held forty jobs in the last twenty years. Once she learned to sew she set up a small business in one room of her home, and is now making a substantial contribution to her family's income. Habitat for Humanity then expanded the Kansas City program into a pilot project in five other cities.

"What started with a chair in a trailer house moved all the way through a sequence of events to where my belief became so great that it flowed into my community," she says. "Now my creative actions have helped other people in the community take other creative actions together, and that has flowed out into the larger world. It's amazing how the process has flourished."

• • •

This story first appeared in the July/August 2002 edition of *DESIGNER/builder* magazine.

Home maintenance and repair are some of the many
services offered to members of Beacon Hill Village.
(Photo courtesy of Beacon Hill Village)

KINGSLEY HAMMETT

AM I OLD YET?

TODAY IN THIS COUNTRY FEW THINGS ENGENDER MORE FEAR THAN growing old. That's why entire industries—entertainment, fashion, pharmaceuticals, cosmetics, plastic surgery, organ and joint replacement, and their handmaidens in advertising and marketing—are dedicated to fooling consumers into believing that they can hold back the tides of time that take their toll on all men and women.

But whatever measures one takes to forestall the inevitable only postpone the moment of truth when one must ask—and ultimately answer—the question "Am I old yet?" Is it when you can no longer see clearly enough to drive a car safely? Is it when you can't remember where you left the car keys? Is it after you've fallen down the stairs and broken your hip and you can't even get into the car? Ultimately that moment arrives and when it does you have to decide how and when you are going to spend your later years.

Susan McWhinney-Morse, a longtime resident of Boston's Beacon Hill, began to think about the unthinkable ten years ago after attending a talk by the geriatric staff at Mass General Hospital, who had just opened a new program for people sixty and older called Senior Health Care. She felt the doctors were somewhat condescending about the elderly (after all, it didn't include them—yet!), and she came away with a feeling of, "Oh well, we're not old enough yet. We don't have to worry about it."

But in a moment of reflection she realized she did have something to worry about. Like 93 percent of all Americans, she wanted to live out her days in her own home. And once that's no longer possible, everyone hopes there will be some assistance available when they need it. But she and her friends knew there would be nothing aside from moving, whether into a retirement community, an assisted living center, or a nursing home.

"I call it warehousing," she says, "which is a curious yet amazingly inadequate

American solution to a growing problem. We do it because we don't know any other choices. No matter what they say about how sensitive they are, it's really being warehoused. You're tucked away somewhere where it's convenient to manage the health care of other people. And I think that's something we all dread."

So she called some people together and they developed a supportive organization tailored to their specific needs. Called Beacon Hill Village, it offers a range of services seniors might find difficult to obtain on their own that help them remain living in their own homes for as long as possible.

"We didn't know what we were doing," she freely admits of their first tentative steps. "I had been head of Beacon Hill Civic Association and I profoundly believe in people power. There were twelve of us and we didn't all know each other. But we shared three things in common: we loved our neighborhood, we wanted to stay where we were forever, and we didn't like any of the options."

McWhinney-Morse loves the urbanity of her neighborhood, where everything she would like to have or need is nearby. Beacon Hill is blessed with an abundance of beautiful houses, has very strong neighborhood connections, and is surrounded by extraordinary cultural amenities, such as the Boston Atheneum, Boston Symphony Orchestra, Boston Public Library, private clubs, and public parks.

"It's ideal," she says. "It is just so rich with life and varied offerings and one can walk so well to most things. The thought of going to a retirement community where I have to be bused to something or can't get there without taking a taxi for $25 or $30 is unacceptable to me."

Their start-up committee talked to everyone in their immediate area who had something to do with elder care, from doctors to developers, and the members realized they already had everything they might need within easy reach—fabulous hospital health care, home health care, intellectual opportunities, and all the lifeline organizations that play some role in aging and helping people stay in their homes. Then the moment came when they thought all they needed was the Rolodex lady, someone to call up and say, "I need a home health care aide or a plumber or a ride downtown."

"There are concierge services in most cities where you can get your dog walked or your laundry brought to you," she says. "But they are very, very expensive. And we thought strongly that if we were to create some sort of organization we wanted it available to everyone in our neighborhood, regardless of income."

McWhinney-Morse and her group decided early on that they wanted to be able to offer what they thought the fancy retirement communities offered, which is a whole way of relating to life—a sense of community, activities, security—but put together in a different way. They didn't know anything about home health care and didn't want to know; they wanted to leave that to the experts. And they didn't want to own any real property, but instead use the spaces already available in the community.

"One of our little genius strokes was creating what we call strategic partnerships with organizations that gave us a believability factor and a strength," she says.

One of them was with Mass General Hospital through its Senior Health Care. Next was with an outstanding home health care provider that was excited about what Beacon Hill Village was doing and offered its members a 10 percent discount. And third was with Rogerson Communities, a company that operates two facilities for low- and moderate-income senior residents on Beacon Hill and other programs for seniors in Boston.

"Their executive director, James Seagle, was very helpful," she says. "In the end he gave us space in one of his facilities to open a little office. And he also does payroll and bookkeeping for our organization. That gave us an anchoring, a believability, a solid look."

Beacon Hill Village got its nonprofit status, hired an executive director, and held a community meeting in February 2002 where about 300 people showed up.

In the first month, seventy people signed up. Then they ran into one of the biggest problems in this country, but something they knew nothing about: the concept of ageism, which, they found, can be profoundly destructive. Nobody wants to be old, and nobody wants to be identified with anything that says old age. But Beacon Hill Village learned what it had stumbled into only after it had set its age threshold for people at sixty and adopted the slogan "Beacon Hill Village: Virtual Retirement Community."

"We soon realized that tag was like death," McWhinney-Morse says. "Nobody got 'virtual' and nobody wanted to have anything to do with retirement or a community that had to do with retirement."

With an eye on the baby boomers, they dropped the age limit to fifty, which made people sixty less afraid to join. Then they rethought their marketing, got rid of the "retirement" tag, and replaced it with "City Living Just Got Easier" and "Plan for Tomorrow, Live for Today." And they redesigned their publications, which had been created pro bono by a woman who does very professional work for retirement communities.

"I looked at these brochures and I thought, 'What! We look like a retirement community,'" she says. "So we took out pictures of very old people and instead focused on where we live. And we began emphasizing what we call our member services, which is the most extraordinary concierge service you could imagine. We can do almost anything for anybody as long as it's legal. And we do."

On one occasion they got someone to help a tiny woman who was not strong enough to put her cat in its carrying case and take it down the street to the vet. Another woman called from the hospital and asked for someone to retrieve her betting slip from the race she had attended prior to going to the hospital.

"Is that necessary? No. She wouldn't have died if she hadn't had it. But it is the little things that keep you going, that keep you feeling you're connected, that keep you happy. So we honor those."

Then there was a woman who wanted her living room furniture rearranged, and a board member said, "We don't waste our time doing things like that, do we? And McWhinney-Morse replied, "Yeah, yeah we do. And it just took finding a nice young man who was strong enough to move the furniture and over he went. These requests just make your life easier. They make you feel like someone's out there. You don't have to do it all yourself. Or give up and not do it."

The core group raised $80,000 in start-up money from the board, the community at large, and a number of prospective members who said, "I really believe in what you are doing. I don't need you now, but I want it there when I do need you."

"That's a very typical response," she says. "And they supported us, not with $10 checks, but with big checks. So we got through a very difficult time with donations from people who just thought, 'Yes, this is the way to go.'"

Beacon Hill Village now has 350 individual members (280 households) whose ages range from fifty to ninety-eight, from the active and healthy to the frail and infirm. And rather than worry about having an upper limit on numbers, McWhinney-Morse and her colleagues are more concerned about spreading themselves too thin geographically.

"It's important that people have a sense of community within this area of central Boston," she says. "And you can't do that if your members live in totally different neighborhoods. They need to do it for themselves."

Apparently many are anxious to do exactly that. Last spring, after an article on Beacon Hill Village appeared in the *New York Times*, the office was flooded with almost 2,000 requests on how to replicate its program. They got calls from non-profit organizations, home care companies, churches, and individuals who live in a neighborhood with older people and want to create something similar. In response, Beacon Hill Village created a professional manual detailing how to adapt its concept to other communities.

For an annual fee of $550 for an individual ($780 for a household), Beacon Hill Village provides members with three distinct categories of service. The first gives them a sense of community through offering trips, events, and programs. It holds a monthly "Conversations with …" where members can meet in an intimate setting with a notable person from the Boston area, such as the head of the Museum of Fine Arts or the library. There's a lunch group that meets once a month at a different restaurant. And a Beacon Hill neighborhood restaurant offers members a discount every night during specific hours.

"This helps ease their social isolation, gives them a chance to meet new friends, and builds a sense of community," says Carol Laibson, Beacon Hill Village's outreach coordinator.

The second area of concentration is health care, giving members a helping hand on a short-term basis. Perhaps they need someone to come in and prepare a meal or ready the house for a member returning from the hospital. For more complicated needs, they can get a reference to hire (at a large discount) a patient advocate or health care manager, typically a licensed social worker.

"Member services directors check in with people routinely," Laibson says. "And members look out for each other. We have an incredible neighbor-to-neighbor volunteer component where neighbors will take a walk with a member, run some errands, read to somebody, play cards, or just make a friendly visit, all at no charge. If someone felt they needed a daily check in, we would find a volunteer who could do that and we would take care of whatever needs arise. This gives families who live out of town or out of state peace of mind that their relative is not alone."

Third is Beacon Hill Village's concierge service, an umbrella term for everything a member might need, from bicycle repair to a referral to a new dentist. The office maintains an extensive resource directory to give recommendations for almost everything, and offers members the opportunity to obtain and give feedback on various services they engage. For example, if a mason comes to do work on someone's front stoop, Village staff checks with the member afterward to see how the service went, and if there was any problem, goes back and deals with it with the provider.

Included in the annual fee is a twice-a-week grocery shopping service where members are picked up at home in a private car with one or two other people (which is especially important within the city where parking is difficult). If they are housebound, the driver will pick up the groceries for them.

In the Village's Rolodex is a five- to ten-page list of different providers who can offer references for homecare aides, personal trainers, massage therapists, errand services, pet sitting, and a home care company that provides a range of home management services, from electricians to plumbers. Members pay à la carte for whatever they need or want, and most of the outside providers the Village deals with offer a discount.

Beacon Hill Village does whatever it can to help people to maintain their independence. And the services it offers have evolved as the organization has grown and members make new requests that then become part of the everyday program. Someone asked for a tai chi class, and people often want alternative means of transportation (one of the biggest challenges facing seniors) so they can avoid using taxis and the long waits typical of senior transport.

"We're like a switchboard operator with many lines," Laibson says. "Some use a lot of our services, others not at all and treat us like an insurance policy so they know we're here when they need us. It's to make members feel safe and connected and give them peace of mind."

• • •

This story first appeared in the January/February 2007 edition of DESIGNER/builder magazine.

AM I OLD YET?

(Photo by Lance Laver)

ACKNOWLEDGMENTS

WE WOULD LIKE TO EXPRESS OUR GRATITUDE TO THOSE WHO helped make this book a reality.

This book would not have been possible without the generous support of both the Graham Foundation for Advanced Studies in the Fine Arts and the Richard H. Driehaus Foundation.

Many thanks to The Canelo Project for administering our grants, and especially Athena Steen who was with us every step of the way. Her support, guidance, and friendship have been invaluable.

Our deep-felt gratitude to Sunny Fischer for her belief in the power of this work.

Thanks to our designer Peter Scholz, whose talent, care, involvement, and support have been with us through the fulfillment of so many outstanding projects.

Gratitude to James Dickinson for his encouragement, and Edward Tenner, for his willingness to help in answering the tough questions.

Special thanks to John Byram, our editor and the director of the University of New Mexico Press, who always believed in us and in this book. And to Beth Hadas, former director, for her guidance, help, and support.

A special acknowledgement to Neil Smith—brilliant geographer, urban theorist, social justice advocate. Gone too soon, and sorely missed. Thanks for your inspiration Neil, the example you set, and all that you taught us.

Thanks to the people who encouraged, mentored, and in so many ways supported us: especially Elizabeth and Dudley Wrigley, Michael Gonzales, Claire Phelan, Michael Winsch, Michael Swier, and the late, greatly missed Margaret Hannigan.

Also a large debt of gratitude to Mary Gray, Ellen Gross, Terry Stout, Hiroki Takeda, and Tico Guerra.

This book grew out of *DESIGNER/builder* magazine and the many dedicated supporters who encouraged us to take the magazine's message of looking at the world in a different way to a wider audience.

We must acknowledge our incredible debt to all the amazing people whose stories and work inspired the magazine and this book. They showed us that change on a small scale adds up, and that we can all begin to transform the world around us into something better.

And of course, our love to Kingsley Hammett, who made all of this possible.

(Photo by Roberta Feldman, courtesy of Roberta Feldman and Susan Stall)